Cooks In Cadence

MARBLEHEAD
P U B L I S H I N G
RALEIGH, NORTH CAROLINA

Published by Marblehead Publishing, Raleigh, North Carolina
Publishing Consultant, Kaye Lasater, Raleigh, North Carolina
Printed in the United States of America
Designed by Denise Riedel, Hays, Kansas
ISBN 0-943335-04-3
Library of Congress Catalog Card Number: 94-74894
This book is a product of the Women In Military Service For America Memorial Foundation, Inc.
Additional copies may be ordered by calling 1-800-222-2294, or writing:

The Women's Memorial
Dept. 560
Washington, DC 20042-0560.

Cooks in Cadence

. . . Dedicated to all women who have served in this nation's defense — past, present and future. We pay special tribute to all those who served with sacrifice and distinction — prisoners of war, casualties of combat, pioneers and groundbreakers. . . .

Acknowledgments

Many gave their time and imagination to this book of culinary delights. Our special thanks for —

• The countless hours of work and total commitment of two extremely dedicated and experienced volunteer editors, Mrs. Norman M. Pritchett and Mrs. William G. Richardson of Florida, both of whom have edited cookbooks previously. Without their meticulous, detailed work in scrutinizing each recipe, we might have had angel food cake without angels and *Cooks in Cadence* would not have been a cookbook of the fine quality that it is.

• The delicious recipes, from snacks to elegant desserts, submitted by servicewomen and WIMSA supporters. Without their input, *Cooks in Cadence* wouldn't have been a WIMSA first!

• The artistic skills of Mr. John Carr, the Memorial's resident architect. His evocative sketches depict various parts of the Memorial and its Education Center, and were derived from the design drawings of our extraordinarily talented architectural team of Ms. Marion Weiss and Mr. Michael Manfredi.

• The keen eyes of Lt. Col. Gloria Lewis, USAF (Ret.) who did the final proofreading.

• The WIMSA Cookbook Committee, chaired by BG Connie L. Slewitzke, USA (Ret.).

Highlights of Women
in the
United States Armed Forces

1775 American Revolution: Women serve on the battlefield as nurses, cooks, laundry women and saboteurs. Deborah Samson Gannett, alias Robert Shirtliffe, disguises herself as a man and serves in the Continental Army.

War of 1812: Lucy Brewer, alias George Baker, serves aboard the *USS Constitution* as a Marine until her disguise is discovered.

1861-65 Civil War: Courageous women such as Dorothea Dix, Clara Barton and Harriet Tubman provide casualty care to Union and Confederate troops.

Women such as Confederate soldier Loreta Janeta Velasquez, alias Harry T. Buford, serve as soldiers on both sides. Belle Boyd is among the women who serve as spies.

Dr. Mary Walker receives the Congressional Medal of Honor, the first and only woman to receive the nation's highest honor.

1898 Spanish American War: More than 1,500 civilian contract nurses volunteer to serve with the Army in Hawaii, Cuba, the Philippines, Puerto Rico and hospitals in the States and on the hospital ship, *Relief.*

1901: Army Nurse Corps is established.

1908: Navy Nurse Corps is established.

1917-1918 World War I: The Navy and Marine Corps enlist more than 12,500 women to "free men to fight" by filling positions such as clerks and telephone operators. A limited number of Coast Guard women also serve. More than 23,000 Army and Navy nurses serve in hospitals in the States and France.

1918: Eighteen black nurses are recruited into the Army Nurse Corps. Segregated from white nurses, black nurses are tasked to care for black soldiers.

The war ends and women are discharged from the services except for those Army and Navy nurses in the regular Corps.

1920: Army Reorganization Act authorizes relative rank for nurses from second lieutenant to major.

1942-45 World War II: Nurses under attack at Pearl Harbor and the Philippines; 88 become prisoners of war in the Pacific; one is held prisoner of war in Europe.

Army establishes Women's Army Auxiliary Corps (WAAC) which soon converts to Women's Army Corps (WAC); Navy recruits women into its reserves as WAVES; Coast Guard establishes the SPARS; and Marine Corps creates its Women Marine Reserves. Army also organizes Women Airforce Service Pilots (WASP).

Charity Adams Early commands the 6888th, an all-black postal unit, in Europe. As in World War I, black women serve on a segregated basis.

More than 400,000 women serve our country at home and overseas in nearly all noncombat jobs.

1947-48: Laws are passed granting women permanent status in the Regular and Reserves of the Army, Navy, Marine Corps and newly created separate Air Force.

Women's components (WAC, WAVES and Women Marines) retain their wartime identifications. Air Force women are identified as WAF.

1949: Air Force establishes its Nurse Corps and the Army and Air Force establish the Medical Specialist Corps.

1950-53 Korean War: Army nurses arrive in Pusan to help set up a hospital — the first of some 540 to serve in the combat zone. Navy nurses serve on hospital ships and Air Force nurses with Air Evacuation units.

Defense Advisory Committee on Women in the Services (DACOWITS) created to advise on recruitment of military women.

1965-75 Vietnam War: Some 7,500 American military women serve tours in Southeast Asia. The vast majority in-country are Army nurses. Lieutenant Sharon Lane dies of shrapnel wounds. Seven others die in the line of duty.

1967: Legal ceilings on women's promotions repealed.

1969: Air Force Reserve Officer Training (AFROTC) goes coeducational.

1970: Army promotes first women, Anna Mae Hays, Chief, Army Nurse Corps, and Elizabeth P. Hoisington, WAC Director, to brigadier general.

1971: Air Force promotes Jeanne M. Holm, WAF Director, to brigadier general.

1972: Decision to end the military draft and recruit more women volunteers.

Navy Chief Admiral Zumwalt publishes Z-116 declaring Navy's commitment to equal rights and opportunities for women.

Hospital ship *USS Sanctuary* sails with mixed male/female crew.

Opportunities expanded for women in nontraditional jobs in all of the services.

Service policies change requiring women to be treated equally with men in all matters of dependency and entitlements.

Alene B. Duerk, Director, Navy Nurse Corps, becomes the first female Navy admiral.

1973: Jeanne M. Holm becomes the first female major general.

1974: Army Lieutenant Sally Murphy becomes the first military helicopter pilot.

Six Navy women are the first military women to earn pilot wings.

1975: Air Force flight nurse Captain Mary T. Klinker is the last American military woman to die in Vietnam when the C-5A Galaxy transport evacuating Vietnamese orphans crashes on takeoff.

Department of Defense policies issued permitting women to raise families and remain in the military.

1976: Women admitted to all the service academies.

Fran McKee becomes the first Navy woman line officer promoted to rear admiral.

1977: Coast Guard ships *Morgenthau* and *Gallatin* welcome women aboard as crew members.

1978: The Coast Guard becomes the first service to open all assignments to women.

Margaret Brewer becomes the first female brigadier general in the Marine Corps.

Judge John Sirica rules the law banning women from ships except transports and hospital ships to be unconstitutional. Congress changes the law to open duty on noncombat ships.

Ensign Mary Carrol joins the crew of *USS Vulcan* repair ship — the first of the women permanently assigned aboard a Navy ship under the amended law.

Women's Army Corps (WAC) is deactivated as its members are integrated into their parent branches.

1980: First women graduate from the service academies.

Hazel W. Johnson, Army Nurse Corps, becomes the first black woman to wear the rank of brigadier general.

1983: Colleen Nevius becomes the first Navy woman test pilot.

Women deploy with forces to Grenada in Operation Urgent Fury.

1989: Women deploy to Panama in Operation Just Cause.

Army Captain Linda L. Bray, commander of the 988th Military Police Company, leads her soldiers in an infantry-style firefight against Panamanian Defense Forces.

Three Army helicopters flown by female pilots encounter heavy enemy fire and are nominated for Air Medals.

1990-91 War in the Persian Gulf: Some 40,000 American military women deploy with the forces on Operation Desert Shield/Storm.

Two Army women, Specialist 4 Melissa Rathbun-Nealy, a truck driver, and Major Rhonda Cornum, a flight surgeon, are taken prisoner by the Iraqis.

Thirteen women die in the line of duty.

1991: Congress repeals laws banning women from flying in combat.

1993: Air Force Lieutenant Jeannie Flynn enters combat pilot training.

Congress repeals law banning Navy women from duty on combat ships; women deploy with *USS Fox*.

Servicewomen deploy with United Nations forces to Bosnia and Somalia.

1994: Navy women join the crew of the carrier *USS Eisenhower*.

Servicewomen deploy with United Nations forces to Rwanda.

Navy servicewomen deploy on combat ships to Haiti and the Middle East.

One of the Navy's first woman combat pilots, Lieutenant Kara S. Hultgreen, is killed in a training accident off the *USS Abraham Lincoln*.

Table of Contents

Hors d'oeuvres

*One of four
pedestrian entry
ways to Court
of Valor*

Dip for Vegetables, Quick & Easy

2 cups mayonnaise
1 cup sour cream
3 tblsps parsley flakes
3 tsps dill seed

3 tsps finely chopped onion
3 tsps Lawry's® seasoned salt
6 drops Tabasco® sauce
1 tsp Worcestershire sauce

Mix well and refrigerate. Good with any raw vegetables.

Piquant Dip for Raw Vegetables

1/2 cup sour cream
1/2 cup small curd cottage cheese
1/2 cup mayonnaise
1/2 cup chili sauce
2 tsps prepared mustard
Few drops Tabasco®

1 tsp Worcestershire sauce
1 tblsp horseradish
1 tblsp cut chives
1 tsp sugar
2 tblsps dry sherry

Combine all ingredients. Blend well. Makes about 2 1/4 cups.

Daffodil Dip

8 ozs cream cheese, regular or light
1/2 cup cottage cheese
1/3 cup mayonnaise
2 tsps parsley, chopped
2 tblsps green onion, chopped

1 small clove garlic, crushed
Dash of pepper
1 tsp lemon juice
1 hard boiled egg, finely chopped
Raw vegetables

Beat together: cream cheese, cottage cheese and mayonnaise. Stir in remaining ingredients, except egg. Mix well; top with chopped egg. Chill and serve with raw vegetables. Makes 2 cups.

Curry Dip

2 cups mayonnaise
3 tblsps chili sauce
1 tblsp Worcestershire sauce
3 tblsps curry powder, or to taste

1/2 tsp garlic powder
1 small onion, grated
Dash of pepper

Combine all ingredients; mix well. Refrigerate 24 hours. Serve with crisp raw vegetables. Makes about 2 1/2 cups.

A Favorite Party Dip, Quick & Easy

1 (8 oz) pkg cream cheese, at room temperature
2 tsps grated onion

1/4 to 1/2 cup French dressing
2 to 3 tblsps catsup

Mix all ingredients in electric mixer until well blended and smooth. Serve with potato chips or crackers. Better if allowed to stand a while before serving.

Bacon Horseradish Dip, Quick & Easy

1 cup mayonnaise
1 cup sour cream

1/4 cup bacon bits
1/4 cup prepared horseradish

Stir all ingredients until well mixed. Cover; chill. Makes 2 cups.

Popeye's Spinach Dip

1 (10 oz) pkg frozen chopped spinach, thawed and squeezed dry
1/4 pkg dry vegetable soup mix
1 3/4 cups plain non–fat yogurt

1/4 cup Kraft® Free® No–Fat mayonnaise
1 (8 oz) can water chestnuts, drained and chopped
2 tblsps chopped chives or green onions
Round loaf of sourdough bread, optional

Thaw spinach, drain and squeeze until fairly dry. Stir dry soup mix before measuring, to ensure that it is evenly mixed. Mix all ingredients together when spinach is ready. Chill and serve with raw vegetables.

For an unusual serving dish, slice top off a round loaf of unsliced sourdough bread and hollow out inside. Fill with cold dip. Save insides to use for bread crumbs, or cube and use for dipping.

Cheesy Avocado Dip, Quick & Easy

1 large avocado, chopped
1 small tomato, diced
3 ozs cream cheese, softened
1/4 green chilies, diced

1 tblsp green onions, finely chopped
2 tsps lemon juice
1/4 tsp salt
Corn chips

Fold avocados and tomatoes into cream cheese. Stir in green chilies, green onions, lemon juice and salt. Serve chilled with corn chips.

Pimiento Cheese Dip, Quick & Easy

2 cups (8 ozs) processed pimiento cheese, shredded
1/2 cup dairy sour cream
1 (3 oz) pkg cream cheese softened
1/2 cup tomato juice cocktail

2 mild green chili peppers, seeded and chopped
3 slices bacon, cooked crisp, drained and crumbled
Raw vegetable dippers and assorted crackers

In small mixing bowl, combine pimiento cheese, sour cream, cream cheese, tomato juice and chilies. Beat with rotary beater until light and fluffy. Stir in bacon crumbs. Chill. Stir by hand just before serving to revive fluffy quality. Serve with vegetables or crackers. Makes 2 cups.

Roquefort Cheese Dip, Quick & Easy

1/2 lb Roquefort or Blue cheese
3/4 lb cream cheese, cut into pieces
3/4 tsp minced garlic

3/4 tsp Worcestershire sauce
3/4 tsp Tabasco® sauce

In electric mixer, beat Roquefort cheese until smooth. Gradually add cream cheese and beat until well combined. Add remaining ingredients and mix until smooth. Serve at room temperature with raw vegetables or crackers.

Con Queso Dip, Quick & Easy

1 lb Velveeta (cubed)
1/2 cup picanté sauce (hot)

1/4 cup milk

Combine in sauce pan over low heat, until melted. Serve warm with tortilla or corn chips.

Hot Cheese and Beef Dip

8 ozs cream cheese
3 tblsps milk
1 (3 or 4 oz) pkg of dried chipped beef (cut up fine)
1/2 tsp pepper

1 dash garlic salt
1/2 cup sour cream
1/2 cup chopped pecan nuts

Mix all except nuts. Sprinkle nuts on top. Bake in oven proof dish 20 minutes at 350°. Serve hot with crackers.

Shrimp Dip I, Quick & Easy

1 can cream of shrimp soup
1 (8 oz) pkg cream cheese, softened
1/4 cup finely chopped green pepper
Dash hot pepper sauce

2 tblsps finely chopped onion
Small pieces of shrimp (optional)
Wheat crackers or corn chips

With electric mixer or rotary beater, gradually blend soup into cheese. Beat just until smooth. Mix in remaining ingredients. Chill. Makes 2 1/2 cups dip. Small pieces of shrimp may be added.

Shrimp Dip II, Quick & Easy

1 can shrimp, cut up (can use 8 to 10 frozen, thawed and cooked)
1 can water chestnuts, chopped finely
1 cup mayonnaise

Dash of lemon juice
1/2 medium onion, finely chopped
Pepper to taste

Mix together and chill. Serve with wheat crackers and corn chips.

Party Clam Dip, Quick & Easy

1 can Campbell's New England Clam Chowder
1 pkg (8 oz) cream cheese, softened
1 can (4 oz) mushrooms, drained and chopped

1 tsp finely chopped onion
Dash of cayenne pepper

In a mixer, gradually blend soup into cream cheese until smooth (do not over–beat; it will get thin). Add remaining ingredients. Chill. Serve with crackers or chips.

Clam Cheese Dip

1 (7 1/2 oz) can minced clams
2 (3 oz) pkgs cream cheese
1/4 tsp salt
2 tsps onion, grated

1 tsp Worcestershire sauce
3 drops Tabasco® sauce
1 tsp parsley, chopped
2 tsps lemon juice

Drain clams, reserve liquid. Bring cheese to room temperature. Combine all ingredients except liquid. Blend into a paste. Add clam liquid one tablespoon at a time and beat after each addition until desired consistency is reached. Chill.

Crab Dip I, Quick & Easy

1 lb crab meat
2 large pkgs cream cheese
8 ozs sour cream
3 shakes garlic powder
1 tblsp prepared mustard

2 tblsps mayonnaise
1/2 tsp lemon juice
3 tsps Worcestershire sauce
1/4 cup grated sharp cheese

Mix all ingredients except grated cheese and place in 9" x 13" baking dish. Bake at 325° for 30 minutes. Sprinkle with 1/4 cup grated cheese and place under broiler to melt cheese.

Crab Dip II, Quick & Easy

8 ozs cream cheese, softened
2 dashes Worcestershire sauce
3 tblsps Miracle Whip salad dressing
1 tsp minced onions

1 tsp lemon juice
1 large tin crab meat, well drained
Paprika

Mix the whole lot except paprika together well. Bake 350° for 15 to 20 minutes. Sprinkle top with paprika.

Salmon Spread or Dip, Quick & Easy

1 (7 3/4 oz) can salmon
1 (8 oz) pkg cream cheese, softened

3 tblsps sliced green onions
1 box crackers

Drain salmon, reserving 2 tsps liquid. Flake. Combine salmon, cheese and onion, and mold. Refrigerate at least 2 hours before serving. Serve with crackers.

Mexican Dip, Quick & Easy

1 can condensed bean with bacon soup
1 (6 oz) pkg garlic flavor cheese food, diced
1 cup sour cream
1/4 cup minced onion

1/4 tsp hot pepper sauce (Tabasco®)
Chili powder
Corn chips

Heat soup and cheese slowly, add sour cream, onion and pepper sauce; heat through, sprinkle chili powder on top. Serve with corn chips. Makes 2 2/3 cups.

4 Layer Mexi Dip

Layer #1: **1 large can refried beans mixed with 1 pkg taco seasoning**
Layer #2: **3 avocados mashed with 4 tblsps sour cream and 2 tblsps lemon juice**
Layer #3: **4 to 5 diced green onions; 1 small can diced green chilies; 3 diced tomatoes, mixed**
Layer #4: **1 1/2 cups shredded cheddar and jack cheese**

Serve with tortilla chips.

Baked Southwestern Dip

1 loaf (16 oz) white peasant or pumpernickel bread unsliced
1/4 cup prepared hot salsa
1 pkg cream cheese

1/2 cup dairy sour cream
1 1/2 cups shredded cheddar cheese
Sliced fresh vegetable sticks

Preheat oven to 400°. Cut 1/4" slice from top of the bread; set aside. Remove center from bread. Set aside and cut in cubes leaving 1/2" shell. Bake cubes until toasted. Beat with electric mixer the salsa, cream cheese and sour cream until smooth. Stir in cheddar cheese, spoon into bread shell. Place reserved slice on top. Wrap in foil. Bake until hot, about 1 1/2 hours. Serve with fresh vegetables and toasted bread cubes.
Editor's note: It might be wise to check the bread in the oven fairly frequently. 400° is rather hot for 1 1/2 hours.

Chili Dip, Quick & Easy

1 (14 oz) can chili without beans
Hot sauce to taste

1 cup shredded cheddar cheese
1/2 tsp cayenne pepper

Combine all ingredients; heat until cheese melts. Serve hot with tortilla chips or corn chips. Makes about 2 cups.

Taco Dip, Quick & Easy

16 ozs cottage cheese
8 ozs cream cheese, softened
16 ozs sour cream
1 packet taco seasoning

Taco chips
Lettuce, finely shredded
Tomatoes, finely chopped
Yellow cheese, shredded

Whip cottage cheese, cream cheese, sour cream and taco seasoning together in a mixer or food processor. Put into serving dish. Top with finely shredded lettuce, finely chopped tomatoes and shredded yellow cheese.

Smoked Salmon Spirals

Slices of smoked salmon
4 ozs cream cheese, at room temperature
1 tblsp fresh dill, chopped fine, or 1 tsp dried dill
1 tblsp fresh Italian parsley, chopped fine

2 tsps drained capers
1 1/2 tsps Dijon mustard
1/2 tsp grated lemon peel
1/8 tsp pepper

Spread creamed mixture on salmon slices, roll up and cut into 1/2" spirals.

Cheese and Shrimp Spread, Quick & Easy

4 ozs cheddar cheese (grate small)
3 green onions (chop fine and include the green tips)
Garlic powder and salt to taste

1 can shrimp
3/4 to 1 cup mayonnaise

Combine all ingredients and refrigerate. May be kept in small crock. Keeps for 2 weeks.

Chutney Cheese Spread

1/2 lb cheddar cheese, grated
1/2 lb Swiss cheese, grated
2 (3 oz) pkgs cream cheese, softened
1/2 stick butter or margarine, softened
1 jar chutney
Dash salt and pepper
Dash cayenne

1/2 tsp curry powder
3 drops Tabasco®
2 tsps Worcestershire sauce
1/4 tsp garlic salt
1 tblsp minced green onion
Paprika

Mix all ingredients except paprika. Roll into a ball and then roll in paprika or spoon into serving bowl and sprinkle with paprika. Cover and refrigerate overnight. Let stand 1 hour at room temperature before serving.

Curry Cheddar Spread, Quick & Easy

2 cups (about 8 ozs) grated cheddar cheese
1 (4 1/4 oz) can chopped black olives, drained
1/2 cup mayonnaise
1/2 tsp curry powder

2 green onions, finely chopped (including green portions)
1 small clove garlic, minced
Crackers or thinly sliced French bread

Combine all ingredients in a bowl with a fork until blended. Refrigerate several hours to allow flavors to blend. Serve cold or at room temperature on crackers or thinly sliced French bread.

Pecan Spread

1 (8 oz) pkg cream cheese
2 tblsps milk
2 tblsps finely chopped chives
1/2 tsp garlic salt
1/4 tsp pepper

1/4 cup finely chopped bell pepper (red, yellow and green)
1/2 cup sour cream
1/2 cup chopped pecans
1 tblsp butter
1/2 tsp salt

Combine softened cream cheese with milk. Blend. Stir in chives, garlic salt, pepper and bell pepper. Mix well. Fold in sour cream. Spoon into a buttered casserole. Heat and crisp pecans in oven in melted butter and salt. Sprinkle over mixture. Bake at 350° for 20 minutes. Serve with melba toast.

Pimiento Cheese

3 ozs Alpine Lace cheddar cheese
2/3 cup cottage cheese
1 (12 oz) jar pimientos, chopped

2 tblsps mayonnaise (low fat)
Dash of artificial sweetener (optional)

Grate cheddar cheese. Add other ingredients. Mix well.
Note: May be placed in blender and blended until smooth.

Russian Cheese Spread

8 ozs Havarti (or other hard cheese), chopped
3 hard boiled eggs, chopped
2 cloves garlic, chopped fine

1/2 cup mayonnaise
Salt and pepper to taste
Parsley sprig

Combine ingredients in a medium size bowl. (Make it in a decorative bowl, and it's ready to serve.) Garnish with a sprig of parsley. Serve with bread or with fresh vegetables.

Salmon Paté Spread, Quick & Easy

8 ozs cream cheese
1 tsp horseradish
1 tblsp lemon juice

2 tsps grated onion
1/4 tsp salt
1 can red salmon

Mix first 5 ingredients together and fold in salmon. Chill.

Cheese Ball

3 ozs cream cheese
8 ozs Velveeta
8 ozs Old English® cheese spread
1 tblsp Worcestershire sauce
1 tsp grated onion
Garlic powder to taste
1/4 cup chopped pimientos

2 tblsps sherry (optional)
1/4 cup chopped green olives

Paprika
Nutmeg
Chili powder
Crackers

Mix the first 9 ingredients and form in the shape of a ball. Roll in a mixture of paprika, nutmeg and chili powder. Chill. Serve with crackers.

Crunchy Cheese Ball

1 (8 oz) pkg cream cheese, softened
1/4 cup mayonnaise
2 cups ground cooked ham
1 tsp minced onion
1/4 tsp hot pepper sauce

2 tblsps chopped parsley
1/4 cup dry mustard
1/2 cup chopped peanuts or pistachios
Crackers

Beat cream cheese and mayonnaise until smooth. Stir in next 5 ingredients. Cover, chill several hours. Form into ball and roll in nuts to coat. Serve with crackers.

Smoky Salmon Cheese Ball

1 (7 oz) can pink salmon
1 1/4 cups (5 ozs) shredded cheddar cheese
1 (8 oz) pkg cream cheese, softened
2 tblsps minced onion
1 tblsp parsley flakes

1 tblsp lemon juice
1/2 tsp liquid smoke (or to taste)
1/2 tsp garlic powder
1/2 cup finely chopped pecans

Drain salmon, remove skin and bones. Flake salmon with a fork, stir in remaining ingredients, except pecans. Chill until slightly firm. Shape mixture into a ball and roll in pecans. Chill several hours or overnight.

Editors note: Liquid smoke has a strong taste. It is advisable to add it little by little to any recipe. Caution doesn't ruin recipes.

Quick Paté, Quick & Easy (food processor style)

8 ozs Braunschweiger
4 ozs sweet butter
1/2 tsp chopped onion
1/4 tsp bay leaf
1/4 tsp allspice
1/4 tsp cloves

1/4 tsp nutmeg
Pepper
1 tblsp brandy
1/2 cup chopped pecans or walnuts
Clarified butter (see Lagniappe)

Put all ingredients except nuts into the food processor fitted with the steel blade. Process until smooth. Put in a bowl and add chopped nuts. Pack into a crock or a wide-mouth jar. Cover with a thin coating of melted clarified butter. Refrigerate.

Note: See Lagniappe for clarified butter.

Chicken Liver Paté

1/2 lb chicken livers
1 tsp salt
Pinch of cayenne pepper
2 tblsps finely minced onion
1/2 cup soft butter

1/4 tsp nutmeg
1 tsp dry mustard
1/8 tsp powdered cloves
Crackers or melba toast

Bring chicken livers to a boil in water, barely to cover. Drain and put hot livers through the finest blade of a meat grinder or purée in a food processor. Mix the paste with all the other ingredients except crackers. Blend well. Pack the mixture in a crock or wide mouth jar, cover with a thin layer of melted, clarified butter and refrigerate. Serve with crackers or melba toast.

Note: See Lagniappe for clarified butter.

Tuna Paté Pyramids

1 (7 oz) can tuna in vegetable oil
1 (3 oz) pkg cream cheese, softened
1/2 tsp minced onion or chives

1/4 tsp Tabasco® sauce
24 triangle shaped crackers

Combine tuna, cream cheese, onion, salt and Tabasco® sauce; mix well. Mound onto cracker; shape into pyramids with edge of knife or spatula.

Cream Cheese and Pickapeppa Sauce, Quick & Easy

1 (8 oz) pkg cream cheese
Pickapeppa sauce

Melba rounds

Pour about 3 or 4 ounces of sauce over cream cheese, and serve with melba rounds.

Chili Squares

1 (3 oz) can chopped green chilies
6 eggs

1/2 lb grated cheddar cheese
1/2 lb grated mozzarella cheese

Remove seeds from chilies and lay flat in well-greased casserole dish. Whip eggs until foamy and combine with cheeses. Pour over chilies. Bake covered 30 minutes at 350°. Lower temperature to 250°; uncover and bake 30 minutes more. Cut into bite size pieces.

Editor's note: When handling chilies, it is wise to use rubber gloves.

Guacamole

2 ripe avocados
1 tblsp lemon
2 tblsps mayonnaise
1/8 tsp cumin powder

1/8 tsp garlic powder
1 tblsp onion, minced
1 tblsp hot sauce (to taste, or omit)
2 tomatoes, diced

Mash avocados in a bowl (or put in a blender). Add lemon juice, mayonnaise, cumin powder, garlic powder, onion and hot sauce. Mix until smooth and creamy. Refrigerate until ready to serve or, if served immediately, add tomatoes. Do not add tomatoes until ready to serve.

Editor's note: Some versions of guacamole call for chopped avocados rather than puréed.

Cream Cheese Hors d'oeuvres, Quick & Easy

1 (18 oz) jar of pineapple preserves
1 (18 oz) jar of jelly
1 (4 oz) jar of horseradish

1 (1 oz) can dry mustard
1 tsp cracked black pepper (or less)
1 (8 oz) pkg cream cheese

Mix first five (5) ingredients and chill in refrigerator. Pour over cream cheese. Serve with crackers.

Lacy Cheese

2 (8 oz) pkgs Monterey Jack cheese

PAM® cooking spray

Thinly slice or cube cheese; spray cookie sheet with PAM®. Place cheese on pan 2" apart. Bake at 400° for 2 to 3 minutes until melted and lacy. Serve with grapes or crackers.

Cheese Puffs, Quick & Easy

1 cup grated cheese
1/2 cup soft butter
1 cup sifted all-purpose flour

1/2 tsp salt
1 tsp paprika
Pimiento-stuffed olives

Blend cheese and butter. Stir in flour and salt. Stir in paprika. Mix well. Wrap 1 tsp mixture around 1 olive to make a ball. Place apart on a baking sheet. Bake 10 to 15 minutes at 400°.

Before cooking, these balls may be stored in the freezer. Place balls on a flat plate or baking sheet, freeze and then store in freezer bags. Defrost and bake at 400°.

Blue Cheese Bites

1 pkg (10) refrigerated biscuits
1/4 cup margarine

3 tblsps crumbled Blue cheese

Cut each biscuit into four pieces. Melt margarine and cheese in baking pan and add cut-up biscuits, coating biscuits well. Bake in 400° preheated oven for 12 to 15 minutes.

Brie in Pastry

1 sheet frozen puff pastry
1 wheel Brie cheese (16 ozs)
1/4 cup sliced toasted almonds

1/4 cup parsley, chopped
1 egg, beaten with 1 tsp water

Thaw pastry 20 minutes; roll sheet out on a lightly floured surface to a 15' circle. Preheat oven to 400°. Slice Brie in half horizontally and layer with almonds and parsley. Reassemble and place in center of pastry. Brush pastry edges with egg wash and pull up sides to enclose Brie. Place seam side down on ungreased baking sheet. If desired, decorate with pastry scraps. Brush with egg wash. Bake for 20 minutes. Let stand 10 minutes before serving. Makes 12 servings.

Editor's note: If pastry scraps are to be used to decorate, brush on egg wash (1 egg beaten with 1 tblsp water) first so the decorations will adhere to the top.

Cheese Sausage Snack

1 lb bulk pork sausage
1 lb Velveeta cheese
1/4 cup catsup, pizza sauce or chili sauce

2 tblsps Worcestershire sauce
2 drops Tabasco® sauce (optional)
1 loaf party rye bread

Cook sausage until browned, drain on paper to eliminate grease. In the same frying pan, put cheese and catsup, pizza sauce or chili sauce. Stir until cheese melts, add drained sausage; cook a few minutes to blend.

Spread on slices of party rye bread, then toast in 400. oven for 7 to 9 minutes, serve hot

Note: Mixture will keep for two weeks in refrigerator, longer frozen for later use.

Sausage Bites, Quick & Easy

1 box brown and serve sausages
6 ozs Classic Coca-Cola®

1 tblsp prepared mustard

Cut sausages into bite size pieces. In a pan, mix Coca-Cola® and mustard. Add sausages and boil until done. Remove sausages and boil liquid down to a syrup. Replace sausages in pan and heat. Serve with toothpicks. They will never guess.

Celia's Chinese Ribs

6 to 8 lbs of pork spare ribs
1 can consommé
1 tblsp salt

1 jar of honey (1 cup)
6 to 8 cloves of garlic, slightly mashed
1 bottle soy sauce (2/3 cup)

Take all fat off ribs and cut them into 2" pieces, sawing through the bones, or have the butcher crack them for you.

Marinate them in the above ingredients for 12 to 24 hours. Drain off and save the liquid. Roast in 350° oven for 1 to 1 1/2 hours, basting frequently with reserved liquid. Turn up oven temperature to crisp, if desired.

Teriyaki Chicken Appetizers

2 lbs chicken wings
1/3 cup water
1/2 cup sugar

1/3 cup soy sauce
Crushed fresh ginger to taste

Cut off the wing tips and save them to make broth for future use. Separate the remaining wing joints. Put chicken pieces in a pot and pour in the remaining ingredients. Bring to a boil, cover and simmer for 45 minutes to an hour. Just before serving, broil for a few minutes to crisp, if desired. Serves 6.

Texas Caviar

2 (14 oz) cans black eyed peas, drained
1 (15 oz) can white hominy, drained
1 (4 oz) can green chilies, drained, chopped
1 (4 1/2 oz) can black olives, chopped
2 medium tomatoes, chopped
4 green onions, chopped
1 medium green pepper, chopped

1/2 cup chopped onion
1/2 cup chopped fresh parsley
2 cloves garlic, chopped
1/2 cup celery, chopped
1 (8 oz) bottle Wish-Bone® Italian salad dressing
1 jar salsa, optional
2 to 3 bags taco chips

Combine all, except for dressing and chips; mix well. Pour dressing over mixture; cover and marinate at least 2 hours in refrigerator. Drain and serve with taco chips.

Marinated Antipasto

2 (9 oz) pkg frozen artichoke hearts
2 (16 oz) pkg mozzarella cheese
2 (7 oz) jars roasted red peppers, drained
1 (6 oz) can (drained wt.) pitted ripe olives, drained
Sliced pepperoni (optional)

1/2 cup salad oil
1/2 cup red wine vinegar
1/2 tsp crushed red pepper
1/2 tsp oregano leaves
1 small garlic clove, crushed

Prepare frozen artichoke hearts as label directs but prepare both packages together; drain. Place artichokes in large bowl; cool slightly. Cut mozzarella cheese into 1" chunks; cut roasted red peppers into 1" pieces, cut olives in half. Slice pepperoni (if used).

To artichoke hearts in bowl, add cheese, roasted red peppers, olives, salad oil and remaining ingredients; toss gently to mix well. Cover and refrigerate at least 8 hours or overnight to blend flavors, tossing occasionally. Makes 12 cups.

Marinated Mushrooms

3/4 cup olive oil
1/3 cup wine vinegar
1 clove garlic, halved
1 bay leaf
3/4 tsp sugar

1/2 tsp salt
1/2 tsp dried basil
6 peppercorns
1 1/2 lbs medium size mushrooms, halved vertical

Combine all ingredients except mushrooms in a skillet; bring to a boil. Reduce heat and simmer ten minutes. Stir in mushrooms and simmer 5 minutes. Let cool. Cover and chill several hours or overnight. Drain before serving, removing garlic and bay leaf. Serve with toothpicks.

Spicy Munchies

Sauce
1/4 cup butter
1/4 cup apple butter (Smucker's)
2 tblsps brown sugar
1 1/2 tsps cinnamon
1/4 tsp allspice

2 cups each of Corn Chex®, Rice Chex®, and Wheat Chex® or 6 cups of Crispex®
1 cup (or pkg) of apple chips (golden)
1 cup assorted raw nuts (cashews, pecans, filberts and almonds)

Melt sauce ingredients in small pan. Place cereals in large baking pan (12" x 17"). Add nuts and mix. Pour spice sauce over all and toss thoroughly. Bake 15 min. at 350°. Stir once. Add apple chips and bake 15 minutes more at 350°. (Break up apple chips if they are too large.) Spread out on foil or paper towels and cool. Store in tin or plastic container. Makes 7 to 8 cups.

Oyster Cracker Snack

3 (8 oz) pkgs small oyster crackers
1 1/2 cups vegetable oil
1 pkg original Hidden Valley® salad dressing (dry)

1 tsp lemon pepper
1 tsp dill weed
1 tsp garlic powder

Empty crackers into a large bowl. Heat oil (do not boil). Add all the dry ingredients, mix well. Pour over the crackers and mix thoroughly until evenly coated. Allow to sit in bowl to cool. Store in plastic container. Keeps well for weeks.

Bologna Wedges, Quick & Easy

6 slices of Lebanon bologna (ham, salami or other lunch meat may be used)
1 (3 oz) pkg cream cheese, softened

1 tblsp horseradish
2 tblsps milk

Mix cream cheese, horseradish and milk together. Spread a layer on bologna slices and make a stack. Top stack with one unspreaded slice of bologna. Chill until cheese is hard. Slice into wedges. Serve with toothpicks.

Ham Appetillas

1 pkg super-size flour tortillas
2 (8 oz) pkgs cream cheese, softened
1/3 cup mayonnaise

2 tblsps green onion, chopped
1/4 cup black olives, chopped
2 (2 1/2 oz) pkgs sliced and pressed, cooked ham

Remove tortillas from refrigerator. Combine cream cheese, mayonnaise, onions and olives. Spread thin layer of mixture on tortilla. Arrange 4 slices of ham over cheese. Roll up tortilla tightly. Wrap individually in plastic wrap. Place in refrigerator at least 3 hours or overnight. To serve, cut into 3/4" slice. Makes about 64 appetillas.

Crab Appetillas: Omit olives and ham. Add 1/4 cup chopped red pepper, 1 cup shredded cheddar cheese and 1 can crab meat (5 oz) to mixture.

Swedish Meat Balls

1 1/2 cup soft bread crumbs (dry with crusts removed)
3/4 cup milk
3 tblsps chopped onion
2 tblsps butter
1 lb ground beef
1/4 tsp nutmeg
1 1/2 tsps salt

1/2 tsp pepper
1 egg, slightly beaten
2 tblsps butter
1 can consommé
1 1/2 tsps flour
1/2 tsp water

Soften bread crumbs in milk. Cook onions in 2 tblsps of butter until brown. Add bread crumbs, meat, seasonings and egg. Form into 1" balls. Sauté in 2 tblsps of butter for 10 minutes. Add consommé and simmer for 5 minutes. Add flour and water mixed together for gravy. Makes approximately 3 dozen.

Hot Sausage Balls

1 lb sharp cheddar cheese, shredded
2 cups biscuit mix

1 lb bulk sausage, hot or regular
Prepared mustard, if desired

Mix cheese with biscuit mix and sausage. Mix like pie dough until mixture sticks together. Form into balls the size of walnuts. Place in baking pan and bake 20 minutes at 375°. They may be accompanied by prepared mustard, if desired. (Can be frozen.)

Artichoke Heart Appetizer

2 (6 oz) jars or 1 (15 oz) can artichoke hearts, drain and reserve juice
1 medium onion, chopped
1 clove garlic
4 eggs

1/2 cup soda crackers, crumbled
1/4 cup chili salsa
1 lb cheddar cheese, grated
Salt and pepper
Grated cheese for topping

Use drained juice from artichokes to sauté onion and garlic. Beat eggs in bowl; add onion, crackers and salsa. Add chopped artichoke, cheddar cheese, salt and pepper. Bake for 25 to 30 minutes. Sprinkle some grated cheese on top for the last 10 minutes.
Editor's note: Suggest 350° oven.

Avocado Shrimp Cocktail

Sauce
1 (3 oz) pkg cream cheese
1 tblsp lemon juice
1 tsp Worcestershire sauce
2 tblsps chili sauce
1 tsp grated onion
1/4 tsp salt

1 large avocado, cubed
8 ozs cooked shrimp, shelled, deveined and chilled
1/2 cup sliced celery

In a small bowl, combine top ingredients and chill. Combine shrimp, avocado and celery. Place in cocktail glasses. Top with sauce. Serves 4.

Sun—dried Tomatoes with Cheese and Basil, Quick & Easy

Sun dried tomatoes, packed in olive oil
Baguette (thin loaf of French bread), thinly sliced

Natural cream cheese
Fresh whole basil leaves or tiny sprigs of watercress

Drain tomatoes and cut in quarters. Spread bread with cream cheese. Garnish with a small whole basil leaf or a sprig of watercress, and a piece of tomato.

Deviled Eggs

6 eggs, hard boiled
2 tblsps mayonnaise
1 tsp vinegar
1/4 tsp salt
Dash of pepper

1/4 tsp paprika
1/2 tsp dry mustard
Garnish (Optional: Olive slices; Jalapeño pepper slices; parsley)

Cut eggs in half length-wise and remove yolks. Set aside white part of eggs. Mash yolks and blend with remaining ingredients. Use this mix to fill in the whites of the eggs. May garnish with olive slices, Jalapeño pepper slices or parsley. Makes 12.

Old Fashioned Cracker Barrel Crackers

2 cups unsifted flour
1 tsp salt
1/2 tsp baking powder

1/4 cup butter
1/2 cup milk
1 large egg, lightly beaten

Combine dry ingredients and blend. With a pastry blender or 2 knives, cut in butter until mixture resembles coarse meal. Add milk and egg and mix to stiff dough. Knead on a lightly-floured board for 5 minutes or until dough is smooth. Divide dough in half. Set one part aside while rolling out remainder.

Heat oven to 400°. Roll dough on a lightly floured board to about 1/8" thickness. Cut into rounds or desired shapes. Place on lightly greased baking sheets. Prick crackers with a fork and bake about 10 minutes until lightly browned. Remove to rack. Crackers will crisp as they cool. Repeat with the other half of the dough. Store in airtight container. Use with soup or as an hors d'oeuvre cracker.

Honey Crisp

1/3 cup margarine
3/4 cup brown sugar

1/4 cup honey
1/2 tsp vanilla

Mix margarine, sugar and honey and boil 5 minutes without stirring. Remove from heat and add vanilla to mixture . While above is boiling, spray 9" x 13" pan with PAM®.
Mix:

6 cups Crispex®
1 cup mini pretzels

1 cup salted nuts
1/2 to 1 cup Cheerios®

Add boiled mixture, put in pan and bake 1 hour at 250°. Stir every 15 minutes. Cool before serving.

Breakfast, Brunch & Lunch

*Decorative urn
atop pylon at
main gateway*

Broiled Grapefruit, Quick & Easy

1 grapefruit
Brown sugar or maple syrup or honey
Butter

Cut grapefruit in half, remove the core and loosen the sections. Pour a little syrup or sprinkle a little brown sugar on each half. Dot each half with a little butter. Put under the broiler and broil until the outer rim of the shell turns brown. Serve immediately.

Breakfast Soufflé

1 1/2 lbs bulk pork sausage
9 eggs, beaten
3 cups milk
1 1/2 tsps dry mustard

1 tsp salt
4 to 5 slices bread, cubed (8 to 10 slices preferred)
1 1/2 cups shredded cheddar cheese

Cook sausage until done, stirring to crumble. Drain well on paper towels. Combine eggs, milk, mustard, and salt. Mix well. Combine with sausage and bread. Pour into greased 13" x 9" x 2" baking pan. Cover and refrigerate overnight. Bake at 350° for 1 hour. Makes 6 to 8 servings.

Egg Casserole

6 slices dry bread, cut into 1" cubes, baked at 250° for 20 minutes or 3 1/2 cups cubes already toasted
1/2 lb grated cheese
Crumbled bacon, chopped onion, chopped olives, mushrooms, or leftover chicken, ham or tuna
6 eggs, beaten

2 cups milk
1 tsp salt
1 tblsp dry mustard
Dash of Worcestershire sauce
1/4 cup melted butter or margarine

In a 13" x 8" baking dish, add 1/2 of bread cubes in bottom of dish. Cover with 1/2 of grated cheese.
Add layer of either or all of the bacon, onion and olives, etc. Repeat with layer of cheese and bread cubes. Beat eggs with milk and seasonings. Refrigerate overnight. Bake at 350° for 30 to 40 minutes.

Morning Casserole

1 lb regular sausage
1 tblsp regular mustard
8 slices bread, no crusts
2 cups grated cheese
6 or 8 eggs

3/4 cup half and half
1 1/4 cups milk
1 tsp nutmeg
Salt to taste
Dash of Worcestershire sauce

Brown and drain sausage; add mustard. Line 9" x 13" pan with bread; top with sausage mixture and top with cheese. Mix eggs, half and half, milk, nutmeg, Worcestershire, and salt. Mix well, pour over casserole. Bake at 350° for 45 minutes or until knife comes out barely moist.
Note: New coffee creamers may be used in place of half and half.

Zippy Cheese Omelet

1/2 can picanté sauce
4 ozs shredded low-fat Monterey Jack cheese (1 cup)
4 ozs shredded low-fat cheddar cheese (1 cup)

6 eggs
8 ozs light sour cream
Additional picanté sauce

Preheat oven to 350°. Lightly spray 9" quiche or pie pan with non-stick vegetable coating. Spread 1/2 cup picanté sauce in bottom of pan. Combine cheeses and sprinkle over sauce. Beat eggs. Add sour cream and beat well. Pour over cheese. Bake uncovered for about 35 minutes or until knife inserted just off center comes out clean. Serve with additional picanté sauce. Garnish with tomato wedges and fresh parsley.

Brunch Strata

1 lb Jimmy Dean® pork sausage
8 slices any choice of bread (trim off crusts)
1/2 cup onion, chopped
1/2 cup green pepper, chopped

1 cup shredded Swiss or cheddar cheese
4 eggs, slightly beaten
1 cup milk
Paprika

Cook sausage, crumbled, until done. Drain off any liquid or grease. In a Pyrex® 8" x 8" x 2" pan, place 4 slices of bread. Layer sausage, onion, green pepper and cheese over the bread. Cover with remaining bread. Mix together eggs and milk. Mix well. Pour over bread, making sure all bread is covered. Sprinkle with paprika. Cover with plastic wrap and refrigerate 4 hours or overnight. Bake at 350° for 30 minutes. Makes 4 servings.

Sausage Breakfast

1 lb bulk sausage
6 slices white bread, crust removed
Softened butter or margarine
1 1/2 cups shredded longhorn cheese

5 to 7 eggs
2 cups half and half milk
1 tsp salt
1 tsp dry mustard

Cook sausage over medium heat until done, stirring to crumble well. Drain sausage on paper towel; set aside. Spread each slice of bread with butter and cut into cubes. Place cubes in a 13" x 9" x 2" baking pan; sprinkle with sausage and top with cheese. Combine remaining ingredients; beat well and pour over mixture in baking pan. Chill for at least 8 hours or overnight, covered with plastic wrap in refrigerator. Bake at 350° for 40 to 50 minutes. This is especially good for quick breakfast for company. Can be made night before. The dish is a complete breakfast.

Sausage Casserole

1 can water chestnuts, diced
1 can cream of chicken soup
1 can cream of celery soup

1 can cream of mushroom soup
1 cup rice, cooked or uncooked
1 lb mild sausage, browned and drained

Combine all ingredients in baking dish. Bake in oven at moderate heat, 350°, until all liquid is absorbed (test with flat knife until comes out clean).

Sausage and Egg Casserole

1 lb sausage, browned and drained
6 slices bread, cubed
2 cups milk
8 eggs, slightly beaten

1 cup cheddar cheese, grated
1 tsp salt
1 tsp dry mustard

Mix together and pour into 9" x 13" pan. Cover and keep in refrigerator overnight or at least 6 hours. Uncover; bake at 350° for 30 to 40 minutes.

Pork Sausage Ring

2 eggs
1/2 cup milk
1 1/2 cups fine cracker or bread crumbs

1/4 cup minced onion
1 cup chopped apple
2 lbs bulk pork sausage

Beat eggs slightly; add remaining ingredients and mix well. Pat into well greased ring mold. Then unmold in a pan 15 1/2" x 10 1/2". Bake at 350° for 1 hour. The ring may be filled with scrambled eggs and sprinkled with sautéed mushrooms.

Quiche Lorraine

1 uncooked pie shell
1 tblsp butter
4 slices Canadian bacon
1 medium onion, chopped
Dash of salt
Dash of pepper
2/3 cup Gruyere or Swiss cheese, grated, halved

2 cups half and half or milk
1/4 tsp dried basil
4 eggs, beaten
Salt
Dash cayenne pepper
1/4 tsp nutmeg
Paprika

Melt the butter and sauté the bacon until golden. Take out of pan and reserve. In the same pan, sauté onion until soft. Spread bacon evenly over pie crust. Spread onion on top of the bacon. Season with a little salt and pepper. Spread with 1/3 cup of the cheese. Mix half and half with the basil, eggs, a little salt and cayenne pepper. Mix well. Add nutmeg and mix. Pour evenly over the pie crust mixture. Dust with paprika. Heat 20 minutes in a preheated 400° oven. Reduce heat to 350° and bake until custard sets. Makes 6 servings.

Potato Pancakes I

4 cups leftover mashed potatoes
2 eggs, beaten lightly
1 tblsp chopped parsley

1/2 tsp onion salt or 1 tblsp chopped onion
1/3 cup flour
1/4 cup shortening or margarine for frying pancakes

Mix all ingredients except shortening/margarine together. Melt shortening or margarine in skillet. Shape potato mix into patties and fry over medium heat, turning once about 5 minutes or until golden brown.

Potato Pancakes II

3 to 4 russet potatoes, about 1 1/2 lbs	Dash salt and pepper
1 medium onion, grated	1 tblsp milk
1 egg	2 tblsps oil

Scrub potatoes, steam until almost tender. Plunge into cold water, then peel. Grate coarsely. Add grated onion. Beat egg with salt, pepper, milk; add to potato-onion mixture. Combine lightly. Preheat oil on cookie sheet. Drop by tablespoonfuls onto sheet and flatten with back of spoon. Bake at 350° until bottoms brown, about 20 minutes. Turn and brown other side, about 15 minutes more. Makes 16 pancakes.

Potato Pancakes with Cheese

1 egg	1 small onion, grated or chopped fine
1/3 cup milk	1/2 cup grated cheddar cheese
1/2 tsp salt	4 medium potatoes
3 tblsps flour	Shortening or salad oil

In bowl, beat egg, then beat in milk, salt and flour. Add onion and cheese. Wash and peel potato, then grate directly into egg mixture working rapidly because grated potato tends to darken. In a heavy skillet, heat shortening or salad oil, using enough to coat surface generously. Add potato mixture by tablespoons and cook until brown and crisp on both sides. Serves 4.

Cottage Cheese Pancakes

1 cup cottage cheese	3/4 tsp salt
1 tblsp sour cream	1/2 tsp baking powder
2 eggs, beaten very light	1/2 cup flour
Few grains of sugar	Butter or margarine

Mix the cottage cheese, sour cream and eggs. Sift the dry ingredients and combine with the cheese mixture. Fry until light brown in butter or margarine.

Sour Cream Pancakes

1 cup flour	4 egg yolks, beaten
1/2 tsp salt	1 cup sour cream
1/8 tsp baking powder	4 egg whites, stiffly beaten
1/4 tsp baking soda	Pinch of sugar

Sift and mix the dry ingredients; add the egg yolks and sour cream. Fold in the egg whites last with the sugar. Cook on greased or non-stick griddle. These are very light. Do not stack them. May be served with a sweet sauce for dessert or with a little sour cream and caviar as a first course.

Whole Wheat Pancakes

1 egg
1 1/2 cups fluid milk
2 tblsps melted fat or oil
2 cups whole wheat flour

4 tsps baking powder
1 tsp salt
2 tblsps sugar

Beat egg in a large bowl. Add milk and fat or oil. Mix flour, baking powder, salt and sugar, and add to egg mixture. Stir just enough to mix. Pour spoonfuls of batter onto heated, greased fry pan. Cook pancakes until top is covered with bubbles. Turn pancakes and brown the other side. Makes about 15 pancakes

Note: This makes a thick pancake; add more milk if thinner pancake is desired.

Fritters (A Pennsylvania Dutch Dish)

1 cup fruit, canned or fresh, or 1 cup corn kernels
1 cup flour
1 tsp baking powder
1 tsp salt

2 eggs, lightly beaten
1/2 cup milk
1 tsp vegetable oil

Peel and dice 1 cup of fruit. Apples or peaches in season may be used. Fritters also may be made with corn kernels to be served as a side dish.

Heat 3" to 4" oil in deep fryer or heavy iron skillet to 375°. Mix ingredients to make fritter batter; add fruit or corn. Drop by tablespoonfuls into hot oil and fry about 5 minutes or until golden brown all over. Drain on paper towels. If using fruit, sprinkle with powdered sugar to serve. If using corn, serve plain or with syrup.

Quick Coffee Cake

2 cups flour
1/2 tsp salt
3 tblsps sugar

4 tsps baking powder
2 tblsps shortening, melted
1 cup milk

Preheat oven to 400°.

Sift dry ingredients into bowl. Add melted shortening and enough milk to make a very stiff batter. Mix well and spread 1/2" thick in a greased pan. Add topping mixture. Bake about 30 minutes.

Topping:

3 tblsps flour
1 tblsp cinnamon

3 tblsps sugar
3 tblsps shortening

Mix dry ingredients. Rub in shortening and spread thickly over the top of dough before baking. Makes one 9" coffee cake.

Cheese Filled Coffee Cake

1 pkg dry yeast
1/4 cup lukewarm water
1 tsp sugar
1 egg, lightly beaten
3/4 cup margarine or butter
2 cups sifted flour

1/4 tsp salt
2 (8 oz) pkgs cream cheese, room temperature
1 cup sugar
1 tsp fresh lemon juice
Powdered sugar

Mix yeast, water and 1 tsp sugar. Let stand 10 minutes; stir in egg. Cut butter into flour and salt; mix to resemble coarse crumbs. Add yeast mixture and mix to dough. Roll dough out on floured wax paper into a 12" x 15" rectangle. Make filling by combining cream cheese, 1 cup sugar and lemon juice. Spread filling on dough to within 1" of edge on all 4 sides. Fold each long edge toward middle, making sure 1" edges overlap, and seal with a dab of water on seam. Fold ends up 1" to 1 1/2", and seal. Flip onto baking sheet, seam down. Bake immediately at 370° for 30 minutes. Cool and sprinkle with powdered sugar.

Sour Cream Coffee Cake I

Batter

3 cups sifted flour
1 1/2 tsps baking powder
1 1/2 tsps baking soda
1/4 tsp salt
1 1/2 cups butter at room temperature

1 1/2 cups sugar
1 1/2 tsps vanilla
3 eggs
1 1/2 cups sour cream

Filling

Mix:

3/4 cup firmly packed brown sugar
1 1/2 tsps cinnamon

1 1/4 cups coarsely chopped walnuts

Topping

Mix:

2 tblsps vanilla

2 tblsps water

Heat oven to 325°. Grease and lightly flour bottom of 9" x 13" pan. Mix sifted flour, baking powder, soda and salt. Set aside. In large bowl, beat butter and sugar until light and fluffy. Add vanilla, then eggs, one at a time, beating well after each. Blend in the sour cream. Gradually add dry ingredients and blend well. Spoon half of mixture into pan (mixture is rather stiff). Sprinkle with half of the brown sugar/nut mixture. Carefully spoon the remaining batter over this, then sprinkle with remaining brown sugar/nut mixture. Spoon the vanilla/water mixture over the top. Bake at 325° for about an hour, or until cake tests done with pick inserted in center. Cool cake on wire rack.

Sour Cream Coffee Cake II

Sugar mix

1/2 cup sugar
2 tsps cinnamon

1/2 cup chopped nuts

Batter

1/4 cup butter
1/4 cup Crisco
1 cup sugar
1 cup sour cream
2 eggs

1 tsp salt
1 tsp vanilla
1 tsp baking powder
1 tsp baking soda
2 cups flour

Mix sugar ingredients together. Beat all batter ingredients together. Grease angel food tin and pour half the batter into the pan; then half of sugar mix over batter; then remaining batter and rest of sugar mix over that. Take knife and cut through batter to mix and marble. Bake 45 minutes at 350°.

Blueberry Muffins

2 1/2 cups flour
4 tsps baking powder
1/4 cup sugar
1/2 tsp salt (may omit)

1 egg
1 cup milk
4 tblsps melted margarine
1 cup blueberries

Sift flour, baking powder, sugar and salt. Save 1/3 of mixture and mix with berries to coat them. Beat egg. Add milk and shortening and beat into flour mixture. Fold in floured berries. Fill greased muffin tin 2/3 full and bake at 425° for 20 or 25 minutes. Loosen with knife after cooling 5 minutes. Makes 1 dozen.

Maine Wild Blueberry Muffins

Preheat oven to 425° and have ingredients at room temperature.

2 cups flour
1/2 to 2/3 cup sugar
3 tsps baking powder
1 tsp salt
1 egg, well beaten
1 cup milk

4 tblsps (1/2 stick) butter or margarine
*1 cup fresh wild downeast blueberries
1/3 cup chopped walnuts, if desired
1 tblsp sugar for topping
1 tsp grated lemon peel

Sift first 4 ingredients together.
Add milk to beaten egg and then add barely melted butter, stirring constantly.
Add liquid to dry ingredients all at once, stirring only to blend (light blending is the secret of fluffy muffins). Add berries while some flour is still showing (and nuts, if wanted). Fold in with a fork or spatula.
Pour into well greased muffin tins to about 2/3 full. Set for 10 minutes. Sprinkle with sugar and lemon peel. Bake about 20 minutes or until golden brown.

*Maine wild blueberries are extra small and sweet. They can be substituted with other blueberries, but add extra sugar. Maine wild blueberries can be found canned or frozen, but if fresh, are in season in August.
Note: If using canned berries, drain well. Toss lightly in some flour and add to batter carefully. If using frozen berries, thaw only half way before adding to batter. Let stand in tins for 20 minutes.

Orange Muffins

1 3/4 cups sifted all-purpose flour
2 1/2 tsps baking powder
2 tblsps sugar
3/4 tsp salt
3 tblsps grated orange peel

1 egg, well beaten
3/4 cup milk
1/3 cup salad oil or melted shortening
12 sugar cubes
Orange juice

Preheat oven to 400°. Grease 12-cup muffin pan (or use PAM®). Sift dry ingredients and orange peel together in mixing bowl. Make a well in the center. Combine egg, milk and salad oil or shortening. Add all at once to dry ingredients. Mix quickly, only until dry ingredients are moistened. Drop batter from tablespoon into muffin pans, filling each 2/3 full. Dip sugar cubes in orange juice until soaked. Use fingers to dip cubes only until they are soaked. Place one cube on top of each muffin. Bake about 25 minutes. Makes 12 muffins.

Molasses Refrigerator Muffins

4 cups sifted flour
2 tsps baking soda
1 tsp salt
1 tsp ground cinnamon
1 tsp ground ginger
1/4 tsp ground cloves
1/4 tblsp dry buttermilk powder

1/4 cup wheat germ
1 1/3 cups shortening
1 cup sugar
4 eggs
1 cup molasses
1 cup water
1 cup raisins (optional)

Sift together dry ingredients. Cream together shortening and sugar until fluffy. Add eggs; beat well. Blend in molasses; add water. Add dry ingredients, stirring just enough to moisten. Stir in raisins, if desired. Store in covered container in refrigerator for up to 3 weeks.

To bake: fill greased muffin pan cups half full. Bake in 350° oven for 20 minutes or until a toothpick comes out clean.

Six Week Muffins

2 cups boiling water
2 cups 100% bran
1 cup shortening
3 cups sugar
4 eggs, beaten

1 quart buttermilk
5 cups flour
1 tsp salt
5 tsps baking soda
4 cups bran buds

Use a large bowl to mix these muffins. Pour the boiling water over the bran and let soak. Cream shortening and sugar. Add beaten eggs, buttermilk and the soaked bran. Sift dry ingredients together and stir into buttermilk mixture. Add bran buds. Stir until moistened. Fill greased or PAM®-sprayed muffin cups 2/3 full and bake at 400° for about 15 to 18 minutes. Fruits and nuts may be added if desired. Recipe may be stored up to 6 weeks in the refrigerator if tightly covered. Makes 6 dozen muffins.

Sour Cream Muffins

1 3/4 cups sifted all-purpose flour
2 tsps baking powder
1/4 tsp salt
3 tblsps sugar

1/2 tsp soda
1 egg
1 1/2 cups commercial sour cream

Preheat oven to 425°. Grease 12-cup muffin pan (or use PAM®). Sift dry ingredients into mixing bowl. Beat egg until foamy, add sour cream and mix well. Stir into dry ingredients until just mixed. Fill muffin pans 2/3 full. Bake about 20 minutes.

Surprise Muffins, Quick and Easy

1 cup self-rising flour

1 cup vanilla ice cream, softened

Preheat oven to 350°. Line miniature pans with paper liners. Combine ice cream and flour. Stir with wooden spoon just until moistened; do not over-mix. Batter will be stiff. Fill pans 3/4 full. Bake about 20 minutes. Makes 12 miniature muffins. If liners are not available, PAM® works very well.

Eggplant Cheddar Muffins

1 1/2 cups all-purpose flour
2 1/2 tsps baking powder
1 tsp instant minced onion
1/2 tsp salt
1 large egg

1/2 cup salad oil
2/3 cup milk
1 1/4 cups bran cereal
1 1/4 cups peeled, shredded eggplant
2/3 cup shredded sharp cheddar cheese

In a small bowl, stir together the flour, baking powder, onion, and salt. In a large bowl, beat egg, oil, milk, cereal, eggplant, and cheese to blend. Add the flour mixture and stir until evenly moistened but still lumpy. Spoon batter equally into 12 greased 2 1/2" muffin cups (fill to rim). Bake in a 350° oven until well browned on top; about 1 hour. Let stand to cool at least 10 minutes, then serve. Makes 1 dozen.

Light as Air Rolls

1 pkg yeast dissolved in
2 cups warm skim milk
1/2 tsp salt
1/3 cup vegetable oil

2/3 cup honey
2 eggs or equivalent Fleischmann's® Egg Beaters
4 to 5 cups flour

Mix all liquid ingredients together. In separate large mix-master bowl or large bowl, beat 2 cups flour 1 minute (this is the secret to these light rolls). Then add part liquid alternately with part of flour (about 4 to 5 cups of flour) until all is added. Knead until dough is sticky and must be pulled off fingers. Rub oil or butter around another large bowl. Place dough in bowl. Let rise 15 minutes in a warm place, covered with a warm, damp cloth. Knead on floured surface. Roll out dough on floured surface. Make your favorite roll shapes (butter, Parker House, etc). Pour melted butter over dough. Grease pans. Let rise about 25 to 30 minutes and bake at 325° for 15 to 20 minutes.

Hard Rolls

2 pkgs dry yeast
2 cups warm water (105° to 115°)
2 tsps sugar

1 tsp salt
4 1/2 to 4 3/4 cups all-purpose flour
1/4 cup butter or margarine, melted and divided, for top

Dissolve yeast in warm water in a large mixing bowl; let stand 5 minutes. Add sugar and salt; mix well. Gradually stir in enough flour to make a soft dough.

Turn dough out onto a floured surface, and knead until smooth and elastic (about 8 to 10 minutes). Place in a well-greased bowl, turning to grease top. Cover and let rise in a warm place (85°) free from drafts, 45 minutes or until doubled.

Punch dough down and divide in half; shape into 18 loaf-shaped rolls. Place on greased baking sheet. Score tops with scissors, making 1/4" deep slashes and brush with 2 tblsps butter. Cover and let rise in a warm place, free from drafts for 25 to 30 minutes or until doubled in bulk. Bake at 400° for 30 minutes or until golden. Brush with remaining butter. Makes 18 rolls.

Irish Soda Bread

4 cups flour
2 tsps baking powder
2 tsps baking soda
1 tsp salt
4 tblsps sugar

1/4 lb margarine (not corn oil or any other oil)
1 cup raisins (or more)
2 cups buttermilk
1 tsp caraway seeds (optional)

Mix dry ingredients together. Add soft margarine. Mix with hands. Rub together to make crumbs. Add raisins. Add buttermilk. Mix with fork until all is moist. Put in a greased round pan. Cut a cross in the top with a knife. Bake at 350° for 1 hour, until brown. For a smaller loaf, use 1/2 recipe.

Irish Soda Bread should be served fresh and hot. It does not keep well.

Kansas Honey Wheat Sunflower Bread

2 cups luke warm water (120° to 130°)
2 3/4 to 3 1/4 cups flour
2 pkgs yeast
1 tblsp sugar
2 cups whole wheat flour
1 cup rolled oats

1/3 cup instant nonfat dry milk
1/4 cup margarine or butter (softened)
1/4 cup honey
2 tsps salt
1 cup unsalted sunflower seeds

In a mixer bowl, combine the water, 2 cups flour, yeast and sugar. Beat on low speed for 3 minutes. Cover and let rise until doubled (30 minutes). It will be spongy.

Stir in wheat flour, oats, dry milk, butter, honey and salt. Mix well. Stir in sunflower seeds, then mix in as much of remaining flour as you can with a spoon. Turn out onto a floured surface and knead in enough remaining flour to make a moderately stiff dough (6 to 8 minutes). Shape into a ball, place in greased bowl, turning to coat. Cover and let rise in warm place until doubled (30 to 45 minutes). Punch down. Turn out onto lightly floured surface. Divide in half. Let rest 10 minutes.

Shape into 2 loaves. Place into 2 greased 8" x 4" x 2" loaf pans. Cover and let rise until doubled. Bake at 375° for 35 minutes, covering with foil the last 15 minutes to prevent over-browning. Remove from pans and cool on rack.

Cinnamon Rolls I

1/2 cup sugar or 6 pkgs artificial sugar
2 tsps ground cinnamon
1/4 cup raisins (optional)

1 (16 oz) loaf frozen bread dough, thawed
Water

Stir together sugar, cinnamon and raisins (if desired). Roll dough out to 12" x 8" rectangle. Brush entire surface lightly with water. Sprinkle sugar mixture over rectangle. Beginning with 12" side, roll tightly in jelly-roll fashion. Cut dough into 12 equal slices. Place slices in lightly buttered 10 3/4" x 7" cake pan or 9" pie pan leaving 1/2" to 1" between slices. Let rise until doubled in size. Bake in preheated 350° oven about 35 minutes or until golden brown. Turn out immediately to cool.

Drizzle with powdered sugar icing:

Icing

1/4 cup powdered sugar

1 tsp water

Mix sugar and water. Drizzle over rolls.

Cinnamon Rolls II

2 cups milk (2%, skim or regular)
2 sticks margarine
4 tblsps sugar
4 tblsps Crisco
1 tsp salt
2 pkgs dry yeast
1/2 cup warm water

2 eggs, beaten
7 cups flour
Cinnamon
Sugar
Powdered sugar
Milk

Scald 1 cup milk. Pour over the margarine, sugar, shortening and salt. Use a whisk to mix evenly together. Let cool.

Add the other cup of milk. Dissolve the 2 packages of yeast in 1/2 cup warm (to wrist) water. Add eggs, then flour. Work all together with hands. Let stand in a warm place until it doubles in size. Divide into 3 parts. Roll out one-third on a lightly floured board to a rectangle.

In a 4-cup Pyrex® cup, melt 1 stick margarine. Spread a little margarine over the rectangle dough. Sprinkle a little cinnamon, then sprinkle sugar lightly over the dough. Roll lengthwise. Cut in approximately 2" slices. Place approximately 1/2" apart on greased cookie sheets.

Prepare remaining two-thirds the same way. Let all rise again. Bake at 350° approximately 20 to 25 minutes until light brown.

To remaining margarine, add powdered sugar and milk to spreading consistency. When rolls are done, place on cooling racks and, with a butter brush, brush each roll with the spread. Let cool.

Makes 48 rolls which can be frozen in bags and reheated in microwave.

Editor's note: If the icing is drizzled on the buns in the shape of a cross, Voilà! Hot Cross buns!

Banana Bread

1/3 cup shortening
3/4 cup light brown sugar
1 cup mashed bananas
2 eggs
1 1/2 cups flour

1 tsp salt
1 tsp baking soda
1/2 cup milk
1/2 cup chopped nuts

Cream sugar and shortening and add eggs. Add all other ingredients and mix well. Bake in greased loaf pan at 350° for 1 hour.

Persimmon Nut Bread

1 cup persimmon pulp
1 cup brown sugar
1 egg
2 1/4 cups flour
1 tsp baking powder
1 tsp soda

1 tsp salt
1/2 cup raisins or chopped dates
1 tsp vanilla
1/3 cup candied orange peel
1 cup chopped nuts

Combine persimmon pulp, brown sugar and egg. Blend well. Dust raisins or dates with a little of the flour. Sift remaining flour, baking powder, soda and salt. Add dry ingredients to creamed mixture. Add raisins, vanilla, orange peel and nuts. Bake in a 9" x 5" loaf pan at 350° for 45 minutes to 1 hour or until bread tests done.

Pineapple Nut Bread

2 1/4 cups sifted all-purpose flour
1/4 cup sugar
1 1/2 tsp salt
3 tsps baking powder
1/2 tsp baking soda

1 cup all-bran
3/4 cup chopped walnuts
1 1/2 cups crushed pineapple, undrained
3 tblsps butter or other shortening, melted

Preheat oven to 350°.
Sift flour, sugar, salt, baking powder and soda together. Stir in remaining ingredients. Bake in a greased loaf pan 9" x 4" x 3" for 1 1/4 hours. If loaf seems to be browning too fast, cover loosely with foil. This bread keeps moist for up to 10 days and slices best when a day or more old.

Orange Marmalade Bread

2 1/2 cups sifted flour
1 tblsp baking powder
1 tsp salt
1/2 cup honey
2 tblsps soft butter

3 eggs, beaten
1 cup orange marmalade
1 tblsp grated orange rind
1 cup finely chopped pecans

Sift flour with baking powder and salt. In a bowl, beat together honey, butter and eggs until smooth. Stir in marmalade and rind. Mix well. Add flour mixture, stirring until well blended. Stir in nuts. Bake in greased loaf pan in 350° oven about 1 hour or until cake tester or toothpick comes out clean. Cool 10 minutes in pan, then remove and cool completely on a wire rack. It won't slice well until completely cooled.

Easy Raisin Loaf

2 cups pancake mix
1/4 cup brown sugar, packed
1/2 tsp powdered cinnamon
1/4 tsp powdered nutmeg
1/4 tsp powdered all spice

4 tblsps shortening
2 eggs, beaten
1 cup milk
3/4 cup seedless raisins

Preheat oven to 350°. Combine pancake mix, brown sugar and spices. Cut in shortening until mixture is coarse crumbs. Add eggs and milk, beating just enough to combine ingredients. Fold in raisins.

Grease one-pound loaf pan (or line it with wax paper, greased lightly). Pour batter into prepared pan. Bake about 50 minutes. If loaf seems to be browning too much before it is done, cover it lightly with foil. Let cool. Store it one day before slicing.

Jalapeño Pepper Corn Bread

1 cup corn meal
1/2 cup buttermilk
2 eggs
1/2 cup bacon dripping
3/4 tsp soda

1 onion, grated
1/2 lb grated sharp cheddar cheese
1 can cream corn
1 small can Jalapeño peppers, chopped

Mix all, except cheese. Grease pan or skillet. Pour in 1/2 of the batter. Sprinkle grated cheese. Add remainder of batter. Bake at 400° for about 30 minutes.

Zucchini Bread

1 3/4 cups sugar
1 cup oil
3 eggs
2 1/2 tsps cinnamon
1/2 tsp salt
2 tsps baking soda
2 tsps vanilla

2 1/2 cups flour
2 tblsps milk
Small can crushed pineapple, undrained
2 1/4 cups shredded zucchini
1/2 cup coconut
1 cup chopped nuts

Mix all together. Pour into 2 greased loaf pans. Bake at 325° for 55 to 60 minutes, until done.

Scones

4 cups flour
1/2 cup sugar
1 tsp salt
4 tsps baking powder

1 cup shortening
2 eggs
1 cup or more milk
1 cup raisins (optional)

Preheat oven to 425°.

Mix together flour, sugar, salt and baking powder. Cut in shortening until mixture looks like coarse meal. Beat eggs and combine with milk. Make a well in the dry ingredients and add egg and milk combination. Add raisins. Stir with a fork until all dry ingredients are moistened. Dough should be soft.

Gather dough into a ball and roll out to 1/4" thickness on a floured board. Cut with a 2 1/2" cutter, place on ungreased baking sheets and bake for about 10 minutes. Makes about 24 scones.

Cheese Straws

1 cup grated American cheese
1 cup flour
1 tsp baking powder
1/2 tsp salt

1/16 tsp cayenne pepper
1/4 tsp paprika
1 egg, beaten
2 tblsps milk

Preheat oven to 450°.

Mix together cheese, flour, baking powder, salt, cayenne pepper and paprika. Add beaten egg. Mix well. Add milk enough to make a stiff dough. Roll out 1/8" thick on floured board. Cut into strips 5" long and 1/4" wide. Bake for 10 minutes. Makes 30 cheese straws.

Puffy French Toast Fingers

1 cup flour, sifted
1 1/2 tsps baking powder
1/2 tsp salt
1 cup milk

2 eggs, well beaten
10 slices white bread
Cooking oil

Sift flour, measure; sift again with baking powder and salt. Stir in milk and eggs, beat well. Trim crusts from bread slices and cut each in thirds, lengthwise. Dip the bread strips in batter and fry in 1/2" of cooking oil in large frying pan until light brown on both sides. As you remove each batch from oil, drain. Put in shallow pan and sprinkle with powdered sugar. Keep warm in oven. Makes 6 to 8 servings. Serve with syrup.

Note: Economical and very good.

Tangerine Toast, Quick and Easy

6 slices of day-old white bread
6 small tangerines
Butter or margarine

Sugar
Vanilla extract

Trim the crusts from the bread. Butter the slices generously and arrange on a buttered baking sheet. Peel tangerines and separate them into sections. Top each slice of bread with tangerines, spacing them evenly and sprinkle heavily with sugar, filling in spaces between fruit. Sprinkle each slice with a drop or two of vanilla and bake the toast in a moderate 350° oven for about 30 minutes or until bread is crisp and fruit is caramelized. Serve hot.

Waffle Cinnamon Toast, Quick and Easy

Sliced Bread
Butter or margarine

Cinnamon and sugar, mixed

Heat the waffle iron. Cut the bread to fit the grids on the iron, cutting off all crusts. Butter the bread on both sides. Make a sandwich of 2 slices of bread, sprinkling the sugar and cinnamon mixture in the middle. Put the sandwiches in the waffle iron with the plain buttered sides out. Press down hard on the waffle iron and cook the sandwiches until brown and crisp. Serve at once.

Toast Cups

Cut crusts off fresh bread slices. Press slices gently down into muffin tins. Put in 325° oven and bake until crisp. Fill with any desired creamed mixture. Fill immediately before serving.

Spoon Bread

3 cups milk
3/4 cup corn meal
2 tblsps butter or margarine
1 tsp salt

2 egg yolks, beaten
1 tsp baking powder
2 egg whites, beaten stiffly

Scald 2 cups milk in top of double boiler. Mix corn meal with remaining milk. Gradually add to scalded milk, stirring constantly. Place over hot water and cook, stirring frequently 30 minutes. Cool 5 minutes. Beat into batter, salt and egg yolks. Stir in baking powder. Fold in beaten egg whites. Pour into greased 1 1/2-quart baking dish. Bake in 375° oven for 30 minutes or until set.

Custard Corn Bread (Spider Pie)

Butter or margarine
2 eggs, beaten
3/4 cup sugar
1 1/3 cups milk
2/3 cup sour cream

3/4 cup corn meal
1 cup flour
1/2 tsp salt
1/2 tsp soda
1 cup heavy cream

Put 2 tblsps of butter or margarine in a 12" cast iron skillet and preheat oven to 350°. Mix all of the batter ingredients and pour into the heated skillet (the batter is not thick). Pour 1 cup heavy cream in the center of the batter. DO NOT STIR. Bake at 350° for 40 to 50 minutes. Let stand 10 minutes before serving.

Pipe Line Hush Puppies

1 cup yellow corn meal
1 cup all-purpose flour
2 tsps baking powder
1/2 tsp garlic powder
1 cup chopped onion

1 cup chopped green pepper
1 or 2 chopped Jalapeños (optional)
or 1/2 can chopped green chilies
1 egg, beaten
1 (#303) can sweet cream corn

Mix well and drop by spoonfuls in hot fish grease. Brown, then turn over to brown other side.

Virginia Ham Biscuits

(For those people fortunate enough to have Smithfield ham)
Preheat oven to 450°.

2 cups sifted flour
4 tsps baking powder
1/2 lb ground Smithfield ham

Pinch of salt (optional)
2 tblsps shortening
3/4 cup milk (or enough to make a soft dough)

Sift flour with baking powder and stir in ham and salt. With two knives or a pastry blender, cut in shortening. With a fork, stir in milk, making a soft dough. Pat the dough out on a lightly floured board, handling the dough as little as possible. Cut into small rounds. Put the biscuits on a buttered baking sheet. Bake for about 15 minutes until golden brown.
Note: An excellent way to use up last scraps of Smithfield ham. They freeze well and can be reheated.

Borscht in a Hurry

Place in a blender:

1 can sliced beets
1 1/2 cups tomato juice
1/2 cup water
5 tblsps lemon juice

2 tblsps sugar
1/2 tsp salt
1 cup sour cream

Heat to boiling, then cool and refrigerate. At serving time, mix with 1/2 cup sour cream. Top portions with 1/2 cup more sour cream. Makes 6 servings.

Cold Cucumber Soup

4 large cucumbers
1 medium onion, chopped
3 tblsps butter
3 tblsps flour
2 2/3 cups chicken broth or bouillon
1 tsp curry powder

1 tblsp lemon juice
2 cups light cream
1 tsp salt
Dash ground pepper
1/4 cup parsley, minced

Quarter cucumbers lengthwise and remove seeds. Cube and sauté in butter until soft - do not brown. Stir in flour, bouillon, curry and lemon juice. Cook until thick. Purée and cool. Stir in cream, add salt and pepper; chill 3 to 4 hours or longer.

Gazpacho Soup

4 tomatoes
1 green pepper
1 bunch green onions

1/2 large cucumber
4 large stalks celery

Chop the above into small pieces. Remove seeds. Set aside, covered in refrigerator, until needed.

3 cups spicy tomato juice or V8® or Bloody Mary mix
1/2 large cucumber, peeled
1 tomato, skin and seeds removed
1 tblsp sugar
1 clove garlic, pressed

1/4 cup salad oil
1/4 cup red wine vinegar
1 tblsp liquid from canned Jalapeño peppers, optional
Dash pepper

Mix the above in a blender until smooth. Chill until needed. Mix chopped vegetables with liquid about 6 to 8 hours before serving.

Hamburger Soup

1 lb ground beef
1 medium onion, chopped
2 medium potatoes, chopped
3 carrots, chopped
2 stalks celery, sliced
1 can tomatoes
1 can tomato sauce
1 1/2 cups cabbage, chopped

1 tsp salt
1/2 tsp pepper
2 tsps Worcestershire sauce
1/2 tsp parsley
Dash celery salt
Dash onion salt
Dash garlic salt

Brown meat. Add rest of the ingredients and enough water to cover. Boil slowly until vegetables are tender.

Hamburger Vegetable Soup

1 lb ground beef, or half turkey and half beef
1 (16 oz) can stewed tomatoes
1 medium onion, sliced
1/4 cup catsup
1 pkg dry onion mix or soup
3 carrots, sliced
2 stalks celery, sliced

1/2 head cabbage, cut
1/2 cup pearl barley
1/2 tsp basil
Peas and green beans, optional
Parsley
Salt and pepper
Grated Parmesan cheese to top

Brown meat in large saucepan, then add remaining ingredients. Cook until vegetables are tender. Peas and green beans may be added. Before serving, sprinkle each bowl of soup with Parmesan cheese.

Venus de Milo Soup

1 1/2 lbs lean hamburger (cooked lightly and drained)   2 medium diced onions (cook with meat)

Add:

2 cans tomato sauce or a 28-oz can of tomatoes   2 tsps hot red pepper
5 beef bouillon cubes   1 handful of macaroni
14 1/2-oz can of mixed vegetables   Salt and pepper to taste
3/4 cup orzo (rice shaped noodles)

Cover well with water. Cook slowly for 45 minutes to 1 hour.

Quickie Bean Soup

1 large can pork and beans
1 large can crushed or chopped tomatoes
1 onion, chopped

Heat on top of stove, or cover and microwave on high until heated through.

Fourteen Bean Soup

1 pkg fourteen bean mix   1 (28 oz) can whole tomatoes, broken up
Water   1 large dry red pepper or 1 to 1 1/2 tsp chili powder
2 qts water   2 cloves garlic, finely minced
Ham or ham hocks, 1 to 1 1/2 lbs   Juice of 1 lemon
1 large onion, chopped   Salt and pepper to taste

Rinse beans carefully and cover with water, soaking over night. Drain. Add 2 quarts of water and bring to a boil, adding ham or ham hocks. Simmer 2 to 3 hours or until beans are soft. Remove ham hocks and cool. Remove bone, fat and gristle. Chop remaining meat and set aside. Add the rest of the ingredients except ham. Simmer 30 to 40 minutes longer. Add ham and heat thoroughly. This soup has a much better flavor if allowed to stand over night in the refrigerator before heating and eating.

Black Bean Soup

1 can black beans   2 stalks celery, finely chopped
2 cups water   2 small carrots, thinly sliced
1/4 cup sun dried tomatoes, chopped   1 cup cooked rice
1/4 cup onion, chopped   1/2 cup dry Sherry
2 tblsps chopped dried cilantro or 1 tblsp fresh, chopped   Sour cream and chives for garnish
1/4 tsp ground cumin

Combine all ingredients except rice, sherry and garnish. Bring to a simmer for 15 minutes. Add cooked rice and Sherry; continue simmering another 5 minutes. Garnish with sour cream and chopped chives as desired. Makes 2 hearty bowls for an entree or 4 soup course bowls.

Tortilla Soup

Cook 1 hen in 2 quarts water with 3 bay leaves and 1/2 chopped onion. Strain and reserve broth. Remove meat from bone and chop.

In large pot, combine:

1/2 meat (reserve other half for other recipes)
1 can black beans
1 can red beans
1 can corn
2 cans chopped green chilies
1 (2 oz) jar chopped pimientos
2 tblsps chili powder
1/2 tsp ground cumin

2 fresh chopped Jalapeño peppers
1 large onion, chopped
Salt and pepper to taste
2 qts chicken broth

Crushed tortilla chips
Cheddar Cheese, grated

Simmer slowly 2 to 3 hours. Can also be cooked in crockpot. To serve: Crush tortilla chips in bowl. Add small amount of grated cheddar cheese. Ladle soup over chips and cheese.

Miso Shiro Soup

1 cup chicken broth
5 cups of water
1/2 cup miso (soybean paste)

3 tblsps green onions, finely chopped
1 egg slightly beaten
1/3 cup tofu in small cubes (optional)

Mix the broth and water together in a large saucepan. Bring to a boil. Add miso, lower heat, and simmer for a few minutes. Stir until all the miso is dissolved. While simmering, slowly drop in the egg. Add onions and tofu. Serve immediately. Serves 6.

Chicken Velvet Soup

3/4 cup butter, melted
3/4 cup flour
2 cups half and half, warm
1 1/2 qts chicken stock, heated
1 1/2 cups cooked chicken, finely chopped

1/8 cup chicken base
1/8 cup parsley, fresh minced
1/4 tsp sage (optional)
1/4 tsp salt
1/4 tsp white pepper

Make a roux with butter. Add half and half, stir until smooth (starts to thicken). Add chicken stock and base. Over low heat, whisk until blended and heated through about 5 minutes. Add chopped chicken; season with white pepper, salt, parsley and sage.

Cabbage and Beef Soup

1 lb lean ground meat (beef)
1/2 tsp garlic salt
1/4 tsp pepper
2 stalks celery, chopped
1/2 cup onion, chopped
1 can (16 oz) red kidney beans, undrained

1/2 medium head of cabbage, chopped
1 (28 oz) can chopped tomatoes, some liquid
1 can water (use tomato can)
4 beef bouillon cubes
1/2 cup parsley, chopped

Brown meat; add all ingredients except parsley; cook for 1 hour. Garnish with parsley. Serve hot.

Cheese Soup

1 quart water (no more)
2 cups diced potatoes
1 cup onion, chopped
1 cup celery, chopped

1 (16 oz) bag frozen vegetables (your choice)
1 (2 lb) box Velveeta cheese, cut small
2 cans cream of chicken soup, undiluted

Combine water, potatoes, onion, celery, and vegetables. Cook in pot until potatoes are tender. Add cheese and soup; cook until cheese is melted. Serve hot.

Potato Soup

4 cups potatoes, cubed
1/2 medium onion, chopped
1/2 cup celery, chopped
2 tblsps butter
3 cubes chicken bouillon

2 cups milk
2 1/2 cups water
1/2 cup milk
1/2 cup sliced or cubed cheddar cheese

Boil first six ingredients in water until potatoes are tender. Remove from heat and purée in blender, return to pan. Add additional 1/2 cup milk and cheese, heat until hot. Do not boil. Salt and pepper to taste. Serves 4.

French Onion Soup

3 lbs onions, peeled
1/2 cup butter or margarine
1 1/2 tsps black pepper
2 tblsps paprika
1 bay leaf
3/4 cup flour

3 quarts canned beef bouillon
1 cup white wine (optional)
2 tblsps salt
1/2 lb Swiss cheese
1 loaf French bread, sliced 3/4" thick and then cut in half

Slice onions 1/8" thick. Melt butter, sauté onions slowly for 1 1/2 hours in large soup pot. Add all other ingredients, except bouillon, wine and salt. Sauté over low heat 10 minutes. Add bouillon and wine, simmer for 2 hours. Season to taste with salt. Refrigerate overnight. Makes 2 quarts of soup.

To serve: Heat soup. Fill oven-proof bowls. Top with 3 pieces of bread and top that with a slice of Swiss cheese. Place under broiler for 5 minutes. Serve immediately.

Easy Luncheon Soup

1 pkg Nissin® Top Ramen Noodles (or similar Oriental mix)
1 1/2 cups water
1/2 cup milk
1 can cream of shrimp soup

Make Oriental noodle soup using 1 1/2 cups water and 1/2 cup milk instead of usual 2 cups water; refer to package instructions. When noodles have cooked, add can of cream of shrimp soup. <u>Do not add water as called for on soup can.</u> Stir until smooth and hot. Serve with crackers.

Clam Chowder

2 slices bacon, chopped
1 large onion, diced
5 potatoes, scrub well, cut out blemishes, diced (makes 3 cups)
Water
Pinch of herbs, any or all of the following: basil, pepper, rosemary, sage, garlic powder
2 large stalks celery, chopped
2 (6 1/2 oz) cans of clams, 1 can chopped; 1 can minced; or 1 lb fresh clams, shelled and chopped.
1 (8 oz) bottle clam juice
2 cups milk
1 cup half and half
Parsley

Sauté bacon and onion in the bottom of a deep, heavy pot. Add potatoes, herbs and celery. Add only enough water to barely cover. Bring to boil, then simmer for 1 hour. Add clams and clam juice and milk. Simmer another 1/2 hour. If it's too thick or sticking to the bottom, add more milk. Add half and half. Ladle into bowls and sprinkle with parsley. Serve hot with buttered, garlicky French bread.
Note: Color may be varied by using red potatoes and Bermuda onion.

Anheuser Soup

1 can Campbell's® tomato soup
1 can Campbell's® pea soup
1 can beef consommé
1 soup can filled with pure cream
2 tsps tomato paste
2 tblsps sherry

Mix; heat on low. Serve immediately.

Canned Soup Variations

1 can condensed cream of chicken soup	**1 can cream of mushroom soup**

Combine and dilute with milk.

1 can condensed vegetable soup	**1 can beef noodle soup**

Combine diluted according to directions on the cans.

1 can condensed tomato soup	**1 can condensed green pea soup**

Combine and add 1 1/2 soup cans of water.

1 can cream of asparagus soup	**1 can cream of celery soup**

Combine and dilute with milk.

1 can vegetable soup **1 soup can milk**	**2 tblsps grated mild processed cheese**

Heat soup to boiling. Reduce heat and simmer 10 minutes. <u>Do not boil.</u> Add cheese, if making vegetable with milk soup, and stir until cheese melts.

Hamburgers

Large hamburger patties	**Sliced cheese**

Divide the patties in two. Roll the two halves with a rolling pin between sheets of wax paper until they are flat. Sandwich a slice of cheese between the two patties. Pinch the edge of the sandwich together very carefully so that the cheese cannot escape. Fry or broil.

Kids' Calzone

1/2 lb lean ground beef	**2 tblsps chopped ripe olives**
1/4 cup chopped onion	**1/2 tsp oregano**
1 (8 oz) can tomato sauce	**1 tsp basil**
1 clove garlic, minced	**4 French rolls, 5" long**
1 tsp sugar	**1 cup shredded mozzarella cheese, about 6 ozs**

In a small skillet, cook meat and onion until meat is brown; drain off fat. Remove from heat and stir in tomato sauce, garlic, sugar, olives, oregano, and basil. Cut a thin slice from the top of each roll. Using a curved grapefruit knife or a melon-baller, hollow out the bottom of the roll, leaving 1/2" thick sides. Sprinkle with about 3 tblsps cheese per roll. Divide the meat mixture among the rolls. Cover each with remaining cheese and replace tops of rolls. Wrap each roll in foil.

May be refrigerated, frozen or baked.

If refrigerated, 3 to 24 hours, bake at 375° for 40 minutes.

If frozen, bake at 375° for 60 to 70 minutes.

If baked immediately, bake at 375° for 20 minutes.

Toasted Cheese Sandwich

1/4 cup grated cheese (sharp or mild)
Mayonnaise to barely mix

Dash cayenne pepper
2 slices bread

Mix cheese, mayonnaise and pepper. Make a sandwich with the bread. Place in a pan and run under a broiler until one side is brown. Turn and toast the other side. Eat while hot. Makes one sandwich.

Cheese Garlic Grits

3 cups water
1 cup quick grits
1 tsp salt (or less)
3 tblsps butter

1 1/4 cups shredded sharp cheddar cheese
2 large cloves garlic, pressed
2 eggs, beaten
1/4 cup milk

Bring water to a boil in a saucepan. Add grits and salt and reduce heat to simmer. Cook and stir for 4 to 5 minutes until thickened, then stir in butter, 1 cup of the cheese and the garlic. Remove from heat and stir until butter and cheese are melted, then fold in eggs and milk. Turn into a greased 1-quart casserole and sprinkle with remaining cheese. Bake in a 350° oven for 45 minutes, or until set. Serves 5 to 6.

Corned Beef Hash

2 tblsps butter or margarine
4 tblsps grated onion
1 can corned beef hash
Salt and pepper

1/4 cup cream or rich milk
Parsley
Green onions or chives

Melt the butter in a skillet and add the onion. Cook 2 minutes, slowly. Add the corned beef hash, breaking it up and tossing lightly. Season to taste and moisten with cream or milk. Empty into a hot serving dish and sprinkle liberally with parsley and chopped chives or thinly sliced green onions.

Editor's note: For a small quantity of cream or milk in an intensely flavored dish, evaporated milk undiluted, serves just as well.

Herbed Tomato Slices

2 large tomatoes
Salt and pepper
Sugar

1/4 cup fine bread crumbs
1 1/2 tblsps mixed dried herbs
3 tblsps butter or oleo margarine

Wash and skin tomatoes. Cut into 3" or 4" thick slices, depending on size of tomatoes. Place slices in a greased shallow baking pan. Sprinkle lightly with salt, pepper and sugar. Add crumbs, herbs and dabs of butter or margarine. Broil under moderate heat, 3" from flame about 3 minutes or until crumbs are brown. Makes 2 to 4 servings.

Variation: Substitute Roquefort or Blue cheese for herbs; omit sugar.

Editor's note: To skin tomatoes, drop them in boiling water for a few seconds. The skins will peel off easily.

Salads

Great Niche of
the Hemicycle

Blue Cheese Dressing

1 cup blue cheese, crumbled
1 cup mayonnaise
1/2 cup sour cream

2 tblsps sugar
1 clove garlic, minced
1/8 cup white vinegar

In electric mixer, whip together all ingredients, using about 1/4 of the blue cheese. Beat until creamy, and then stir in remaining blue cheese by hand. May be stored in refrigerator for 2 weeks in a large jar.

French Dressing

1 cup sugar
1 cup salad oil
1 cup vinegar
1 (15 oz) can tomato sauce
4 tblsps catsup
2 tsps salt
1 tsp Worchestershire sauce

1 tsp paprika
1 clove garlic, chopped very fine = 1 tblsp
1 small onion, chopped very fine = 4 tblsps
1/4 tsp onion powder
1/4 tsp garlic powder
1 tsp parsley flakes
1/4 tsp Kitchen Bouquet®

Mix all the above and shake well. Store in refrigerator.

Old Fashioned Salad Dressing

2 tblsps flour
6 tblsps sugar
1/4 tsp celery seed
1/2 cup water
1/4 tsp salt

1/4 tsp dry mustard
1/2 cup vinegar
Dash of hot pepper flakes
1/2 cup evaporated milk

Mix in order given, except milk. Heat to boiling, stirring constantly. Cool. Add milk, stirring well. Add more sugar or vinegar, if needed.

Orange Salad Dressing

1/2 tsp grated orange peel
1/4 cup orange juice
2 tblsps sugar
2 tblsps wine vinegar

1 tblsp lemon juice
1/4 tsp salt
1/2 cup oil

Mix first 6 ingredients in blender. Add oil slowly.

Salt-Free Salad Dressing

1 tblsp "salt substitute"
1/3 cup white vinegar

2/3 cup vegetable oil

Combine and mix well.

Turmeric Cabbage Slaw

1 large head cabbage, shredded
4 sweet red peppers, shredded
4 sweet onions, shredded
1 tsp salt

1/4 tsp turmeric
1 cup sugar
1 cup vinegar
1/2 tsp white mustard seed

Toss vegetables. Combine and bring to a boil the salt, turmeric, sugar, vinegar and mustard seed. Pour over vegetables and mix. Put in a tightly covered bowl and refrigerate. Keeps indefinitely.

Superb Cole Slaw

1 medium head cabbage, sliced
1 green pepper, finely chopped
4 stalks celery, grated
1 medium size onion, sliced (or 1 tsp dried onion soaked in hot water)
1 tsp dried onion soaked in hot water and drained

1/2 cup sugar
1/2 cup vinegar
1/2 cup salad oil
1 tsp dry mustard
1 tsp celery seed
Salt to taste

Place sliced cabbage in a bowl in layers along with celery, green pepper, alternating with onion rings and sugar. Bring vinegar, oil and mustard and celery seed to a boil in a sauce pan. Pour over cabbage while still hot. Cover and refrigerate 4 to 6 hours. Mix and serve, or store in refrigerator. The slaw is better after 2 or 3 days and will keep for 2 or 3 weeks. Add salt to taste before serving.

German Cole Slaw

1 head cabbage (medium to large), sliced
2 medium size onions, sliced in rings
1 green pepper, chopped
1 medium jar pimiento, chopped
1 cup sugar

1 tblsp celery seed
1 cup vinegar
3/4 cup vegetable oil
1 tblsp salt

Use large bowl and make day before serving. Combine first 4 ingredients. Mix in sugar and celery seed thoroughly. Put vinegar, oil and salt in pan; bring to rolling boil; pour over cabbage mixture. Stir well. Refrigerate, stirring several times. The longer it marinates, the better it tastes. Has been kept in refrigerator for 3 weeks.

Sweet and Sour Cole Slaw

1 pkg cole slaw mix
2 bunches green onions, chopped
1 cup slivered almonds, lightly toasted

1 cup salted sunflower seeds
2 pkgs beef Nissin® Top Ramen Noodles, chopped not too fine

Dressing

1/2 cup vegetable oil
1/2 cup sugar
1/3 cup white wine vinegar

2 silver pkgs (flavor packets) from Nissin® Top Ramen Noodles

Mix dressing ingredients together. Add rest of ingredients except noodles. One-half hour before serving, add noodles. Mix well. Serves 8 to 10.

Crunchy Cole Slaw

4 tblsps sesame seeds (toasted)
1 cup slivered almonds (toasted)
8 green onions, chopped

1 or 2 bunches cilantro
2 pkgs chicken Nissin® Top Ramen Noodles (broken)
1 large head of cabbage, chopped

Dressing

4 tblsps sugar
6 tblsps rice vinegar
1 cup oil
2 tsps salt

1 tsp pepper
1/4 tsp Chinese Five Spice
1 or 2 Nissin® Top Ramen Noodles flavor packets

Combine all ingredients except noodles. Mix dressing and add to slaw. Add broken noodles just before serving.

Cabbage Slaw

1 head cabbage, shredded
1 large onion, shredded
3 to 4 ribs of celery, shredded

1 green pepper, shredded
3 to 4 carrots, shredded
1 sweet red pepper (if available), shredded

Dressing

2 cups white sugar
1 cup vinegar
1/2 cup water

1 tblsp salt
1 tblsp dry mustard

Mix vegetables in a very large bowl. In a sauce pan, over low heat, mix dressing ingredients. Let it come to a boil. Watch carefully; it boils over very quickly. Cool and pour over vegetables. Refrigerate. Best served the next day. Will keep in the refrigerator for several weeks. Makes about 50 servings.

Editor's note: If a very large bowl for mixing is not available, a nice clean dish pan will serve. The salad then may be packed into several bowls to be refrigerated.

Chicken Curry Salad

2 cups diced, cooked chicken (turkey or ham may be substituted)

1 can bean sprouts, drained
1 can water chestnuts, drained and sliced

Salad Dressing

1/2 cup salad dressing (or to taste)
3 small green onions chopped, or 1 tsp dried onion
1 tsp curry powder (or to taste)

1 tsp soy sauce
Salt to taste
Sliced almonds for garnish

Pour salad dressing mixture into bowl with all other ingredients and mix well. Refrigerate over night or at least 4 hours. The longer it is refrigerated, the more the taste improves. Garnish with sliced almonds.

Hot Chicken Salad

2 cups diced cooked chicken
1 1/2 cups cooked rice
1/2 cup mayonnaise
1/2 cup chopped celery

1 can cream of chicken soup
3 hard-boiled eggs, chopped
1/2 tsp minced onion
Rice Krispies®

Mix all the ingredients together, except Rice Krispies®. Place in the refrigerator overnight. Next day, put the salad in a casserole and cover with Rice Krispies®. Bake at 275° for 45 minutes.

Hot or Cold Chicken Salad

2 cups chicken, cooked and diced
2 cups celery, diced
1/2 cup hickory smoked almonds (Blue Diamond®)
2 tblsps onion, chopped

2 tblsps lemon juice
3/4 cup mayonnaise
1 cup mild cheddar cheese, grated
1 cup crushed potato chips for topping

Mix well and pour into greased casserole. Top with potato chips. Bake for 20 minutes at 350°. May be served hot or cold. May be made ahead of time and refrigerated.
Editor's note: Chicken and mayonnaise, mixed and kept any length of time, have been known to be unhealthful. It would be wise to not risk it.

Italian Vegetable Potato Salad (Microwave)

1 1/2 lbs tiny new potatoes, quartered
1/4 cup water
1/2 lb green beans, cut in 2" pieces
1/2 lb young carrots, sliced diagonally
1/2 lb baby yellow summer squash
1/4 cup vinegar, divided
2 tblsps Dijon mustard
1 tblsp olive oil

1/2 tsp salt
1/8 tsp pepper
8 oz reduced fat mozarella cheese, cubed
1 cup red onion wedges, thin
2 tblsps fresh basil leaves, chopped
2 tsps fresh oregano leaves, chopped
Small amount of water, if desired

Place potatoes and water in a 3-quart microwave safe casserole. Microwave on high for 5 minutes. Add the beans and carrots. Microwave 5 more minutes. Add squash, cover and microwave 5 to 8 minutes. Drain. Toss with 2 tblsps of the vinegar. Cool to room temperature.
Mix remaining 2 tblsps vinegar, mustard, oil, and salt and pepper. Add onion, cheese cubes, basil leaves and oregano leaves. Toss all together. Serve refrigerated or at room temperature. (A little water may be added to the dressing mixture, if desired.) Makes 4 servings.

Yogurt Potato Salad

8 medium potatoes
1 bay leaf
1 tsp caraway seeds
1 medium sliced onion
6 hard boiled eggs, chopped
1 medium chopped onion
2 cups chopped celery
1 tsp salt

Pinch of pepper
1 tsp celery salt
1 (8 oz) container plain yogurt
1/2 cup mayonnaise
1 tsp prepared mustard
Hard boiled eggs, sliced, for garnish
Green pepper rings for garnish

Cover potatoes with water. Add bay leaf, caraway seeds and onion slices. Cover and cook until potatoes are tender. Drain and cool. Peel and cut into cubes. Add eggs, chopped onion, celery, salt, pepper and celery salt. Blend yogurt, mayonnaise and mustard together. Add to potato mixture and toss lightly until well mixed. Chill several hours. Garnish with hard boiled egg slices, green pepper rings and paprika.

Spaghetti Potato Salad

1 1/2 cups cooked spaghetti
2 boiled eggs (whites only)
1 cup celery, chopped fine
1/2 cup grated fat free cheese
1 cup tart apple (Granny Smith), chopped

3 boiled potatoes, cut in cubes
1/2 small jar pimientos, chopped
1/4 cup chopped purple onion
Salt and pepper to taste

Russian Dressing

1 cup Kraft® Free® No-fat mayonnaise

1/2 cup chili sauce

Mix together first nine ingredients. Combine dressing ingredients. Pour over salad and toss.

Bloody Mary Aspic

5 (5 oz) cans Bloody Mary mix
2 envelopes unflavored gelatin
1/2 cup cold water
Oiled mold or 8 individual oiled molds

2 (3 oz) pkgs cream cheese
1 medium cucumber, unpeeled, finely chopped
Half and half (optional)

Heat mix to boiling. Soften gelatin in cold water. Add to hot mix, stirring until gelatin is completely dissolved. Pour into oiled 1 1/2 quart mold or 8 individual oiled molds. Cover with plastic wrap and chill until firm. Unmold on lettuce and serve with cucumber dressing. Beat cream cheese until smooth and fold in cucumber. If the dressing is too thick, stir in a small amount of half and half. Chill.
Editor's note: When only this small amount of cream is needed, undiluted evaporated milk will suffice.

Christmas Jell-O Ring

1 small pkg lemon Jell-O®
1 small pkg raspberry Jell-O®
1 1/2 cups boiling water

1 can jellied cranberry sauce
1 pkg frozen raspberries
1 1/2 cups lemon-lime soft drink

Dissolve gelatins together in boiling water. Melt cranberry sauce carefully. Add cranberry sauce and frozen raspberries to gelatin. Stir until the mixture is melted. Refrigerate until partially set. Add lemon-lime soft drink. Pour into a ring mold. Chill until firm.

Editor's note: Stiffly whipped, sweetened cream might be placed inside the ring.

Gelatin Fruit Salad

2 cups boiling water (divided)
1 (3 oz) pkg lemon flavored gelatin
2 cups ice cubes (divided)
1 (3 oz) pkg orange flavored gelatin
1 (20 oz) can crushed pineapple, drained (reserve liquid)

2 cups miniature marshmallows
3 large bananas, sliced
1/2 cup shredded cheddar cheese (nuts may be used in place of cheese)

Cooked Salad Dressing

1 cup reserved pineapple juice
1/2 cup sugar
1 egg, beaten

2 tblsps corn starch
1 tblsp butter or margarine
1 cup whipped topping

In mixing bowl, combine 1 cup boiling water and lemon gelatin. Add 1 cup ice cubes, stirring until melted. Add pineapple. Pour into 13" x 9" x 2" baking pan. Refrigerate until set. Repeat with orange gelatin, remaining water and ice. Stir in marshmallows. Pour over lemon layer. Refrigerate until set. For dressing, combine pineapple juice, sugar, egg, corn starch and butter in a sauce pan. Cook over medium heat, stirring constantly, until thickened. Cover and refrigerate overnight. The next day, arrange bananas over gelatin. Combine dressing with whipped topping, spread over bananas. Sprinkle with cheese or nuts. Makes 12 to 15 servings.

Editor's note: Sometimes there may be problems with cooking salad dressing containing egg and corn starch over direct heat. If there are any doubts, cook in a double boiler over boiling water which does not touch the top pan. Always safe, although continuous stirring still is necessary.

Blueberry Salad

2 (3 oz) pkgs blackberry Jell-O®
3 cups boiling water
1 (8 1/4 oz) can crushed pineapple (drain and reserve juice)
1 (15 oz) can drained blueberries

1/2 pint sour cream
1/2 cup sugar
1 (8 oz) pkg cream cheese, softened
1/2 cup pecans

Mix Jell-O® and boiling water. Dissolve. Stir in pineapple juice. Add pineapple and blueberries. Chill until syrupy. Beat sour cream, sugar and cream cheese and together. Spread topping over Jell-O®. Top with nuts. Refrigerate.

Cinnamon Applesauce Salad

1 tblsp red cinnamon candies
1 cup hot water
1 pkg cherry gelatin

1 lb (2 cups) sweetened applesauce
1/2 cup chopped celery
1/2 cup chopped walnuts

Melt cinnamon candies in hot water, heating further if necessary. Pour over gelatin and stir to dissolve. Add applesauce; chill until partially set. Fold in celery and nuts. Pour into individual molds and chill until firm. Makes 6 to 8 servings.

Molded Cranberry Salad

2 cups cranberries, picked over
1/2 cup sugar
1 cup water
1 pkg lemon Jell-O®

1 tblsp plain gelatin
1 cup boiling water
1 cup celery, chopped
1 cup nut meats, broken

Cook cranberries in sugar and 1 cup water until the berries pop. Dissolve Jell-O® and gelatin in 1 cup boiling water. Add to cranberries. Stir until dissolved. Chill. When partially set, add the celery and nut meats. Stir and chill until firm.

Frozen Cranberry Salad

1 (3 oz) pkg cream cheese
2 tblsps mayonnaise
2 tblsps sugar
1 can whole cranberry sauce

1 (8 or 9 oz) can crushed pineapple or pineapple tidbits
1/2 cup nut meats, crushed
1 cup whipped cream or Cool Whip®

Mix cream cheese, mayonnaise and sugar together. Add cranberry sauce, pineapple, nut meats and whipped cream or Cool Whip®. Blend, put in a serving bowl and put in the freezer. Keep frozen. Remove from the freezer 15 or 20 minutes before serving.

Grapefruit Salad

3 large cans grapefruit, drained and juice reserved
1 can crushed pineapple, drained and juice reserved

15 marshmallows
2 envelopes unflavored gelatin

Add the gelatin to the juices and cook 5 minutes or until gelatin is dissolved. Add marshmallows and dissolve off the heat. Let cool. Add the fruit and pour into a mold that has been rinsed in cold water. A simple bowl may be used and the salad spooned out. Chill and serve.

Iced Walnut Lime Salad

1 pkg lime Jell-O®
1 cup boiling water
1 large can crushed pineapple (reserve 1 tsp juice)

1/2 cup celery, finely chopped
1 cup cottage cheese
1/2 cup black walnuts, finely chopped

Icing

1 pkg cream cheese
1 tsp pineapple juice

Maraschino cherries
Walnut halves

Mix Jell-O® into boiling water. Stir until dissolved. Chill until syrupy. Stir in pineapple, celery, cottage cheese and walnuts. Pour into 8" square pan and chill until firm. Mix cream cheese with pineapple juice and spread on top of mixture. Garnish with cherries and walnut halves.

Editor's note: If black walnuts are difficult to obtain, regular walnuts might be used.

Jellied Gazpacho Salad

2 envelopes unflavored gelatin
3 1/2 cups tomato juice
2 tblsps lemon juice
2 tblsps vinegar
1 pkg Lawry's® Italian Dressing mix
1 cup finely chopped cucumber, well drained

1 cup finely chopped tomato, well drained
1/2 cup minced green pepper, well drained

1/2 cup mayonnaise
1/2 cup sour cream
Small amount of lemon juice (optional)

Sprinkle gelatin over 2 cups of the tomato juice in sauce pan. Place over low heat and stir constantly until dissolved, about 3 minutes. Remove from heat and add remaining 1 1/2 cups of tomato juice, lemon juice and vinegar. Stir gently. Add Italian dressing mix and blend. Cool and refrigerate until slightly thickened. Add vegetables to tomato mixture and stir gently. Turn into a 6-cup fish mold or ring mold. Chill until set, preferably overnight. Unmold and garnish with parsley or lettuce.

For salad dressing, use 1/2 cup mayonnaise and 1/2 cup sour cream. Blend and thin with a little lemon juice as desired. This salad may be molded in 12 individual molds of 1/2 cup size.

October Salad

1 (3 oz) pkg apricot Jell-O®
1 cup boiling water
1/2 cup cold water

1/2 cup chopped dates
1 cup diced red apples (not pared)
1 cup diced pears

Dissolve gelatin in boiling water. Add 1/2 cup cold water. Chill slightly. Add other ingredients and pour into a wet mold. Chill until firm. Serve with ginger salad dressing.

Ginger Salad Dressing

1/3 cup mayonnaise
1/3 cup whipped cream or topping

2 tblsps chopped candied ginger

Mix mayonnaise and whipped cream. Fold in ginger. Serve with October Salad.

Orange Salad

1 small (8 oz) carton cottage cheese
1 can mandarin orange sections, not drained

1 small pkg orange Jell-O® (use dry)
1 small (8 oz) carton Cool Whip®

Mix all ingredients thoroughly. Chill until firm.

Sparkling Ribbon Pineapple Salad

1 (6 oz) pkg raspberry Jell-O®
2 (10 oz ea) pkgs frozen raspberries
1 (13 1/2 oz) can crushed pineapple

1/4 tsp salt
1 pint sour cream (divided)

Dissolve Jell-O® in boiling water as per package instructions. Add raspberries, undrained, pineapple and salt. Pour about 1 1/2 cups gelatin mix into 6-cup ring mold; chill quickly until firm. Let remaining gelatin stand at room temperature. Carefully spread 1 cup sour cream over chilled gelatin. Spoon half of remaining gelatin over top; chill until firm. Layer with remaining sour cream. Top with remaining gelatin. Chill several hours or overnight. Unmold on serving plate. Makes 8 to 10 servings.

Strawberry Salad I

Topping

1/2 cup sliced almonds

2 1/2 tblsps sugar

Cook in a small skillet over low heat, stirring constantly, until sugar is melted and almonds are coated. Cool and break apart. Store at room temperature.

Salad

1/3 large head iceberg lettuce, torn in bite size pieces
1/3 large bunch romaine lettuce, torn in bite size pieces
2 stalks celery, slivered

2 to 3 green onions, thinly sliced
2 1/2 cups fresh strawberries, sliced
1 (11 oz) can mandarin oranges, drained.

Combine in a large bowl.

Dressing

1/2 cup vegetable oil
4 tblsps sugar
4 tblsps white vinegar

1/2 tsp salt
Dash of pepper
Dash of Tabasco®

Combine well.
Add the dressing slowly to the salad. You may not need all of the dressing. Toss thoroughly and sprinkle with almonds.
Variations: Fresh spinach may be substituted or combined, if desired. Amount of greens used is flexible. Also good with fresh orange or grapefruit sections

Strawberry Salad II

2 pkgs strawberry Jell-O®
2 cups boiling water
1 (10 oz) pkg frozen strawberry halves and juice (may be cut up if too large)

1 (#2 can) Del Monte crushed pineapple and juice
Crushed pecans (optional)
1 carton sour cream

Combine Jell-O® and boiling water. Stir until dissolved. Add strawberries and pineapple. Add crushed pecans. Pour 1/2 of this mixture into a square Pyrex® pan. Chill until set. Beat sour cream until fluffy. Spread over Jell-O®. Carefully spoon remaining Jell-O® over sour cream to cover. Chill mixture until firm.

Yum Yum Salad

2 1/2 cups water
3 tblsps sugar
1 large pkg orange Jell-O® or
2 small pkgs sugar free orange Jell-O®
1 pkg unflavored gelatin

1 large can crushed pineapple in its own juice
1 cup grated cheddar cheese (optional)
3/4 cups pecans, chopped
1 large tub Cool Whip®

Bring 2 cups water and the sugar to a boil. Add Jell-O®. Soak remaining gelatin in remaining water. Add to boiling Jell-O®. Mix until gelatin is dissolved. Cool. Chill until syrupy. Add pineapple, cheese, nuts and Cool Whip®. Refrigerate until firm. Serves 12.

Corned Beef Salad

1 (3 oz) pkg lemon Jell-O®
1 cup boiling water
3/4 cup cold water
1 small can green peas
1 (12 oz) can corned beef (shredded)

1 cup mayonnaise
1 cup diced celery
1 (2 oz) jar chopped pimiento
Egg slices (optional)
Lettuce (optional)

Dissolve Jell-O® in hot water. Add cold water and cool until slightly thickened. Add remaining ingredients. Pour into lightly oiled mold or 8" square pan. Chill until firm. May be garnished with egg slices and lettuce, if desired.

Shrimp Mold

1 (8 oz) pkg cream cheese
1 regular can tomato soup
1/2 cup chopped celery
1/2 cup chopped onion

1 cup mayonnaise
1 envelope Knox® plain gelatin
2 small cans shrimp, drained

Mix cream cheese and tomato soup. Heat until boiling. Combine all other ingredients. Pour hot soup mixture over other ingredients. Pour in mold and chill.

Louisiana Shrimp Salad

1 lb medium shrimp, cooked, peeled and deveined
2 hard cooked eggs, chopped
1 cup chopped celery
1/2 cup chopped onion
2 tblsps chopped dill pickle

1/2 cup mayonnaise
1 tblsp catsup
1/2 tsp Worcestershire sauce
Salt and pepper to taste

Combine all ingredients, mix well, chill. Serve on lettuce leaves. Serves 4.

Shrimp Noodle Salad

1 cup chopped celery
4 green onions, chopped
1 cup sliced water chestnuts
2 pkgs cooked Nissin® Top Ramen Noodles (without

seasonings), broken before cooking
1 1/2 cup mayonnaise
2 cans (or 2 cups cooked fresh or frozen) shrimp
1 pkg dry ranch dressing mix

Mix together. Keeps one week.

Salmon Salad

1 (1 lb) can salmon, drained. Remove bones and skin
10 round Ritz crackers, crushed
4 tblsps sweet pickle relish
3 hard cooked eggs, chopped
1 cup diced celery

1/3 cup mayonnaise
1/8 tsp pepper or more to taste
1 tsp lemon juice
1 tsp onion, finely minced

Mix all together and chill. Serve on lettuce leaves.

Tuna Fish Salad

1 can tuna fish
2 large stalks of celery, chopped

Mayonnaise, to taste

Drain tuna fish and combine with celery and mayonnaise.
Consider these variations:
1. Sweet pickle relish, to taste
2. Chopped bread and butter pickles, to taste.
3. Chopped pimiento stuffed olives, to taste.
4. Chopped pineapple tidbits, to taste.
5. Halved seedless grapes, to taste.
6. Chopped pecans or walnuts, to taste.
7. A combination of pineapple, grapes and pecans, to taste.
If the pickles or olives are used, a very small amount of prepared mustard might be added.

Olde Thyme Cranberry Conserve

1 qt (1 lb) cranberries
1/2 lb (1 cup) walnuts, chopped
1 pkg seeded raisins

1/2 cup water
2 cups sugar

Combine all ingredients in large sauce pan over medium heat. Stir constantly to dissolve. When mixture starts to boil, turn heat to low and cook 1/2 hour, stirring occasionally. Turn into glass or earthenware bowl.

Ham Twirl Salad

2 1/2 cups macaroni rotini (pasta twirls)
2 cups diced cooked ham or SPAM®
1 1/2 cups chopped celery (optional)

1/2 cup chopped sweet pickles or pickle relish
3/4 cup mayonnaise (additional may be required)
1 tblsp grated onion

Cook macaroni as directed; drain; rinse with cold water to cool. Drain again. (May be refrigerated until time of serving and then add remaining ingredients.) Combine with ham, celery and pickle. Blend grated onion with mayonnaise. Add to macaroni mixture. Toss lightly and chill. Before serving, add additional mayonnaise to moisten, if necessary. May be spooned into lettuce cups if served immediately. Serves 6 to 8.

Marinated Macaroni Salad

1 lb rotini
Water
1 pint jar Hellmann's® mayonnaise (no other)
1 cup water
1/2 cup cider vinegar
1 cup sugar

1/2 tsp turmeric
1 medium onion, chopped
2 carrots, shredded
1 cup celery, diced
Salt and pepper to taste

Cook rotini in water 10 to 12 minutes. Rinse and drain. Mix mayonnaise, water, vinegar, sugar and turmeric. Beat well with whisk. Add the vegetables and rotini. Mix well. Cover and refrigerate at least 12 hours. It appears watery at first but will absorb the dressing. Uncover and stir 2 or 3 times during refrigeration.

Spaghetti Salad

1 lb spaghetti, broken and cooked until tender. Rinse and drain.
2 cucumbers, diced
1 small onion, chopped

4 tomatoes, diced
1 (2.75 oz) bottled McCormick Salad Supreme® (in the spice department)
1 (16 oz) bottle Italian dressing

Combine all ingredients. Refrigerate. It is better after 24 hours.

Crunchy Crucifer Salad

1 head cauliflower, cut into bite size flowerettes
4 stalks broccoli, cut into bite size pieces
1 cup chopped green onions

1/2 cup golden raisins
1/2 cup coarsely chopped walnuts
4 heaping tblsps bottled bacon chips

Dressing

1 cup mayonnaise (low fat, cholesterol free)
1/4 cup sugar

2 tblsps vinegar
1 tsp salt

Mix, pour over salad and refrigerate 2 hours.

Layered Salad

Lettuce in bite size pieces (1st layer)
1/2 cup sweet red onions, chopped (2nd layer)
1 cup celery, chopped (3rd layer)
1 (5 oz) can sliced water chestnuts (4th layer)
1 pkg frozen green peas (unthawed) (5th layer)

Mayonnaise (may use Miracle Whip™ mixed with yogurt) (6th layer)
Small amount of lemon juice
Grated cheddar cheese (5 oz)
Imitation bacon chips

Layer the salad in a 2 quart casserole. Cover well the last layer of peas with mayonnaise mixed with lemon juice. Sprinkle on the grated cheese. Cover with plastic wrap. Set over night in refrigerator or may use in 3 to 4 hours. Sprinkle with bacon chips before serving.

Lettuce with Hot Bacon Dressing

1/2 lb bacon, fried crisp
1 egg, beaten
6 tblsps vinegar

6 tblsps sugar
6 tblsps water
1/2 to 1 head lettuce, chopped

Fry bacon until crisp. Crumble bacon slices. Cool bacon fat so egg mixture doesn't harden. Mix beaten egg, vinegar, sugar and water together and stir into bacon fat over low heat, stirring constantly until thickened.
Clean and chop lettuce and put in serving dish. Pour thickened dressing over lettuce. Add crumbled bacon. Toss lightly. Also good over endive, dandelion, green beans or spinach.

Sauerkraut Salad

1 large can sauerkraut, well drained
1 large onion, chopped (Bermuda red onion is best)
1 cup chopped celery
1 green sweet pepper, chopped

1 red sweet pepper, chopped
1 cup vinegar
2 cups sugar

Mix all the vegetables (first 5 ingredients) in a bowl. Boil vinegar, add sugar, stir until sugar is dissolved. Pour hot vinegar over the vegetables. Cover and refrigerate at least 24 hours. A sweet/sour salad, it stays crunchy and fresh for several weeks.

Spinach Salad

1 (10 oz) pkg fresh spinach
Lettuce (bibb, leaf or iceberg)
1/4 lb fresh mushrooms, sliced

Sunflower seeds
1 (8 oz) can water chestnuts, sliced
2 (11 oz) cans mandarin oranges

Remove stems from spinach. Tear into pieces. Add desired lettuce, torn into pieces. Mix all ingredients together.

Sliced, boiled eggs and crumbled bacon may be used instead of the oranges.

Editor's note: This might be tossed with French dressing.

Ice Cream Salad

2 scoops vanilla ice cream
2 apples, diced
1 pear, diced

1/2 tblsp nuts, crushed (mixed nuts preferred)
1 tsp carrot, grated (for color)

Leave ice cream in carton on counter for about 20 minutes to soften. Add apples, pear, carrots and nuts. Mix and serve.

Michigan Bean Salad

1 lb dry Navy beans (6 cups cooked)
6 cups water
1 tsp salt
1 1/4 cup celery, diced
1/2 cup onion, chopped
1/2 cup green pepper, chopped
1/2 cup oil
1/2 cup vinegar

1/2 cup sugar
1 tsp dry mustard
1/2 tsp garlic granules
1/4 tsp paprika
1/2 tsp salt
1/2 cup carrots coarsely grated
1/4 cup pimiento, chopped

Rinse and sort beans. Combine beans, water and salt in a large sauce pan. Cover and let stand over night. Bring to a boil, lower heat and cook until beans are just tender. Add more hot water to cover beans as necessary. Drain well and chill. Combine remaining ingredients and pour over beans. Stir gently. Chill at least 4 hours before serving. Serves 10 to 12.

Hot 5 Bean Salad

8 slices bacon
2/3 cup sugar
2 tblsps corn starch
1 1/2 tsps salt (may use less)

Dash of pepper
3/4 cup vinegar
1/2 cup water

In a large skillet, cook bacon until crisp; drain, reserving 1/4 cup drippings. Return reserved drippings to skillet.

Combine sugar, corn starch, salt and pepper, blend into drippings. Cook a minute or two. Stir in vinegar and water. Cook and stir until boiling.

Drain:

1 (15 oz) can dark red kidney beans
1 can cut green beans
1 (1 lb) can lima beans

1 (1 lb) can cut wax beans
1 (15 oz) can garbanzo beans

Add to skillet. Cover and simmer 15 to 20 minutes. Turn into serving dish. Crumble bacon over top. Makes 10 to 12 servings.

Rice Salad

4 cups cooked rice, cooled (not instant rice)
1 (16 oz) can pineapple tidbits, well drained
2 (6 1/2 oz) cans chunk tuna, drained
2 cups celery, chopped

1/2 cup toasted slivered almonds
1 cup frozen baby green peas. Cover with boiling water and let stand 1 minute, drain.
Miracle Whip™

Mix all together and moisten with Miracle Whip™. Chill several hours before serving.

Wild Rice Salad

1/2 cup wild rice
3 cups water

3 chicken bouillon cubes

Bring above ingredients to a boil and simmer for 20 to 30 minutes until rice kernels have puffed out and absorbed most of broth. Drain and place in a large bowl.
Add:

1 (4 to 5 oz) jar small, whole mushrooms, drained
1 (2 oz) jar pimiento, drained
1/2 cup celery, sliced
1/3 cup green onions, sliced (white part only)
1/3 cup green pimiento stuffed olives, cut in halves
1 (8 oz) can sliced water chestnuts, drained

1 cup Italian dressing
1 (11 oz) can mandarin oranges, drained
1/3 cup pecans, coarsely chopped
More dressing, if desired
Sprig of parsley

Marinate wild rice, mushrooms, pimiento, celery, onions, olives and water chestnuts in dressing 6 to 8 hours or over night. Before serving, fold in oranges and pecans. Place in serving bowl and decorate with parsley. Makes 8 generous servings.

Beef

Cornice detail of
the Great
Niche

Roast Prime Ribs of Beef

Rub a rib roast of beef with salt and spread it generously with shortening. Put it on a rack of a roasting pan, resting beef on the bone ends. If it lacks a thick layer of natural fat, lay a slice of beef suet on top. Sear the beef in a very hot oven (450°) for about 20 minutes. Reduce the heat to moderate (350°) and continue to roast the meat until it is done. If it is a large roast, put a few tablespoonfuls of water in the bottom of the pan to keep the fat from burning.

Rule of thumb:
16 minutes a pound for rare
20 minutes for medium
23 minutes for well done

A safer way:
Plunge an ice pick into the thickest part of the roast, avoiding bone or fat. In the hole, place a meat thermometer:
140° for rare
160° for medium
170° for well done
Remove the meat to a large platter and let it stand for about 10 minutes before carving.

Editor's note: Many professional chefs use the instant meat thermometer or just their fingers to check the doneness of meat, but for the amateur the old-fashioned meat thermometer is safer.

Boiled Beef

4 lbs brisket of beef (flank steak or chuck roast may be substituted), all fat removed
2 cans consommé
5 soup cans water
2 medium onions, sliced
2 cloves garlic, chopped
6 whole cloves
1 tsp thyme
2 bay leaves
2 tsps salt
5 small potatoes, pared
3 small carrots, in 2" pieces
5 wedges from 1 medium head of cabbage

Brown meat in hot frying pan and place in Dutch oven. Add consommé, water, onion, garlic and seasonings. Simmer about 3 hours. Remove meat from liquid, add potatoes and carrots. Cook 10 minutes. Add cabbage and cook 20 minutes. Carve meat while vegetables cook. Cut across the grain in thin slices. Serve hot or cold. Makes 6 servings.

London Broil

1 1/2 lbs flank steak
3/4 cup red wine
1/4 cup vegetable oil
1 small onion, chopped
1 tblsp oregano, crumbled
Salt and pepper

Early in the day, mix wine, oil, onion, oregano and salt. Marinate the steak in this mixture until ready to cook. Remove, pat dry with paper towels. Preheat the broiler. Broil 1 1/2" beneath the broiling element 4 to 5 minutes each side for medium; 3 to 4 minutes for medium rare. Remove, sprinkle with salt and pepper, and slice thinly across the grain.
Leftovers make great sandwiches.
Editor's note: When broiling, leave the oven door slightly ajar. If not, when the temperature in the oven reaches "broil," the flame or electric unit will cut back.

Broiled Beef Tenderloin with Mushroom Stuffing

1/2 cup butter or margarine
3/4 lb mushrooms, finely chopped
1 (4 or 6 oz) pkg sliced cooked ham, diced
1/2 cup minced green onions
1/4 tsp salt

1/4 tsp pepper
3 cups white bread cubes (6 slices)
2 tblsps water
2 (1 1/2 lbs) beef loin tenderloin roasts (center pieces)

1 1/2 hours before serving:

Make mushroom stuffing. In a 12" skillet over medium heat, melt butter; add mushrooms, ham, green onions, salt and pepper. Cook until vegetables are tender, stirring frequently. Remove skillet from heat. Add bread cubes and water, toss gently to mix well; set aside.

Make a lengthwise cut, about 1 1/2" deep, along center of each beef loin tenderloin roast. Into cut section of each tenderloin roast, spoon half of the mushroom mixture; pack mixture firmly. With string, tie each tenderloin securely in several places to hold cut edges of meat together.

Preheat broiler; place both tenderloins, cut-side up in broiling pan; broil 15 minutes. (If necessary, cover stuffing with foil to prevent it from browning and drying out.) Turn tenderloins carefully, cut side down, and broil 15 minutes longer for rare or longer until desired doneness.

To serve: place tenderloins on cutting board, let stand 10 minutes for easier slicing, remove string, slice meat. Arrange on **warm platter**, garnish with watercress sprigs and tomatoes. Serve any gravy in boat. Makes 10 servings.

Flank Steak with Vegetables

1 1/2 to 2 lbs flank steak
2 tblsps flour
1 tsp salt
2 tblsps shortening
4 potatoes, scrubbed, pared and sliced

1 large onion, peeled and sliced
1 green pepper, sliced
1 tsp salt
1/4 tsp pepper
1 (1 lb 3 oz) can tomatoes, chopped

Preheat oven to 325°.

Make shallow cuts in surface of steak diagonally across grain. Mix flour and salt together. Rub into both sides of steak. Melt fat in heavy, flameproof casserole. Brown steak on both sides over high heat. Heap potatoes, onion and green pepper on top of steak. Season with salt and pepper. Pour tomatoes over all. Cover casserole. Bake 2 hours or until vegetables are cooked and tender. Makes 4 servings.

Editor's note: Always slice flank steak across the grain.

Minute Steaks

3 minute steaks
1/4 cup flour
1/8 tsp salt
Dash black pepper
1/4 cup salad oil
1 (4 oz) can mushrooms, sliced

1 envelope French's® Onion Gravy Mix
1 envelope French's® Brown Gravy Mix
1 1/2 cups water
1/4 cup onion, sliced
1/4 cup green onion, sliced

Dredge steaks in flour, salt and pepper. Heat oil until hot, and fry steaks until well browned on both sides. Drain grease. Mix in the rest of the ingredients. Cover and simmer for about an hour.

New England Boiled Dinner

6 lbs corned brisket of beef
Cold water to cover beef
1 medium turnip, quartered
5 small parsnips
6 small carrots

8 small onions
6 medium potatoes, peeled
1 medium cabbage, quartered and cored
6 beets

Cover meat with cold water and boil gently for 3 to 5 hours, until done. Skim the excess fat off the liquid. While meat is cooking, scrape the carrots and parsnips; peel onions and potatoes. Add vegetables to meat. Boil uncovered for 20 minutes. Add cabbage and continue cooking until the cabbage is soft. Place meat on a large plate and surround with vegetables including the beets which have been cooked separately.

Editor's note: Beets take a long time to cook. Canned beets, heated, are just as good.

Beef Stew Casserole

2 lbs meat, cut in cubes
6 carrots, cut in quarters
6 potatoes, cut in quarters
4 tblsps tapioca

1 onion, sliced
1 (1 lb) can tomatoes
Salt and pepper to taste

Put all ingredients in a covered casserole or roasting pan and bake 5 hours at 250°. It makes its own gravy.

California Casserole

2 lbs ground beef
1 medium green pepper, chopped
3/4 cup chopped onion
1 (16 1/2) oz can cream-style corn
1 (8 oz) can tomato sauce
1 (10 3/4 oz) can condensed tomato soup, undiluted
1 (4 oz) can mushrooms, undrained
1 (10 oz) can tomatoes with green chilies, undrained

1 (2 1/4 oz) can sliced ripe olives, drained
1 (4 oz) jar chopped pimiento, drained
1 1/2 tsps celery salt
1/2 tsp chili powder
1/2 tsp dry mustard
1/4 tsp pepper
8 ozs wide egg noodles, cooked and drained
2 cups (8 oz) shredded cheddar cheese

In a large skillet, cook ground beef with green pepper and onion until the meat is browned and the vegetables are tender; drain. Add next 11 ingredients; mix thoroughly. Add noodles; mix well. Pour into a Dutch oven or large baking dish. Cover and bake at 350° for 50 minutes. Sprinkle with cheese; return to the oven for 10 minutes or until the cheese melts. Makes 12 to 16 servings.

Hamburger Casserole

1 lb hamburger or ground turkey
1 tsp salt
1 tblsp minced onions
2 tblsps brown sugar

3/4 cup tomato catsup or barbecue sauce
1 (16 oz) can pork and beans.
1 box cornbread mix

Brown ground meat, onions, salt. Add brown sugar and catsup or barbecue sauce. Remove from heat. Add baked beans. Pour into casserole. Mix cornbread mix (or the real thing). Spread over top of casserole mixture. Bake until cornbread is done, 20 to 25 minutes. Can be frozen and reheated in microwave or oven. Makes 6 to 8 servings.

Meat Ball Casserole

Mix together:

1 lb ground beef
1/2 lb ground pork
1 small onion, chopped
1/2 cup uncooked rice (not instant)
1/2 cup cracker crumbs

1 egg
1/2 tsp salt
1/4 tsp pepper
1 can condensed tomato soup
1 can water

Shape ground beef and other ingredients, except soup and water, into 1" meat balls, and place in greased casserole. Mix together condensed soup and water. Pour over meat balls. Cover and bake 1 hour at 350°.

Variation: After placing meat balls in casserole, cover with 1 pound of sauerkraut. Pour tomato soup mixture over all. Cover and bake 1 hour at 350°.

Reuben Casserole

1 large can or 2 lb bag of sauerkraut, drained
1 1/2 lbs Swiss cheese, grated
1 lb corned beef, cooked and chopped

1 large bottle thousand island dressing
7 slices rye or pumpernickel bread, cubed
1/2 cup margarine, melted

Place drained sauerkraut in the bottom of a 9" x 13" pan. Add 1/2 of the grated cheese. Place corned beef on top of the cheese and then the remainder of the cheese. Pour dressing over top. Cube the bread and place on top. Pour melted margarine over the bread. Bake at 350° for 30 minutes.

Tater Tot® Casserole (Crock Pot)

1 lb hamburger (or ground turkey)
3 cans cheddar cheese soup

2 soup cans milk
Bag of Tater Tots®

Fry hamburger, and drain grease. Add cheese soup. Add milk. Add milk. Stir and place into crock pot. Place bag of Tater Tots® on top of the mixture. Turn setting of crock pot to low and cook 6 hours.

Beef and Gravy

(This is a crock pot recipe but may be modified for use in a slow oven.)

4 lbs roast (rump, cross-rib, top or bottom round will do)
1 cup hot water
1 bouillon cube (or granular equivalent)

1 chopped onion (optional)
1 pkg brown gravy mix (may substitute light gravy mix)
Salt and pepper to taste

Trim fat off roast; place roast in crock pot. Dissolve bouillon in hot water. Pour bouillon over roast, add onion and any other desired seasoning. Cover and cook for 8 to 9 hours, using the low setting of the crock pot. Just prior to serving, prepare gravy mix according to package instructions, but instead of adding plain water to gravy mix, add 1 to 1 1/2 cups of liquid from the crock pot. **Carefully** remove roast from crock pot, slice thinly and arrange on a platter. Pour gravy over slices and serve. Liquid remaining in the pot may be used for gravy.

Beef Roulin

4 slices bacon, cooked dry and diced
3 tsps pickle relish
1 large minced onion
1 tsp mustard
2 lbs thin beef or sandwich steaks

Pinch marjoram
2 to 3 tblsps sauce flour
Hot fat
2 cups or 2 cans beef broth

Combine bacon, relish, onions and mustard and spread on beef slices. Sprinkle with marjoram. Roll, dredging in flour and secure with wooden toothpicks. Sauté in hot fat until brown. Transfer to a casserole. Add remainder of flour to pan drippings and slowly add broth. Simmer until thick, pour over meat, cover the casserole and simmer in a slow oven for 1 to 1 1/2 hours or until tender. Makes 4 to 6 servings.

Sherried Beef Onion Bake

3 tblsps margarine
2 tblsps sauce flour
Dash pepper
1 cup water
1/4 cup dry sherry
2 tsps instant beef bouillon granules
1 lb stew meat, cut in 1" cubes

1/4 tsp A.1. Sauce®
2 large onions, cut in wedges
3/4 cup plain croutons
1/3 cup shredded Swiss cheese
2 tblsps Parmesan cheese
Parsley flakes

In a medium size saucepan, melt margarine. Stir in flour and pepper. Add water, sherry and bouillon granules to saucepan. Cook and stir until mixture is thickened and bubbly. Cook and stir 1 more minute; remove from heat. Stir in stew meat and A.1. Sauce®. Place onion wedges in a 1 1/2-quart casserole and spoon mixture over onions. Cover the casserole. Bake in a 375° oven for 1 3/4 hours to 2 hours or until the meat is tender. Arrange croutons on top. Sprinkle with cheeses and parsley. Return casserole to the oven and bake uncovered for about 5 minutes. Makes 4 servings.

Effortless Five-Hour Stew

2 lbs lean stewing beef
1 cup chopped celery
6 carrots, cut in 1" pieces
2 (8 oz) cans tomato sauce
1 1/2 tsps salt

12 small white boiling onions
2 potatoes, cut in eighths
1 slice white bread, cubed
1 cup water
1/8 tsp pepper

Cut beef into bite-size pieces. Combine all ingredients in casserole; cover and bake at 250° for 5 hours.

Substitutions: A large onion cut in wedges may be used. More celery and carrots may be added. 3 tblsps tapioca may be substituted for bread cubes. Red wine may be substituted for water.

Oven Stew

2 1/2 lbs lean boneless beef, cut into 3/4" to 1" cubes
12 small white onions or chunks of regular onions
4 large carrots, 1" slices or even thinner
3 large ribs celery, 1" slices or even thinner
1 1/2 cups canned, chopped tomatoes
1/2 cup red wine
2 tblsps sauce flour

2 tblsps water
2 small bay leaves
1 tsp dried basil
Pepper to taste
1 medium size potato, partially cooked (optional)
Frozen peas (optional)

Preheat oven to 300°. Mix all ingredients in a heavy 3-quart oven-proof pan. Cover and bake, stirring 3 times, for 3 hours or until meat is tender and the sauce is thickened. Partially cooked potato may be added in the last hour; frozen peas in the last 20 minutes. Remove bay leaf before serving. May be prepared ahead; is better the second day.

Oven Beef Stew

2 heaping tblsps tapioca
1 can beef bouillon
2 lbs cubed beef
2 stalks celery, cubed
6 to 7 carrots, cubed
2 onions, diced

1 can stewed tomatoes
4 to 5 potatoes, cubed
2 tsps salt
1 can green beans
1 tblsp brown sugar

Mix tapioca with bouillon. Mix everything else together with it and put in a large roaster. Tightly cover the roaster. Bake at 325° for 3 1/2 hours. Do not open the roaster until ready to serve. Serves 6.

Harvest Beef Stew

2 lbs boneless beef, cut into 1" cubes
3 tblsps oil
2 1/2 tsps salt
1/4 tsp pepper
1/4 tsp thyme
1 tsp paprika
2 bay leaves

1/2 cup chopped onion
1 (1 lb 13 oz) can tomatoes, or 6 medium fresh
2 carrots, cut into 1/2" pieces
1 green pepper, cut into 1/2" strips
1/2 lb green beans, cut into 1" pieces
3 small zucchini, cut into 1/2" pieces

Brown beef cubes in the oil. Pour off drippings. Add salt, pepper, thyme, paprika, bay leaves, onion and tomatoes. Cover tightly and simmer for 1 hour. Add carrots, cover and cook for 30 minutes. Add green pepper, green beans and zucchini and continue to cook another 30 minutes. Thicken cooking liquid for gravy, if desired.

Rib Stew with Dumplings

2 lbs short ribs
1/4 cup flour
1 tblsp salt
1/4 tsp pepper
2 tblsps fat
2 (1 lb) cans tomatoes, chopped

1/2 clove garlic, peeled and minced
1 tblsp Worcestershire sauce
4 carrots, scraped and sliced
2 medium onions, peeled and sliced
1 potato, pared and sliced
Parsley dumplings

Use ribs that are in serving pieces. Combine flour, salt and pepper. Dredge meat on all sides. Brown meat in hot fat in Dutch oven or heavy kettle. Combine tomatoes, garlic and Worcestershire sauce. Pour over meat. Cover kettle and simmer 1 1/2 hours. Add vegetables, cover and simmer 45 minutes longer or until meat and vegetables are done. Skim fat off top. Taste for seasoning. Add salt and pepper.

Parsley dumplings: Use the recipe for dumplings on the Bisquick® box, halving the recipe, and adding 1/4 cup finely chopped parsley. Should make 6 dumplings. Do not lift the lid while the dumplings are cooking. Mix gently with the stew. Makes 4 to 6 servings.

Bar-B-Q I

5 lbs ground chuck
1 envelope dried onion soup
1 cup sugar
1/2 cup cider vinegar
2 tblsps mustard

4 tblsps Worcestershire sauce
2 tsps salt
1/4 tsp pepper
1/4 cup dried parsley flakes
1 (14 oz) bottle of catsup

Sauté ground beef. Drain off fat. Add other ingredients and simmer for 1/2 hour or until flavors blend.

Barbecue II

3 medium onions
1 stalk celery
2 tsp fat
1 cup catsup
1/4 cup Worcestershire sauce

2 cups water
1 tsp vinegar
1 tsp sugar
1 tsp salt
1 can corned beef, chopped

Brown onions and celery in fat. Add the rest of the ingredients. Cook over low heat until thick. Serve on buns.

Meat Loaf

1 lb ground beef (preferably lean)
1/2 cup uncooked oatmeal (quick or regular)
1/2 tsp salt

1 (8 oz) can tomato sauce
1 egg, beaten

Topping

1 tblsp vinegar
1 tblsp prepared mustard

1 1/2 tblsps brown sugar
Remaining 1/2 can tomato sauce

In bowl, mix ground beef, oatmeal, salt and half the can of tomato sauce. Shape into loaf, place in loaf pan and pat down. Mix topping well and pour over meat loaf. Bake 1 hour in 350° oven.

Special Meat Loaf

3 lbs ground lean chuck
1 cup oatmeal (uncooked)
4 tblsps Worcestershire sauce
1 (8 oz) can tomato sauce
1 tsp onion powder

1 tsp garlic powder
1 tsp salt
1/2 tsp black pepper
2 eggs
1/2 cup catsup for top (if desired)

   Mix all ingredients except catsup thoroughly. Shape into 2 equal sized loaves. Use pan with rack covered with foil. Pierce foil with fork so grease can grain away. Place the loaves on foil-covered rack and bake in 350° oven for 1 hour or until done. Catsup may be spread over top before baking if desired. Makes 8 to 12 servings.

Meat Loaf Supreme (Microwave)

1 1/2 lbs lean ground beef
1 (12 oz) roll Jimmy Dean® sausage (hot or sage-seasoned)
1 cup Stove Top® seasoned cornbread stuffing
1 tsp minced garlic

1 medium chopped onion
1 or 2 ribs chopped celery
2 beaten eggs
Pepper and pinch of thyme

   Mix well, put in microwave-safe ring mold, or use an inverted custard cup or whiskey glass in the center of a 2-quart casserole. Cook on high 16 to 18 minutes, or medium 25 minutes. Let stand 5 minutes to finish cooking.

Porcupine Meat Balls

1 1/2 lbs ground beef
1/3 cup uncooked rice
1 medium onion, chopped
1 egg
1 1/2 tsps salt

1/8 tsp of pepper
4 tblsps milk
1 can cream of mushroom soup
2 cups water

   Combine all ingredients except soup and water. Mix well. Form into small balls, drop into heated mixture of soup and water. Simmer, covered, for 1 1/2 hours. Add water if needed.
   Note: **Do Not Brown Meatballs.** The recipe may be doubled and golden mushroom soup may be added. Freezes very well. Gravy may be served over potatoes or cooked rice.

Baked Barbecue Meat Balls

3 lbs hamburger
1 1/2 cups dry oatmeal
6 tblsps chopped onion

1 1/2 tblsps pepper
1 tblsp salt
2 cups milk

Mix and shape into balls the size of tennis balls. Bake about 3/4 hour on a cookie sheet at 350°.

Sauce

1 large bottle catsup
3/4 cup water
3 tblsps Worcestershire sauce

3 tblsps vinegar
3 tblsps sugar

Put meat balls in a casserole. Mix sauce and pour over meat balls. Bake at 350° for 1 hour or until oil comes to the top. Spoon oil off. Serve either cold or hot. Freezes well. Makes 24.

Meat Balls in Gingersnap Sauce

1 lb ground beef
1 egg
3/4 cup soft bread crumbs
1/4 cup water
1/4 cup finely chopped onion
1/2 tsp salt
Dash pepper

1 1/2 cups water
2 beef bouillon cubes
1/3 cup brown sugar
1/4 cup dark seedless raisins
2 1/2 tblsp lemon juice
1/2 cup coarse gingersnap crumbs

Combine meat with next 6 ingredients; shape in 1" balls (makes about 25). In large, heavy skillet, bring 1 1/2 cups water to boiling. Stir in bouillon cubes, sugar, raisins, lemon juice, and crumbs. Add meat balls, cook uncovered over low heat 10 minutes. Turn meat balls, spooning sauce over. Cook 10 minutes longer, stirring occasionally. Makes 5 or 6 servings.

Enchilada Pie

1 lb ground beef
1 large onion, chopped
2 (8 oz) cans tomato sauce
1/2 tsp chili powder
1 can chopped ripe olives (save a few whole olives)
1 small can creamed corn
Salt and pepper

1 large can red chili sauce
12 plain tortillas
8 ozs jack cheese, grated
8 ozs cheddar cheese, grated
3 hard cooked eggs, cooled and grated
Extra tomato sauce if pie is reheated
Whole ripe olives

Brown beef and onion 5 minutes. Add tomato sauce, chili powder, olives, corn and cook slowly 30 minutes. Add salt and pepper to taste. Cool. Put a small amount of chili sauce in the bottom of a large pan. Cover bottom. Dip six (6) tortillas in the unused sauce and place evenly over the bottom of the large pan. Cover with 1/2 of cooked meat sauce. Grate jack cheese over this. Add the remaining six (6) tortillas, dipped in sauce. Add the rest of the meat sauce. Top with grated cheddar cheese and grated eggs. Dot with whole olives. Bake 1 hour at 350°. If reheating, add more tomato sauce.

Tamale Pie

1 lb ground beef
1 large onion, chopped
1/4 cup olive oil
2 eggs, well beaten
1 quart solid tomatoes (canned or fresh)
1 (2 lb) can creamed corn
1 cup milk

1 green pepper, chopped
1 clove garlic, chopped
1 scant cup yellow corn meal
1 can ripe olives
1/4 tsp chili powder
Salt and pepper

Simmer ground beef and onion in olive oil. Add to mixture of eggs, tomatoes, corn, milk, green pepper and garlic. Add corn meal and mix well. Add olives, salt, and pepper. Add chili powder and mix. Bake 45 minutes at 400° until done.

Hamburger Pie

1 lb hamburger
1 can French style green beans, drained
1 small can tomato sauce

1 pkg crescent rolls
1 egg
1 half moon cheddar cheese, grated

Cook hamburger, drain and cool. Add the beans and tomato sauce to the meat. Mix well. Push rolls together and roll out to make a pie crust. Fit into a 9" pie pan. Beat the egg and a little cheese together and place on top of pie crust. Add the meat mixture and top with cheese. Bake, covered, for 45 minutes at 350°. Remove cover and brown (about 5 minutes). Ground turkey may be substituted for hamburger.

Savory Chuck Roast

1 slab of chuck roast (any size)
1 pkg onion soup mix

Heavy duty foil

Put the roast on a square of heavy duty foil large enough to cover the roast completely. Sprinkle onion soup mix over the meat. Cover the meat completely with the foil and roast in a 350° oven until it is tender.

Savory Oven Pot Roast

3 lbs beef, bottom round or rump
Salt, pepper, pinch of nutmeg
2 tblsps flour
1 tblsp oil
4 large onions, sliced
1 clove garlic, crushed
2 cups hot beef bouillon

2 tblsps tomato paste
1 tblsp sugar
1 tblsp vinegar
1 tsp thyme
4 sprigs parsley, 2 celery tops, 1 bay leaf (tied together in a bouquet)

Dust beef with combination of seasonings and flour. Heat oil in heavy oven-proof pan; brown meat, then remove. Brown onions and garlic lightly in pan. Replace meat; add remaining ingredients. Cover, bake at 350° until meat is tender (about 2 1/2 hours). Discard herb bouquet. Serve with pan gravy. Makes 10 servings.

Pot Roast

1 tblsp vegetable oil
3 lbs beef rump roast
2 bouillon cubes with 1 cup water
1 or 2 large onions, peeled
2 to 4 large carrots, cleaned

2 to 4 potatoes quartered
1/4 tsp ground thyme (or 2 sprigs of fresh)
1/4 tsp basil
Salt and pepper to taste

Put the oil into a large, heavy pot and heat. When hot, add the roast and turn the meat until all surfaces are brown. Add the bouillon cubes and water, onions, carrots, potatoes, herbs and seasoning. Stir to blend the flavors. Cover the pot and place in a preheated 350° oven. Cook about 1 hour covered and 1/2 hour uncovered until the meat is 160°, or medium well done. Remove meat and vegetables from the liquid but cover the vegetables to keep them warm. Allow the meat to "set" awhile before carving.

Make gravy from the liquid, using a favorite gravy making method and Wondra® flour which guarantees "lumpless" gravy. Red wine may be used to replace part of the water. Vegetables such as turnips, celery, peas or green beans may be added. Leftovers are very good.

Teriyaki Pot Roast

2 tblsps flour
1 1/2 tsps salt
1/8 tsp pepper
1/2 tsp curry powder
3 to 4 lbs beef armor blade roast

1/4 cup water
1/4 cup honey
1/4 cup soy sauce
2 tblsps chopped candied ginger or 1/4 tsp ground ginger
1/4 cup flour

Combine flour, salt and pepper and curry powder. Dredge meat in mixture and brown in a large skillet. Add water, honey, soy sauce, and ginger. Cover tightly and cook slowly 3 to 3 1/2 hours or until tender. Add water to cooking liquid to make 2 cups. Thicken with 1/4 cup flour to make gravy.

Sauerbraten with Gingersnap Gravy

3 to 3 1/2 lbs beef round or rump cut in one piece
Salt and pepper
4 bay leaves
1/2 tsp pepper corns
8 whole cloves
2 medium onions, sliced

1 carrot, sliced
1 rib celery, slice
1 1/2 cups red wine vinegar
2 1/2 cups water
Butter or margarine

Rub meat with salt and pepper. Place in a crock with all the spices and vegetables. Heat the vinegar and water to a boil and pour while hot over the meat. Cool. Cover crock and refrigerate. Let marinate about 48 hours, turning the meat twice a day. Remove meat from marinade and pat dry. Brown in butter or margarine in a Dutch oven. Strain the marinade and pour over the meat. Cover and simmer 3 hours until fork-tender. Serve with Gingersnap gravy.

Gingersnap Gravy

2 tblsps sugar
1 1/2 cups marinade
1/2 cup water

2/3 cup gingersnap crumbs
1/2 cup sour cream (optional)

Stir sugar into hot marinade and water. Add gingersnap crumbs and stir until mixture thickens. If desired, add sour cream but do not let mixture boil. Serve over meat or in a gravy boat.

Saucy Oven Steak

1 1/2 lbs round steak, cut 3/4" thick
1/4 cup whole wheat flour
1/2 tsp salt
1 tblsp salad oil
2 tblsps prepared horseradish or to taste

2 tsps honey
1 can cream of mushroom soup
1 small can evaporated milk
1 can mushroom stems and pieces

Trim fat from steak and cut into serving-size pieces. Dredge with flour and salt and brown meat in oil over medium heat. Remove from skillet and arrange in 2-quart baking dish. Spread steak with horseradish and honey. Add remaining flour to skillet and add remaining ingredients. Cook, stirring, until bubbly. Pour over meat. Bake covered in 325° oven for 1 1/2 hours or until fork-tender. Makes 4 to 6 servings. Serve with mashed potatoes, rice or noodles.

Swiss Steak with Mozzarella Cheese

4 lbs round steak, 1/2" thick
3/4 cup flour
5 tblsps shortening
1 tblsp salt
1/4 tsp pepper
1/2 tsp dried savory

2 cups water
1 cup chopped celery
1 cup chopped green pepper
2 (1 lb) cans tomatoes
1/2 lb mozzarella cheese, sliced thin

Cut steak in serving pieces, coat with 1/2 cup flour. Heat shortening in large skillet and brown steak. Remove and place in shallow baking pan. Add remaining flour, salt, pepper and savory to meat drippings. Stir until smooth. Add water, celery, green pepper and tomatoes to skillet. Cook until mixture is thick. Pour over steak. Bake, uncovered in 325° oven 2 to 3 hours or until tender. Top with cheese slices and continue to bake until cheese melts (about 3 minutes). Makes 8 servings

Pigs in Blankets

2 lbs round steak (thin)
Bacon
Onion, sliced
Salt and pepper
Toothpicks
Fat for browning

1/2 cup tomato juice
3/4 cup water
Beef bouillon cube
2 tblsps corn starch
2 tblsps water

Cut round steak into 4" squares. Lay a 3" slice of bacon and a slice of onion on top of each square. Salt and pepper. Roll up the squares and secure with toothpicks. Brown the rolls in a skillet, adding any leftover onion which has been chopped, tomato juice, water and bouillon cube. Cook over low heat or in the oven 1 1/2 hours. Combine corn starch and water, and add to the gravy to thicken.

Editor's note: Mixtures thickened with flour or corn starch need to be cooked for 2 extra minutes.

Beef Stroganoff

1 1/2 lbs round steak
1/4 cup flour
Dash of pepper
1/4 cup butter or margarine
1 (4 oz) can mushrooms, drained

1/2 cup chopped onion
1 clove garlic, chopped
1 can beef broth
1 cup sour cream
Egg noodles

Cut steak into thin strips. Dust with flour and pepper. In a large skillet, melt the butter, brown the meat. Add sliced mushrooms, onion and garlic. Brown lightly. Stir in beef broth. Cover and cook until meat is tender (about 1 hour). Stir occasionally. When meat is tender, add the sour cream, cook for 5 minutes. Serve over cooked egg noodles.

Poor Man's Stroganoff

1 lb extra lean ground beef
1 medium onion, chopped
1 clove garlic, minced
Salt and pepper to taste

1 can cream of chicken soup
1 (4 oz) can sliced mushrooms with juice
1 (8 oz) carton sour cream
Noodles or mashed potatoes

Brown meat; crumble while browning. Add onion, garlic, salt, pepper. Sauté until onion is limp. Add soup and mushrooms. Blend well, cover and simmer 20 minutes. Add sour cream, heat. Serve over noodles or mashed potatoes.

Beef Parmesan

1 to 2 lbs round steak, cut 1/2" thick, trimmed and cut into serving pieces
3/4 cup flour, divided
5 tblsps shortening
1 tblsp salt
1/2 tsp pepper

1/2 tsp dried savory
2 cups water
1 cup celery, chopped
1 cup green pepper, chopped
2 (1 lb) cans tomatoes
1/2 lb mozzarella cheese, sliced thinly

Coat meat with 1/2 cup flour. Heat shortening in skillet and brown steak. Remove and place in shallow baking pan. Add remaining flour, salt, pepper and savory to meat drippings. Stir until mixture is smooth. Add water, celery, green pepper and tomatoes to skillet. Cook, stirring until mixture is thickened. Pour over steak.
Bake, uncovered, 325° for 2 1/2 hours. Top steak with cheese slices and continue to bake until cheese melts. Makes 4 servings.

Beef Chop Suey

1 1/2 lbs beef strips (1 1/2" long), or 1 1/2 lbs ground beef
1 cup celery, sliced
3/4 cup green pepper, diced
1 medium onion, cut in small wedges
1/2 cup mushrooms, sliced
2 tblsps butter, melted

2 tblsps soy sauce
2 cups water
2 tblsps corn starch
3/4 tsp salt
Dash black pepper
2 cups cabbage, shredded

Brown the beef, celery, green pepper, onion and mushrooms in the melted butter in a large skillet. Stir the soy sauce, water, corn starch, salt and pepper into meat mixture and cook, stirring frequently, until thickened. Add cabbage and cook over low heat until vegetables are tender, covered, about 10 minutes. Serve with hot cooked rice and additional soy sauce, if desired.

Beef Sukiyaki

2 tsps butter
1 small onion, halved and sliced 1/4" thick
1 lb sirloin, filet mignon or lean ribeye
1 tblsp sugar
1/2 cup soy sauce
1/2 cup mushrooms, in 1/4" slices

1 cup bamboo shoots, in 1/4" slices
1 cup celery, in 1/4" slices
1/2 pkg bean threads (optional)
1/2 block firm tofu, cubed
1 cup green onions, cut slices 1 1/2"

Slice meat on the diagonal into 1/4" slices. Then cut any longer slices so they measure no more than 2" long. Slice vegetables as indicated above. Soak bean threads in hot water for about 30 minutes.

Heat a large cast iron pan or a wok and add the butter. Add a few slices of onion, stirring to prevent burning. When transparent, remove from the pan. Add the meat and stir until it is nearly cooked. Cover with sugar and soy sauce, and bring to a boil without stirring.

Push meat to the side of the pan and add vegetables, except green onions, keeping them neatly grouped in the pan. Add bean threads and simmer. When bean threads are transparent, add the tofu. Add green onions last. Cover and simmer for a few minutes.

Chicken may be substituted for the beef; or use more tofu for a vegetarian meal. Makes 6 servings.

Stir-Fry Beef

1 lb beef sirloin
1/2 cup celery
1 cup carrots
1 cup onion, sliced
1/4 cup oil
1 (8 oz) can tomato sauce
1/4 cup soy sauce

1 tsp sugar
1 tsp ginger
1/4 cup corn starch
1 cup green pepper, chopped
1 cup fresh mushrooms, sliced
Water chestnuts, if desired
Cooked rice

Cut sirloin into 2" strips. Cut celery and carrots diagonally and green pepper into strips. Slice onion and separate into rings. Heat oil in wok or large frying pan. Stir fry beef quickly and push aside. Add celery, carrots and onion, stir fry until crisp-tender. Mix tomato sauce, soy sauce, sugar, ginger and corn starch and add to pan. Push beef back into the vegetable mixture and continue stirring. Lower heat and add green pepper and mushrooms. Continue to cook until glossy. Serve over rice. Chicken may be substituted. Water chestnuts, sliced, may be added.

Southern Wet Hash

1 cup leftover beef, cut in small cubes
1 or 2 onions, cut fine
2 tblsps butter or margarine
2 cups boiling water

1 cup raw potatoes, cut in small cubes
1 green pepper, cut fine
Salt and pepper

Brown beef and onions together in butter. Add boiling water and potatoes and green pepper. Salt and pepper to taste. Cover and cook slowly until all ingredients are tender. A little sauce flour may be added gradually until thickened as desired. If so, cook for 2 more minutes to cook the flour. Serve on toast. Many Southerners prefer serving with soft grits.

Editor's note: This should be a wet hash, so it may be necessary to add a little hot water during the cooking. An economical dish may be made by substituting 1 1/2 cups ground beef, instead of the leftover beef.

Lasagna

3/4 cup minced onion
1 clove garlic, minced
1 tsp oil
1 lb ground beef
1 (6 oz) can tomato paste
1 (#2 1/2) can tomatoes
1/4 tsp pepper

2 tsps salt
1/4 tsp basil
1/2 tsp oregano
1/2 lb lasagna noodles
1/2 lb mozzarella cheese
3/4 lb ricotta cheese
1/2 cup grated Romano cheese

Sauté onion and garlic in oil until tender. Add the beef and brown. Add tomato paste, tomatoes, pepper, salt, basil and oregano. Simmer for 1 hour.

Cook lasagna noodles in boiling water until tender. Drain. In a deep casserole, put a layer of meat sauce (about 1 cup). Sprinkle with grated Romano cheese. Add a layer of noodles. Add a layer of mozzarella cheese. Add a layer of ricotta cheese. Repeat layers until all ingredients have been used. Bake in a 350° oven for 30 to 40 minutes. Remove from the oven and let sit for 20 minutes.

Editor's note: Lasagna is often cooked in a large shallow casserole. In this case, the dish is cut into squares with a sharp knife and placed on plates.

Sloppy Joes

1 1/2 lbs ground beef
1 tsp salt
Small amount of onion (optional)
2 tblsps brown sugar

2 tblsps mustard
2 tblsps Worcestershire sauce
1/2 cup catsup
Few drops of liquid smoke (optional)

Brown beef and salt (onions if desired). Add the rest of the ingredients. Simmer a few minutes before serving. Serve on hamburger buns.

Chili Con Carne

3 lbs lean beef cut into 1/2" to 3/4" cubes
4 onions, chopped
1 tblsp minced garlic (or to taste)
1/2 cup Wesson Oil®
4 qts hot water
1 large can tomatoes

1 tblsp all spice, powered
2 tblsps salt
3 tblsps paprika
3 tblsps chili powder (or to taste)
2 cans red kidney beans, drained

Brown beef, onions and garlic in oil. Add water, tomatoes and seasonings. Simmer 4 hours, stirring occasionally. Add kidney beans. Simmer 20 minutes Makes about 10 servings.

Unstuffed Peppers

1 lb lean ground beef
1 medium onion, diced
4 large green bell peppers
1 large chili pepper, cut in small pieces (optional)
1 stalk celery, chopped fine, or 1/2 tsp celery seed

1/2 tsp garlic powder
1 (15 oz) can tomato sauce
1 can tomato soup
2/3 cup Minute® Rice (uncooked)

In Dutch oven, brown ground beef. Drain and add onion. While mixture is simmering, remove stem and seeds from peppers. Cut into large chunks (1 1/2" to 2"). Add pepper and all other ingredients to pan. Cover and cook for 30 to 40 minutes or until peppers are tender. This is even better the next day.

Syrian Stuffed Zucchini

1 lb extra lean ground beef
1 (10 oz) can diced tomatoes
1/4 cup uncooked rice (not instant)
1/2 cup water
1/4 cup finely chopped onion
1 1/4 tsps dill weed, divided

1 tsp salt, optional
1/4 tsp mint flakes, crushed
Dash of black pepper
6 medium size zucchini
1 (15 oz) can tomato sauce

In large skillet, brown beef, stirring to crumble. Drain. Add tomatoes, rice, water, onion, half the dill weed, salt, mint, and black pepper. Bring to boil.

Cover and reduce heat to simmer until rice is tender, 15 to 20 minutes, stirring occasionally.

Preheat oven to 350°.

Trim off ends of zucchini, cut thin lengthwise slice from top of each zucchini and hollow out to leave 1/4" shells. Fill shells with tomato-beef mixture. Place in shallow casserole. Combine tomato sauce with remaining dill weed. Pour over zucchini. Bake covered, until tender, 40 to 45 minutes.

Tallarene

1 medium onion, chopped
2 heaping tblsps butter
1 lb ground round steak
1 can tomato sauce
1 cup water

2 heaping cups uncooked noodles
Salt to taste
1 can whole kernel corn
1 can mushrooms
1 cup sharp cheese, grated

Chop and fry onion in butter until brown, Add meat, stir and cook until brown. Add tomato sauce and water. Add noodles; stir and cook noodles until they are tender. More water may have to be added to keep mixture moist. Salt to taste. Add corn and mushrooms. Pour into large buttered casserole. Sprinkle with cheese. Cook 45 minutes at 350°. Let stand in oven with heat off about 15 minutes before serving. Can be prepared the day before and baked when needed.

Homemade Salami

2 lbs ground round
1/8 tsp black pepper
1/4 tsp garlic powder
1/4 tsp onion powder
1 tsp liquid smoke
1/2 tsp dry mustard (powdered)

2 tblsps Morton® Tender Quick Salt
3/4 to 1 cup of water or dry red wine
1/2 tsp ground cumin
1 tblsp brown sugar
1 tsp chili powder

Mix thoroughly. Roll in 1 1/2-inch diameter size. Wrap in aluminum foil. Refrigerate for 24 hours. Bake on rack in a 325° oven for 90 minutes. Put 1/4" water in pan under rack. Cut slits in underside of foil to allow meat to steam. Slice to serve. Keeps well frozen for future use.

Medley of Meats

Chicken Coating

1 large Shake 'N Bake®
1 large Cheese-It® Crackers
1 tsp salt

1/2 tsp pepper
1 tsp onion salt
1/2 tsp garlic powder

Run crackers through food processor until fine, mix in Shake 'N Bake®; add salt, pepper, onion salt and garlic powder.

Chicken for Late Arrivals

2 sticks of butter or margarine
4 chicken breasts

1 1/2 cups bread crumbs
3/4 cup Parmesan cheese

Roll chicken in butter, then in the crumb mixture which has been mixed with the cheese. Put in a baking dish in a single layer. Put the residue of the butter over the top of the chicken. Bake at 350° for 1 1/2 hours if necessary to hold, turn oven to warm. It will keep up to 3 hours.

Fried Chicken with Sherry or White Wine

6 boned chicken breasts (or 2 breasts, 2 thighs and two drumsticks)
Flour for dredging
4 to 6 tblsps vegetable oil
Salt to taste

1/2 tsp rosemary
1/4 tsp thyme
1/2 cup chicken bouillon (more if necessary)
1/4 cup dry sherry

Dry chicken with paper towels. Dredge with flour and brown in hot vegetable oil (use a heavy skillet). Crush rosemary and thyme with fingers. Sprinkle chicken with salt and herbs. Add bouillon. Cover and cook on top of the stove, using simmer heat and adding more liquid if necessary. Requires about 1 1/2 hours. After 1 hour test for doneness. Add 1/4 cup dry sherry or dry white wine and continue simmering for 10 minutes.
Note: It may be baked in oven at 350° (covered) until done. Can be prepared the day before and re-heated.

Chicken Cacciatore

1 large chicken, cut up
2 tblsps butter or margarine
2 tblsps olive oil
1/2 lb mushrooms, sliced
1 medium onion, chopped
2 green peppers, seeded and chopped
2 cloves garlic, minced
1/2 cup white wine, or 1 cup chicken broth

1/2 cup water
1 can tomato paste
1 1/2 tsps salt
1/4 tsp each marjoram, oregano, thyme
1 tsp chicken base or chicken bouillon cube
2 tblsps minced parsley
Spaghetti or rice

Pat chicken dry. Heat margarine and olive oil in a 12" fry pan, over medium heat. Put in chicken and brown on all sides. Remove from pan, and set aside. Add mushrooms, onion, peppers and garlic to the pan juices and sauté until onions are soft. Stir in wine, water, tomato paste, salt, marjoram, oregano, thyme, stock base and parsley. Mix well. Return chicken to pan. Bring to boil, cover and simmer until meat is tender. Serve with spaghetti or rice.

Chicken Sauté

4 to 5 large pieces chicken
2 tblsps flour
1/2 cup margarine
3/4 cup sauterne
1/2 tsp rosemary, thyme or basil or Italian seasoning

1/4 cup chopped onions
1 cup sliced mushrooms
2 tblsps finely chopped parsley
1 cup sour cream (optional)

Dust chicken pieces with flour. Heat 1/3 cup margarine until bubbly in skillet. Add chicken and brown on all sides turning frequently. Add wine and spices, turn heat to low, cover tightly and cook 12 to 20 minutes. Meanwhile, sauté onions and mushrooms in remaining margarine until soft and add sour cream if desired. Add to chicken, cover and continue cooking until tender 10 to 15 minutes. Sprinkle with parsley.

Chicken Maria

Butter
4 ozs shredded ham
5 whole chicken breasts, boned, skinned and halved
10 slices lean bacon

1/2 cup sour cream
1 cup undiluted mushroom soup
1 cup sliced, fresh mushrooms

Butter a 13" x 9" baking dish lightly and sprinkle shredded ham over bottom. Wrap chicken half with a slice of bacon. (Do not use picks.) Place over ham. Combine sour cream and soup. Pour over chicken. Sprinkle with fresh mushrooms.
Cover lightly with foil. Place in 350° oven. Bake 1 1/2 hours. <u>Uncover</u> and bake additional 1/2 hour. Serves 10.

Sesame Chicken

Toast 4 tblsps sesame seeds in heavy hot skillet (takes 90 seconds).

4 tblsps sesame seeds, toasted
1 tblsp oil
1/2 tblsp sherry, if desired
4 tblsps soy sauce

4 tblsps lemon or lime juice
2 cloves of minced garlic
2 lbs of skinned chicken parts

Mix first 6 items well. Marinate chicken parts 1 hour in mix. Broil 5" to 8" from broiler, for 7 minutes.

Yorkshire Chicken

1 1/3 cups all–purpose flour, divided
1 1/2 tsps salt, divided
1 tsp poultry seasoning
1/4 tsp pepper
1 broiler–fryer, about 3 pounds, cut up

1/2 cup butter or margarine, divided
1 tsp baking powder
3 large eggs
1 1/2 cups milk

Mix 1/3 cup flour, 1 tsp salt, the poultry seasoning and pepper. Coat chicken pieces with the mixture and brown on all sides in 1/4 cup butter in large skillet. Arrange chicken pieces in 13" x 9" pan and bake in preheated 350° oven for 30 minutes. Remove chicken and make gravy in pan, using drippings. Pour off into saucepan. Put chicken back in pan.
In electric mixer, beat together remaining flour, 1/2 tsp salt, baking powder, eggs and milk. Add remaining butter, melted, and beat until smooth. Pour over chicken and bake 45 minutes. Reheat gravy and serve with the chicken. Makes 4 servings.
Note: Gravy may be omitted if preferred.

Gourmet Chicken

1 envelope dry onion soup
4 skinless, boneless chicken breasts
2 cans mushroom soup

1 can dry vermouth
1 small can mushroom pieces

Spread onion soup on bottom of large baking dish. Put chicken breasts on top. Mix mushroom soup, dry Vermouth and mushrooms and spread on top of chicken. Bake covered at 325° for 25 minutes. Uncover and continue to bake for another 25 minutes.

Chicken Diable

1/4 cup butter
1/2 cup honey
1/4 cup prepared mustard

1 tsp curry powder
1 tsp salt
1 broiler-fryer chicken, cut-up

Melt butter in a shallow baking pan and stir in honey, mustard, curry powder and salt. Roll chicken in this mixture. Arrange chicken, skin side up in a single layer in the pan. Bake uncovered at 350° oven for 1 hour or until tender. Serves 2.

Land O' Pleasant Livin' Chicken

1 lb crab meat
1 (7 oz) jar Old English® cheese spread
1 (4 oz) jar Kraft® Cheez Whiz
4 tblsps mayonnaise

1 tblsp garlic salt
1 tsp Baltimore Spice Old Bay Seafood Seasoning
8 chicken breasts, boned
1 (8 oz) bottle of spent beer (no fizz)

Mix together first 6 ingredients to make the stuffing. Cut pockets in chicken breasts by cutting from the edge where the bone was toward the outside, but not all the way through. Open up to enlarge the cavity. Do the same on the opposite side. Fill with a generous handful of stuffing, fold chicken over the stuffing and skewer in place. Put in roasting pan and pour beer over all. Sprinkle with salt and pepper and bake at 375°, 45 minutes to an hour, or until chicken is tender and the beer has evaporated. Also may be placed in crock pot for about 5 to 6 hours.

Chicken with Mushrooms and Spinach

3 to 4 garlic buds, chopped
4 boneless, skinless, chicken breasts
Flour to coat chicken
3 tblsps olive oil
1/2 lb sliced mushrooms

1 cup dry white wine
1 lb tomatoes, peeled, seeded and chopped
2 cups packed, fresh spinach leaves
2 tsps fresh rosemary or 1 tsp dried
3 tblsps unsalted butter or margarine

Slowly cook garlic in 1 tblsp olive oil until tender, but not brown. Remove from pan and set aside.

Using meat mallet or rolling pin, pound chicken between sheets of plastic wrap to 1/2" thickness. Coat chicken with flour, shake off excess.

Heat remaining 2 tblsps olive oil in skillet over medium heat. Add chicken and sauté until cooked through, about 3 minutes per side. Transfer chicken to plate; tent with foil to keep warm.

Add mushrooms to skillet and sauté 4 minutes. Add wine to skillet and boil until liquid is reduced to one half, about 4 minutes. Add tomatoes, spinach, rosemary, garlic, and sauté until spinach wilts, about 3 minutes. Add butter and mix until melted. Spoon mixture over chicken.

Chicken Mozzarella

5 or more boneless, skinned chicken breasts
1 egg, beaten
1 cup Italian style bread crumbs

1/2 stick margarine
1/2 cup chicken broth
8 ozs shredded mozzarella cheese

Dip chicken breasts in egg and coat with bread crumbs. Melt margarine in skillet and brown the coated breasts. When browned, place in 9" x 13" pan. Pour broth over the chicken, top with cheese, cover with foil and bake at 350° for 20 minutes. Remove foil and bake another 15 minutes. Serve.

Perky Picnic Chicken

1 egg
2 tblsps milk
1 (1 1/2 oz) envelope French's® Spaghetti Sauce mix
1/4 cup flour

2 tblsps grated Parmesan cheese
Frying chicken, cut up
Oil

Combine egg and milk in shallow bowl, mix lightly. In a separate bowl, combine spaghetti, sauce mix, flour and cheese; mix well. Dip chicken pieces in egg mixture and then spaghetti sauce mixture. Fry in hot oil in large skillet for about 20 minutes, turning to brown evenly. Cover. Cook for 20 to 30 minutes longer or until tender. Chill and serve cold.

Szechuan Style Chicken

1/4 cup vegetable oil
3 cloves minced garlic
2 chicken breasts, boned and skinned, cut into strips
2 tblsps soy sauce
2 tblsps dry sherry
1 tsp sugar

1 tsp corn starch
3/4 tsp ground ginger
1/2 tsp hot pepper sauce
2 cups julienned carrots
1 (8 oz) pkg frozen peas
Cooked rice

Heat oil in a wok or large skillet. Add garlic and sauté (for about a minute). Add chicken strips and sauté until meat turns white. Combine soy sauce, sherry, sugar, corn starch, ginger and hot pepper sauce. Add to skillet with carrots. Stir fry 3-4 minutes. Add peas and stir fry 2 more minutes. Serve with cooked rice and add more hot sauce, if desired.

Mexican Chicken

1 (10 oz) pkg tortilla chips
4 chicken breasts (cooked, skinned, boned and broken into pieces)
1 (10 3/4 oz) can cream of mushroom soup
1 (7 oz) can whole Ortega® chilies (mashed)
3 cups sour cream

6 green onion tops, chopped (use onion part also, if desired)
1/2 cup milk
Garlic salt and seasoned salt to taste
1/4 lb jack cheese (grated)
1/4 lb cheddar cheese (grated)

Place tortilla chips in the bottom of a 9" x 13" baking dish or pan. Break up a little. Mix together all other ingredients except cheese. Pour mixture over chips, sprinkle on cheeses. Bake in 350° oven for 30 minutes.
(For extra heat, salsa or Japaleño pepper may be added to taste.)

Fast Kung Pao Chicken

1/4 cup canned chicken broth
1/4 cup soy sauce
1/4 cup dry sherry
1 tblsp cornstarch
1 garlic clove, minced
1/2 tsp bottled chili sauce

1 whole boneless chicken breast, skinned and cut into 1/4" thick strips
1 tblsp cornstarch

2 tblsps peanut oil or vegetable oil
4 to 5 dried hot red chilies, seeded for less heat or crushed for more heat
2 garlic cloves, minced
6 to 7 green onions, cut into 3" pieces
1/2 cup snow peas
1 (8 oz) can water chestnuts, drained
1/2 cup dry-roasted unsalted peanuts
Freshly cooked rice

Blend first six ingredients in a bowl. Set sauce aside.

Mix chicken with 1 tblsp cornstarch until well coated. Heat oil in wok or heavy large skillet over high heat. Add chilies and 2 minced garlic cloves and cook until aromatic, about 30 seconds. Add chicken and cook until browned, stirring frequently, 1 to 2 minutes. Remove chicken using slotted spoon. Add green onions and snow peas and stir fry 1 minute. Add chicken and water chestnuts and stir fry 30 seconds Mix in peanuts. Stir sauce and add to wok, stirring until thickened. Serve immediately with rice. Makes 2 to 4 servings.

Swiss Chicken & Stuffing

4 whole chicken breasts, skinned, boned and split
8 slices Swiss cheese
1 can creamed chicken soup

1/4 cup water
1/2 cup margarine
2 cups Stove Top® Dressing

Place one slice of Swiss cheese on each breast. Dilute soup with water and pour over chicken. Melt margarine and mix with dressing. Sprinkle over breasts. Bake at 325° for 1 1/2 hours, uncovered.

Chicken Casserole

1 can cream of chicken soup
1 can milk
1 (10 oz) package frozen peas and carrots
1/2 cup processed American cheese

2 cups diced, cooked, chicken or turkey
3 cups cooked rice
2 tsps pimiento, chopped and drained

Bring soup and milk to a boil, stirring constantly. Add peas and carrots. Stir until mixture comes to a boil. Add cheese and stir until melted.

Mix rice and pimiento thoroughly and pour over chicken. Heat in a 350° oven until heated through, about 40 to 50 minutes.

Chicken—Wild Rice Casserole

1 (6 oz) box each long grain and wild rice mix (Uncle Ben's®)
1 (10 1/2 oz) can cream of celery soup
1 (10 1/2 oz) can cream of mushroom soup

2 (6 oz) cans evaporated milk
1 envelope dry onion soup mix
1 (2 to 3 lb) chicken, cut up

Combine rice (both packs), soups, milk and dry onion soup mix. Pour into 3-quart casserole. Lay cut-up chicken on top. Bake, covered, 1 1/2 hours at 350°.

Silver Spoon Wings

1/2 cup sugar
1/2 cup water
1/2 cup dark soy sauce
1/4 cup pineapple juice

2 tblsps vegetable oil
1 tsp grated fresh ginger
1/2 tsp garlic powder
2 to 3 lb chicken wings, cut at the joints, tips discarded.

Combine sugar, water, soy sauce, pineapple juice, oil, ginger and garlic powder. Stir until sugar is dissolved. Pour over chicken wings in bowl small enough so that all are covered. Cover and refrigerate. Marinate at least one day (two is preferable), stirring occasionally. Preheat oven to 350°. Lift wings from marinade and place on cookie sheet. Bake 40 minutes or until tender, basting twice with the marinade. Makes 6 to 8 servings.

One Dish Dinner

8 chicken thighs or whole chicken, cut up
Water
1 lb package mixed frozen vegetables
Salt and pepper

2 1/2 cups Bisquick®
1/8 tsp poultry seasoning
3/4 cup milk or enough to make a stiff dough

Put chicken in a Dutch oven and cover with water. Cover pot and bring to a boil. Boil 10 minutes. Add the frozen vegetables, salt and pepper. Bring to a boil. Mix Bisquick® with poultry seasoning and milk. Drop by spoonfuls on top of chicken. Cook uncovered for 10 minutes. Cover and lower the heat. Cook for about 20 minutes, or until chicken is done. Serve chicken and dumplings covered with vegetables and gravy or juice in the pot. Makes 4 servings.

New England Boiled Dinner

1 cabbage (1 lb)
1 1/4 lbs smoked pork shoulder
6 medium Washington or Idaho potatoes, peeled
6 carrots, trimmed and scraped
2 leeks, trimmed and well washed
4 ribs celery, trimmed and tied
1 onion peeled and stuck with 2 cloves

2 tsps allspice
2 sprigs fresh thyme (or 1 tsp dried)
1 bay leaf
6 peppercorns
4 chicken legs and thighs
Salt to taste

Quarter cabbage and remove core. Combine cabbage, pork, potatoes, carrots, leeks, celery, onion, allspice, thyme, bay leaf, and peppercorns. Cover with water; add salt. Cover and bring to a boil; simmer for 20 minutes. Add chicken and simmer until chicken is done.

Chicken and Rice

2 cups rice (may be part brown rice)
1 can cream of mushroom soup
1 can cream of celery soup
1/2 cup milk
1/2 cup chopped onion

1 cup diced celery
1 (2 1/2 to 3 lb) frying chicken, in parts
Salt
Pepper
Paprika

Sprinkle rice evenly over bottom of 9" x13" baking pan. Heat soups, milk, onion and celery together and pour over rice. Lay chicken parts atop this mixture, and sprinkle with salt and pepper and or paprika, as desired. Cover tightly with foil and bake two hours at 325°. Serves 6 people.

Rice with Chicken

Chicken giblets
2 chickens
3 cloves garlic, crushed
Juice of 1 sour orange
1/3 cup oil
1 large onion, chopped
1 green pepper, chopped
1 can tomato sauce
2 cans red peppers
1 can petits pois
1 can asparagus tips

1 tblsp salt
1/2 tsp pepper
1 bay leaf
Saffron to color
Water
3 1/2 cups dry white wine
2 cups broth
Water, as needed
2 cups rice
Sliced hard boiled eggs

Prepare broth with chicken giblets. Cut chickens into quarters and cover with crushed garlic and sour orange juice and leave to stand for awhile. Heat oil in large skillet and brown chicken. Add chopped onion and green pepper, tomato sauce, 1 can of red peppers and the liquid from both cans of peppers, the liquids from the peas and the asparagus, salt, pepper, bay leaf, saffron, wine and broth.

Wash and soak rice. When chicken is half cooked, add water, if needed to make 2 cups of liquid. Add the rice and allow to cook over low heat until rice is loose and soft. Add the petits pois, and garnish with remaining red peppers, asparagus and hard boiled eggs. Should be soupy. Makes about 8 servings.

Chicken with Apricots

1 1/2 cups flour
Salt and pepper
Ginger
4 pairs chicken breasts
1 1/2 sticks of butter or margarine

3/4 cup water
2 tblsps minced onion
Chicken stock made from cube
2 tblsps cornstarch
1 (16 oz) can apricot halves

In paper bag, mix flour with salt and pepper; add ginger. Shake chicken breast until well-coated, preferably one at a time. Sauté in 1/2 stick of butter at a fairly brisk heat until golden brown. Remove from heat and place in oven proof casserole, big enough so that each lies by itself with no overlapping. Add the water and stick of melted butter. Bake 1/2 hour at 375°, basting frequently.

Sauté onion in the butter in which the chicken was browned. Drain apricots, retaining juice. Measure juice and add enough chicken stock to make two cups. Blend cornstarch with this liquid. Add to the onion and bring to a boil, stirring constantly. Add apricots. Serve over or surrounding the chicken. Makes 4 to 6 servings.

Chicken Tetrazzini

1/2 cup chicken broth
1/2 cup milk
2 cups grated cheese (may use 3 to 4 kinds not too strong cheese, if desired)
6 cups cooked spaghetti (12 ozs uncooked and broken into pieces)

4 cups boned, cooked, chicken breast
1/2 cup canned mushrooms
1/2 cup toasted, slivered almonds (skins on)
Parmesan cheese
Paprika

Blend broth and milk. Heat and then stir in cheese until cheese is melted, stirring constantly. In a separate large bowl, mix cooked spaghetti, chicken, mushrooms and almonds. Pour in heated liquid, and mix well until spaghetti is coated. Turn into greased 9" x 13" casserole. Sprinkle with Parmesan and paprika. Bake at 350° about 30 minutes or until bubbly on top and slightly brown. If it seems gooey, it will dry as it is cooking. Can be prepared in advance and frozen. Defrost before heating. Makes 8 to 10 servings.

Casserole Chiz—Broccoli

6 boned and skinned chicken breasts, cut into pieces
1 (20 oz) pkg broccoli cuts, frozen
1 can cream of mushroom soup
1 can cream of chicken soup

2 cups cheddar cheese, shredded
2 cups herb–seasoned croutons
3 tblsps butter for croutons

Place cut pieces of chicken into a 9" x 13" baking dish. Put broccoli cuts over chicken. Combine soups and spread over chicken and broccoli. Sprinkle cheddar cheese over soups. Sprinkle croutons, tossed with melted butter, on top. Bake uncovered at 350° for 1 hour. Finished when bubbly.

Green Chili Chicken Casserole

1 can cream of chicken soup
1 can diced green chilies
1 (5 oz) can chicken with broth
1 soup can milk

1 dozen corn tortillas
Small amount hot oil
10 ozs longhorn cheese, grated
1 medium onion, diced

Mix chicken soup, chilies, chicken with broth and 1 soup can of milk. Stir well. Cook tortillas in a small amount of hot oil. Drain well. Put small amount of cheese and onion on each tortilla and roll tight. Place in oven proof casserole. Pour chicken mixture over tortillas. Sprinkle remaining cheese over casserole. Bake at 325° for 40 minutes. Let cool 5 to 10 minutes before serving.

Chicken Livers in Wine Sauce

1/2 lb chicken livers
2 slices of bacon, diced
2 tblsps butter
1/2 tsp salt

Pinch black pepper
Pinch ground sage
1/4 cup sherry

Wash, pat dry and cut chicken livers in half. In a skillet, sauté diced bacon until it is lightly browned, then pour off drippings. Add butter and when it is bubbling, add livers. Sauté for 2 minutes; season with salt, pepper and sage. Turning any undone sides over, sauté for 2 more minutes. Stir in wine and scrape bottom of brown bits. Cook another minute and serve. Makes 2 servings.
May be served over toast triangles, noodles, steamed rice or rice pilaf.

Sherry-Marinated Cornish Hens (For the Grill)

1/2 cup soy sauce
1/4 cup sherry
1/4 cup water
1/4 cup honey

2 tblsps minced fresh ginger root
1 clove garlic, minced
2 (1 1/2 lb) Cornish hens, split
Garnishes: onion fans and cherry tomato halves

Combine soy sauce, sherry, water, honey, ginger root and garlic in small bowl. Place hens in shallow dish, pour marinade over hens and cover. Chill 3 hours, turning occasionally. Place on upper rack of grill which should be set on low. Place skin side down first. Cook for a total of 1 hour.

Fantastic Crock Pot Cheese Chicken

4 to 6 chicken breasts
1 pkg Italian Good Seasons® dry salad dressing
2 cans undiluted golden cream of mushroom soup

1 (8 oz) pkg cream cheese
1/2 cup white wine or water
(Sliced water chestnuts and sliced mushrooms, optional)

Layer chicken breasts and dry seasoning in crock pot. Cook 4 hours on high. Mix well mushroom soup, cream cheese and wine. Pour over chicken and cook one more hour. Serve over noodles.

Make—Ahead Turkey Tetrazzini

1/2 (16 oz) package spaghetti
2 cups sliced fresh mushrooms
1/4 cup margarine or butter
3 tblsps flour
2 cups chicken broth
3/4 cup half and half
1 to 3 tblsps sherry, if desired

1/4 cup chopped fresh parsley
1 tsp salt
1/8 tsp nutmeg
Dash of pepper
3 cups cubed, cooked turkey
1 cup grated Parmesan cheese
Chopped fresh parsley, if desired

Cook spaghetti to desired doneness as directed on package. Set aside. In Dutch oven, sauté mushrooms in margarine until tender. Stir in flour. Add chicken broth; cook, stirring constantly until sauce is thickened. Remove from heat; stir in half and half, sherry, parsley, salt, nutmeg and pepper. Toss turkey and cooked spaghetti into sauce. Turn mixture into 13" x 9" pan. Cover and refrigerate overnight. Heat oven to 350° When ready to bake, sprinkle with Parmesan cheese. Bake 45 to 55 minutes or until thoroughly heated. Garnish with parsley before serving, if desired. Makes 8 servings.
Tip: To bake immediately after preparation, bake for 30 to 40 minutes.
Editor's note: Sauce flour for thickening is easier.

Broiled Lamb Chops

Have loin, rib or shoulder chops cut 1" thick. Preheat broiler. Place chops on greased broiler rack about 2" below heat. Broil until brown. Season with salt and pepper. Turn chops with tongs. Brown other side and season. Serve hot. Cook a total of 15 minutes, slightly less for thinner chops.
Editor's note: To maintain the broil, leave the oven door slightly ajar. If the door is closed, the broiler will turn down when temperature reaches "broil."

Braised Lamb Shanks

3 to 4 shanks (3 lbs)
3 to 4 tblsps flour
2 tblsps oil
1 clove garlic
1 tsp dried oregano leaves (Italian seasoning OK)

1/4 tsp pepper
1 cup chicken broth, or 1 chicken bouillon cube in 1 cup water
1 tsp salt (omit salt if using chicken bouillon cube)
1 tblsp lemon juice

Remove excess fat from shanks, coat with flour and brown in hot oil in Dutch oven. Turn to brown on all sides. Add garlic, oregano, pepper, broth or bouillon, salt and lemon juice. Cover and cook over low heat until tender (about 2 hours), or bake in covered pan at 350° for 2 1/2 hours. Serve with broth over rice.

Braised Lamb Shanks with Italian Sauce

2 meaty lamb shanks
1 jar favorite spaghetti sauce
1 clove garlic, chopped (optional)

1 medium onion, chopped
1 cup water
Salt and pepper to taste

Put lamb shanks in a large kettle or Dutch oven. Add garlic and onion to spaghetti sauce. Pour over shanks. Add water.

Take a piece of foil a little larger than the circumference of the kettle. Push down into kettle all the way to the shanks. Cover the kettle closely and put in a 350° oven. Braise. At the end of an hour, open kettle and foil and check for doneness. If it is not done, put the foil and cover back on and braise until done. Put the shanks on a warm platter and pour the sauce over. Serve with cooked rice or noodles. Makes 2 generous servings.

Lamb Shanks with Sour Cream Sauce

6 lamb shanks
Salt and pepper to taste
3 tblsps butter or margarine
1 1/2 cups dry white wine
1/2 cup beef bouillon

1 large onion, chopped
2 tblsps flour
3 tblsps water
3 tblsps fresh dill, chopped, or 1 tblsp dried dill
8 ozs sour cream

Trim excess fat from lamb shanks. Wash and pat dry. Rub meat with salt and pepper. Heat the butter in a frying pan and brown lamb shanks on all sides. Transfer shanks to a deep kettle or Dutch oven and add wine and bouillon. Add onion to the pan drippings and fry until tender. Pour onion and drippings over shanks. Simmer, covered, for about 1 1/2 hours or until tender. Remove shanks to a hot platter. Strain stock and return it to the kettle.

Mix flour and water to a smooth paste and stir it into the stock. Cook until smooth and thickened, stirring constantly. Stir in dill and sour cream. Return lamb shanks to the sauce and heat **but do not boil**. Makes 6 servings.

Editor's note: If dill is not desired, it may be omitted. If there are not enough drippings in the pan to fry the onions, add a little butter or margarine.

Roast Leg of Lamb

1 leg of lamb (any size desired)
Garlic cloves, slivered
Water
Meat thermometer

Gravy
Ice cubes
Chicken broth or water, if necessary
Sauce flour

Place lamb in a roasting pan with skin side up. With a small, sharp knife, make deep slits in the top and insert garlic slivers. Put water in the bottom of the pan, enough to keep the meat from burning. Punch a hole in the roast and insert a meat thermometer into the thickest part of the meat, avoiding the bone. Roast at 350°. At the end of an hour, inspect the roast. If the water is evaporating, add a little more.

For a well-done lamb, roast 30 to 35 minutes per pound OR until the thermometer registers 170°. Remove from the pan.

To make the gravy: Check the liquid in the pan. If there isn't enough, add water or chicken broth to the desired level. Tilt the pan and add several handfuls of ice cubes. The fat will coagulate on the ice cubes. Remove the cubes. The remainder is fat-free. Heat the liquid in the roasting pan on top of the stove. When it is simmering, add sauce flour, little by little, stirring constantly until the desired thickness is reached. Simmer 2 more minutes to cook the flour.

Editor's note: The timing of the roasting naturally depends on the size of the roast. Watch the thermometer.

Moussaka (MOO-sah-kah) (Greek Casserole of Lamb, Eggplant & Tomato)

Oblong baking pan 11" x 16" or equivalent.
2 lbs lean lamb, ground chili-size
Salad oil or margarine
2 medium onions, finely chopped
2 large cloves garlic, crushed or chopped
2 tsps Lawry's® Seasoned Salt
1 tsp Lawry's® Seasoned Pepper
1 1/2 tsps thyme

1 1/2 tsps basil
2 large cans tomatoes, sliced or cut up, well drained
2 large eggplants, about 1 lb each
Flour
4 to 6 zucchini, cut in circles (1 quart)
1/2 lb pork sausage links, browned and cut in circles
3/4 lb mozzarella cheese, shredded
1/2 cup grated Parmesan

2 cups béchamel sauce: Make a cream sauce using part chicken broth, rich milk, 2 egg yolks, 2 tblsps Parmesan and a good pinch of nutmeg. (See The Ditty Bag for additional white or béchamel recipe.)

Brown lamb, using a small amount of salad oil or margarine. Add onions, garlic, salt, pepper, thyme, basil, and tomatoes. Bring to boil. Cover and simmer about 15 minutes. Set aside.

Slice unpeeled eggplant about 1/2" thick, crosswise. Spread on cookie sheets, salt both sides, and let stand about 30 minutes. Drain well; dust with flour; and bake on oiled cookie sheets at 400° about 5 minutes, each side. Drain on paper towels; cool; cut pieces in half.

Steam zucchini about 5 minutes, drain and cool. Make béchamel sauce in double boiler.

To assemble: Oil baking pan lightly and layer ingredients, starting with eggplant then meat sauce, zucchini, sausage and mozzarella. Repeat. Top with béchamel sauce and sprinkle with Parmesan.

Bake at 350° about 45 minutes, longer if taken from refrigerator. Makes 8 generous servings.

Editor's note: The French classic béchamel is complicated and uses ground veal. Béchamel may be a simple cream sauce with minced onion. This béchamel is in-between and contains no flour. The egg yolks must be beaten well, and a little of the hot liquid should be mixed into the yolks before adding to the liquid. **Do not overcook or it will curdle.**

Lamb Stew with Vegetables

1 1/2 lbs boneless lamb shoulder
3 tblsps flour
2 tblsps salad oil
2 onions, peeled and diced
2 cups hot water

1 tsp salt
1/4 tsp pepper
3/4 tsp marjoram
6 carrots, scraped and quartered
6 small potatoes, pared and halved

Cut lamb in serving pieces. Dredge meat evenly in flour. Heat oil in Dutch oven or heavy kettle. Brown meat well on all sides. Add onions during last 5 minutes of browning. Stir to mix well. Add water, salt, pepper and marjoram. Add vegetables. Reduce heat. Cover kettle. Continue cooking about 30 minutes or until vegetables are done. Makes 4 servings.

Lamb Curry

3 tblsps butter or margarine
1/2 cup chopped onions
1 small tart apple, peeled, cored and diced into 1" chunks
1 clove garlic, crushed
1 cup chicken broth

1/2 cup raisins
Curry powder to taste
2 cups leftover cooked lamb, ground or diced small
Sauce flour

Melt the butter. Add the onions, apple and garlic. Cook until onions and apples are tender. Add broth and raisins. Add curry powder. Add lamb. Shake in a little sauce flour, stirring constantly until mixture is slightly thickened. Serve over hot rice. Serves 2.

Editor's note: This is a simple, easy-to-prepare dish. Purists contend that curry powder should be lightly sizzled in a little butter to take away the raw taste.

Leftover Roast Lamb with Oregano

1 bouillon cube
1 cup water

1/2 tsp oregano

Melt bouillon cube in water; add oregano. When steaming, lay in slices of lamb. Cover and heat until steaming hot. Makes hot sandwiches or may be served with vegetables.

Leftover Roast Lamb with Currant Jelly

2/3 cup currant jelly
1/2 cup prepared mustard

6 thick slices leftover roast lamb

Heat jelly in wide saucepan or frying pan over low heat. Mix and stir until jelly is melted. Lay lamb slices in mixture and turn heat low. Cover pan and let heat only until lamb is hot. Makes good hot lamb sandwiches.

Veal Cutlets Parmigiano

3 veal cutlets
1 egg, beaten
1/4 cup flour
1/4 cup Parmesan cheese

Salt and pepper
Olive oil
2 buds garlic
Cooked spaghetti

Pound the cutlets rather thin. Beat the egg and dip the cutlets in it and then in the flour mixed with grated cheese. More cheese and flour may be necessary for more than 3 cutlets. Slice the garlic buds in the oil. Heat the oil and remove the garlic if desired. Brown the cutlets and then cook slowly until well done, about 15 minutes. Remove the cutlets to a hot serving dish. Add 2 or 3 tblsps of hot water to the pan they cooked in, let boil up and pour over the meat. Chopped parsley may be added to the sauce. Serve cutlets and sauce with spaghetti.

Editor's note: It would probably be desirable to pour off most of the oil in the pan before adding the water for the sauce. More generally, cutlets are moved to the hot platter, ignoring the sauce.

Veal Scaloppini

1 lb very thin veal cutlets
1/2 cup flour
4 tblsps butter
1/2 cup Marsala wine or sherry

1 tsp salt
Quick grind black pepper
1 lemon, thinly sliced

Place veal between 2 or 3 thicknesses of wax paper and pound with a wooden mallet or edge of a heavy plate until it is very thin. Cut veal into 4 pieces. Roll lightly in flour. Heat heavy skillet. Melt butter. Brown cutlets quickly, but thoroughly on both sides, using a pancake turner to turn. Add wine, cover pan. Simmer over low heat for about 5 minutes or until meat is tender. Season with salt and pepper. Serve at once on a hot platter garnished with lemon slices. Makes 4 servings.

Have all vegetables and other foods ready to serve as soon as the meat is done. It should be eaten a few minutes after it is cooked.

Editor's note: In this simple dish, butter is essential for the flavor.

Veal Marsala

4 veal cutlets
Flour
Salt and pepper
4 tblsps butter or margarine

1/2 lb fresh mushrooms, sliced
1/2 cup dry Marsala wine
1/2 cup beef broth
3 tblsps fresh parsley, chopped

Dredge veal with flour, seasoned with salt and pepper. Sauté in butter until lightly browned on both sides. Remove to a heated platter. This part can be done ahead of time by covering meat to keep it from getting dry and placing it in oven on warm.

Add the mushrooms to the same skillet that the meat was cooked in. Sauté until tender. Add wine and broth, and cook for a few minutes over high heat. Pour contents of pan over veal and garnish with parsley. Makes 2 to 4 servings.

Veal Stew

2 lbs lean, boneless veal, cubed
Salt, pepper, and nutmeg
Flour
1 tblsp salad oil
3 tblsps butter or margarine

1 cup dry white wine
2 tblsps fresh lemon juice
1/3 cup heavy cream
1 egg yolk, beaten

Sprinkle veal with salt, seasonings and flour. Heat oil and butter in a large skillet. Brown veal, a few cubes at a time. Remove from pan and when all are browned, return to the pan and add wine, lemon juice and cream. Bring to a boil, reduce heat, cover and simmer for 1 hour. Stir a small amount of the mixture in the egg yolk and then back into the stew. Serve with noodles. Makes 4 servings.

Quick Veal Parmesan

Prepare frozen breaded veal cutlets as instructed on box. Place heated cutlets in large pan. Place slices of Mozzarella cheese on top of cutlets. Pour tomato sauce over all (Prego is good). Bake at 400° for 15 minutes.

French Veal Stew (Blanquette de Veau)

2 lbs stewing veal
1 large onion, peeled and studded with 2 whole cloves
1/4 cup carrots, scraped and chopped
1 bay leaf
1/2 tsp dried thyme
4 peppercorns
Salt to taste
1 quart boiling water
12 small onions, peeled

5 tblsps butter or margarine
1/4 cup sauce flour
3 cups veal stock
Juice of 1/2 lemon
2 egg yolks, slightly beaten
1 (6 oz) can sliced mushrooms
2 tblsps finely cut parsley
Cooked onions
Hot cooked rice

Cut veal in 2" pieces. Combine veal with onion, carrots, bay leaf, herb, peppercorns, and salt in a large kettle. Add boiling water and return to a boil. Reduce heat and simmer 1 hour or until meat is tender.

Cook small onions in 2 tblsps butter or margarine over low heat in a covered heavy sauce pan or skillet 20 to 30 minutes until tender. Drain veal. Measure 3 cups stock. In a separate pan, melt remaining 3 tblsps of butter. Stir in flour, blend smoothly. Strain 3 cups stock and add to butter and flour. Cook, stirring constantly over moderate heat until mixture boils and thickens. Stir lemon juice and egg yolks into a little of the thickened sauce. Stir into rest of sauce. Add to the veal in the kettle, and add mushrooms and parsley. Stir all together and reheat just to the boiling point. Serve on a hot platter with mounds of cooked onions. Serve a bowl of hot cooked rice. Makes 6 servings.

Editor's note: This is not an every day dish, but distinctly elegant and gala. It proves what the French can do with a piece of stew meat. Veal is more common and cheaper in Europe.

Calf's Liver and Onions I

3 tblsps oil
2 1/2 to 3 cups sliced onions
Salt
4 slices calf's liver, 3/8" thick (about 1 lb)

Freshly ground pepper
Flour for dredging
1/4 cup chicken broth

Heat half the oil in a frying pan over moderate heat, put in the onions and salt. Cover and cook until tender. Stir occasionally. Uncover and cook until lightly brown. Remove from pan. Season the liver with salt and pepper. Heat the rest of the oil in the pan. Flour liver lightly and cook 1 minute on each side. Return the onions to the pan, pour in broth and cook rapidly until thickened, about 30 seconds.

Calf's Liver and Onions II

3 tblsps oil
2 slices of liver about 1/2" thick

3 cups chopped onions
Salt and pepper

Heat the oil. Put in the liver slices and just sear on either side. Remove from pan. Add the onions. Cook until tender. Remove onions from pan. Put the liver back in the pan, cover with the onions. Cover the pan, turn the heat to low and simmer until the liver has reached the desired state of doneness. (Some people prefer it slightly rare.)

Editor's note: Beef and pork livers have much stronger tastes, but they are less expensive and some people like them better.

Apricot/Sausage Loaf

2 eggs, beaten
1/2 cup fine dry bread crumbs
1/4 cup sliced green onions
3/4 tsp salt
1 lb pork sausage
1 lb ground veal or hamburger
1 cup water

1/2 cup dried apricots
1/2 cup brown sugar
1/8 tsp ground cloves
1/4 cup water
1 tblsp corn starch

In a bowl, combine eggs, bread crumbs, green onions, and salt to the sausage and veal or hamburger. Mix well. In a shallow baking pan, shape mixture into a loaf and bake 1 1/2 hours at 350°.

Meanwhile in a saucepan, combine 1 cup water, apricots, brown sugar, and cloves. Cover and simmer for 20 minutes.

Combine mixture of 1/4 cup water and cornstarch into apricot sauce and cook until thick and bubbly. Pour over cooked sausage loaf and serve

Baked Ham Slices

2 slices tenderized ham, 1 1/2" thick
Prepared mustard
Peanut butter
2 cups fruit juice (apricot, pineapple or orange)

1 cup sherry
1/2 cup honey
Canned apricots, halved

Spread ham slices with prepared mustard and peanut butter. Put 1 slice on top of the other. Pour fruit juice over ham. Bake 1/2 hour at 325°. Add wine Bake another hour. Place apricot halves on top and cover with honey. Bake 20 minutes longer.

Hot Ham Loaf

1/4 butter or margarine
4 tblsps flour
1 cup milk
1/8 tsp pepper

1/8 tsp nutmeg
2 eggs (slightly beaten)
2 tblsps grated Parmesan cheese
3/4 pound boiled or baked ham (chopped)

Melt butter in saucepan and blend in flour. Add milk, stirring constantly, and cook over low heat, continuing to stir until thickened. Add pepper and nutmeg, no salt. Remove sauce from heat and cool. When cold, add eggs, Parmesan and ham. Mix well. Grease and flour a mold and pour in the mixture. Place mold in a pan with 1 1/2" of water in it and bake in a 350° oven for 1 hour. When done, let pan rest a little while, then remove from mold onto serving dish. Serves 4.

Ham Soufflé

1/2 lb butter or margarine
2 tblsps flour
2 cups milk
2 cups cooked ham, diced fine

2 tblsps Parmesan cheese
3 egg yolks, lightly beaten with fork
3 egg whites, beaten stiff

Melt butter in saucepan, blend in flour until smooth, add milk and cook slowly, stirring constantly until thickened. Remove from fire. Add ham, cheese and egg yolks and fold in egg whites. Grease a 1-quart casserole, pour in soufflé mixture, smooth with knife and bake in moderate oven (350°) for 20 minutes. Serve immediately. Serves 4.

Decorative Baked Ham

1 (10 to 12 lb) precooked ham
Cloves (whole)
Pineapple slices, glacéed

Cherries, glacéed
3 cups sugar
Toothpicks

Bake the ham for about two hours in a 350° oven. Remove any skin on ham. Cool completely. With a very sharp knife, score the fat into squares. Push in one whole clove to each square. Decorate the top of the ham with glacéed pineapple slices, wholes or halves. Use toothpicks to secure the slices, pushing into ham until fruit is secured but picks do not show. Finish with glacéed cherries using the same method. The design is up to you.

In a large frying pan, place sugar. Heat sugar slowly until completely melted but not brown. Stir constantly. It must be clear. Grasping the handle of the pan with both hands, pour the glaze over the outside of the ham, covering the fruit. The ham is cold, so the glaze will set immediately.

Note: Be very careful when dealing with melted sugar. It can cause a severe burn.

Scalloped Ham and Potatoes

Slice of ham, 1 1/2" to 2" thick
1 large onion, chopped
3 cups sliced potatoes

Freshly ground pepper
1 small can evaporated milk
1 cup milk

Freshen the ham by pouring boiling water over it, then drain it. Make a bed of half the onions and half the potatoes in a heavy iron skillet with a tight lid, or a Dutch oven. Sprinkle with pepper. Lay the ham on the vegetables, then cover with the rest of the vegetables and more pepper. Pour the small can of evaporated milk and the cup of milk over the mixture. Cover and simmer about an hour. The sauce should have body and the ham be tender. Taste before adding salt. Lift ham onto a hot plate and pour the sauce over it.

Ham and Cheese Casserole

1 cup finely chopped onions
1 cup chopped celery
2 tblsps butter or margarine
4 cups finely chopped cooked ham
6 eggs, well beaten

3 cups (12 oz) grated sharp cheddar cheese
1 1/3 cups cracker crumbs
3 cups milk
1/4 tsp pepper

Sauté onions and celery in butter until soft. Stir in remaining ingredients. Line two 10" x 6" x 1 1/2" baking pans with heavy duty aluminum foil. Grease foil generously. Divide ham mixture evenly between the two pans. Bake one batch uncovered in 350° oven for 45 to 50 minutes, or until brown and firm in the center. Freeze second batch. When frozen solid, lift from pan. Wrap tightly with heavy duty foil, return to freezer. When ready to bake, replace frozen block in original pan. Bake covered in 400° oven for 1 hour; uncover and bake until brown and firm, 30 minutes. Each batch makes 6 servings.

Ham and Broccoli Casserole, Quick and Easy

1 pkg Betty Crocker® Au Gratin Potatoes
1 (10 oz) pkg frozen chopped broccoli, partially thawed

1 1/2 cups cooked ham, cubed

Prepare potatoes as directed on package. Stir in broccoli and ham. Pour into an ungreased casserole. Bake at 350°, uncovered, 45 to 50 minutes or until golden brown and potatoes are tender.
Note: Make sure all of the potatoes are down in the liquid so they don't dry out.

Glazed Pork Chops and Yams

6 pork chops, 3/4" to 1" thick
3 tblsps sugar
2 tsps flour
1 tsp salt
1/2 cup orange juice

1/2 cup water
2 tblsps lemon juice
2 (17 oz) cans yams, drained
2 oranges, thinly sliced
1 (10 oz) pkg frozen peas

Brown chops and remove from pan. Blend sugar, flour and salt to pan drippings. Stir in orange juice, water and lemon juice. Return chops to pan and simmer until chops are tender (45-50 minutes). Add yams, cover and heat 10 to 15 minutes, or until yams are hot. Garnish with orange slices and cooked, hot peas.

Hong Kong Pork Chops

8 loin pork chops
2 to 3 tsps salad oil
1 medium onion, thinly sliced
1/4 cup low-salt soy sauce
1/4 cup orange juice
2 tblsps lemon juice

1/2 tsp ground ginger (or grated fresh)
1 (4 oz) can sliced mushrooms (undrained)
1/4 tsp garlic powder
1/2 large green pepper, cut in rings
1/2 cup sliced water chestnuts
1 lemon, thinly sliced

Season chops, brown in oil and drain or broil until just lightly browned. Place chops in shallow casserole. Cover with onion slices. Combine soy sauce, orange juice, lemon juice, ginger, mushrooms, and garlic powder. Blend well. Pour over chops. Cover and bake at 350° for 35 minutes. Add green pepper slices, water chestnut slices and lemon slices. Bake uncovered for 15 minutes. Serves 8.

Pork Chop Casserole

4 to 6 pork chops
1 box Uncle Ben's® rice with herb seasoning
1 1/4 cups water

1 small can or jar of mushrooms, drained (optional)
1 can golden mushroom soup
Salt and pepper

Mix all together except chops in large casserole 13" x 9". Place chops on top and sprinkle with salt and pepper. Cover and bake at 350° for 1 hour and 20 minutes.

Sweet & Sour Pork Chops

4 pork chops, 1/2" to 3/4" thick
1 1/2 tsps salt
1/4 cup water
1 chicken bouillon cube
1 cup hot water
1/2 tsp Worcestershire sauce
1 tsp soy sauce
1/3 cup pineapple juice from can of pineapple
1 tblsp vinegar

1/4 tsp prepared mustard
2 tblsps corn starch
2 tblsps cold water
1 (9 oz) can pineapple chunks
1/2 green pepper, sliced in thin strips
1 tomato, cubed
1/2 cup celery, sliced
4 cups hot cooked rice

Brown chops, both sides. Salt. Add 1/4 cup water. Cover and simmer 30 minutes. Remove chops and pour off fat. In skillet, melt bouillon cube in the hot water and add Worcestershire, soy sauce, pineapple juice, vinegar and mustard. Combine corn starch with 2 tblsp water. Stir into skillet mixture and simmer until thick, stirring constantly. Add chops and remaining ingredients except rice, and simmer 5 minutes. Serve over steamed rice. Makes 4 portions.

Stir Fry Pork with Pineapple

1 tblsp peanut oil
1/2 tsp salt
1 lb lean pork, thinly sliced
1/4 cup sliced green peppers
1 cup chunk pineapple; drain and reserve juice
1/4 cup peeled and sliced water chestnuts

1/4 cup sliced sweet pickles (optional)
1 cup chicken broth
2 tblsps corn starch
1 tblsp sugar
2 tsps soy sauce
1/2 cup pineapple juice

Heat peanut oil in large skillet or wok and add salt and pork. Stir fry until pork is brown. Add pepper to pork and stir fry 2 minutes. Combine pineapple, water chestnuts and pickles with pork and pepper and stir fry for 1 minute. Pour chicken broth over pork mixture and boil 1 minute. In a separate bowl, combine the corn starch, sugar, soy sauce and pineapple juice. Add corn starch mixture to pork and stir fry until gravy thickens. Serve over rice.

Editor's note: As with so many Oriental type recipes, if the ingredients are ready in order, on the counter, this recipe may be cooked very quickly.

Chinese Baked Spareribs

3 lbs pork spareribs, cut in serving pieces
1/4 cup prepared mustard
1/4 cup light molasses
1/4 cup soy sauce

3 tblsps cider vinegar
2 tblsps Worcestershire sauce
2 tsps Tabasco® sauce

Place ribs in shallow baking dish. Combine remaining ingredients and pour over ribs. Chill, covered, 3 hours or longer.

Heat oven to 350°. Bake ribs about 1 1/2 hours until tender and done, basting frequently with sauce in pan. Turn ribs once during baking. When brown and crusty, serve at once.

Note: Finger food. Furnish plenty of paper napkins.

Oriental Pork and Rice

1/2 lb boneless pork sirloin, in 1/2" diced pieces
1 tblsp oil
1 cup celery, finely diced
1 medium onion, minced
1 cup carrots (2 large), sliced and peeled

1/2 tsp pepper
3 tblsps soy sauce
1 cup white rice
1/2 cup salted peanuts, coarsely chopped

In heavy 3-quart saucepan, sauté pork in hot oil over high heat 10 minutes until lightly browned, stirring frequently. Add celery, onion, carrots, pepper, soy sauce and 1/4 cup water. Bring to a simmer, cover and cook over low heat 25 minutes, stirring often. Meanwhile cook rice in 2 cups boiling water 15 minutes until tender. Add to pork mixture with the peanuts and toss lightly. Makes 4 large servings.

B—B—Q Pork (For a Group)

6 to 7 lb eye of round pork roast or pork loin (trim bone and fat)
1 bunch celery, chopped
3 large onions, chopped
1 large green pepper, chopped
1 quart bottle catsup
1/4 cup barbecue sauce

1 1/2 to 2 cups water
3 tblsps vinegar
1 tsp Tabasco® sauce
2 tblsps chili powder
2 tblsps salt
1 tsp pepper
3/4 cup molasses

Cut meat into 6 chunks, put in a roaster. Combine all remaining ingredients and pour over the meat. Bake at 300° for 6 hours. When done, using 2 forks, shred the meat apart. Serve on buns.
Note: Works great in a large electric roaster. If baked in oven, cover for the first 3 hours.

Cantonese Sweet—Sour Pork

2 lbs lean pork shoulder
2 tblsps peanut oil
1/4 cup hot water
1 (#2) can pineapple chunks
1/4 cup brown sugar, packed
2 tblsps corn starch

1/4 cup cider vinegar
1 tblsp soy sauce
1/2 tsp salt
1 green pepper, cut in thin strips
1/4 cup onion, peeled and thinly sliced
2 cans chow mein noodles (about 5 cups)

Cut meat into strips about 2" long and 1/2" wide. Brown pork slowly in hot oil. Add water. Cover and simmer about 1 hour until tender.

Drain pineapple. Save syrup. Combine sugar and corn starch in saucepan (not aluminum). Add pineapple syrup, vinegar, soy sauce and salt. Cook, stirring, over low heat until thick and clear. Pour over hot cooked pork. Let stand 10 minutes or longer. Add pineapple, cut into cubes, green pepper and onion. Bring to a boil. Boil 3 minutes stirring occasionally. Serve over chow mein noodles, made crisp in a hot oven. (May not be necessary if noodles are already crispy.)

Note: As with most Oriental type dishes, preparation is important. If the ingredients are readied ahead of time, the cooking is easy.

Pork Chops with Mustard

4 pork chops, 1/2" thick
1 tblsp butter or margarine
1 small onion, chopped
1 tblsp flour
1/2 cup dry white wine

1/2 cup stock or water
1/2 tsp prepared mustard
1 tsp capers
1/2 tsp salt
1/8 tsp pepper

Braise pork chops in skillet with butter, browning nicely about 20 minutes on each side. Remove chops from skillet. Place onion in skillet, brown slowly, blend in flour, add white wine and stock (or water) and boil gently until mixture is slightly thickened. Return chops to skillet and simmer 10 minutes. Add mustard, capers, salt and pepper, mix well and serve.

Tropical BBQ (Microwave and standard oven)

1 1/2 lbs country style pork ribs
1/4 cup undiluted frozen orange juice
1/2 cup shredded coconut
1/2 pkg onion soup mix
1 tblsp minced garlic

1/4 tsp ginger, fresh or powdered
Pinch of pepper and rosemary
1/2 cup white wine
2 tblsps herbed vinegar

Place ribs in an 8" baking dish (glass, not plastic). Add remaining ingredients. Marinate 1 to 2 hours. Cover with plastic wrap. Cook for 20 minutes on high in microwave. Remove plastic. Bake in 350° oven for another 20 minutes. Serves 2.

Spareribs—Mexican Style

3 to 4 lbs meaty spareribs
1 cup catsup
1/3 cup Worcestershire sauce
2 tsps chili powder

1 tsp salt
1/4 Tabasco® sauce
2 cups water

Start oven at hot (450°). Place ribs on shallow roasting pan, meaty side up. Roast 30 minutes. Combine remaining ingredients in a saucepan. Bring to a boil, pour over meat in roasting pan. Lower heat to moderate (325°). Baste ribs with sauce in roasting pan every 15 minutes. (If sauce gets too thick, stir a little hot water into pan.)
Continue roasting about 1 hour or until meat is tender. Total time should be 40 minutes per pound.
Note: Finger food. Furnish plenty of paper napkins.

Pork Loin Casserole

4 pork loins (or pork chops)
Approx 2 tblsps cooking oil
4 potatoes, peeled and sliced
2 large onions, peeled and sliced

2 (10 3/4 oz) cans cream of mushroom soup
2 soup cans water
Salt and pepper

Fry pork in oil until brown. Arrange alternate layers of potatoes and onions in large, greased casserole. Top with pork. Combine soup, water, salt and pepper in bowl or saucepan. Pour soup mixture over all ingredients. Cover and bake at 300° for about an hour. Remove cover and cook another 1/2 hour.

Smoked Pork with Kraut

1 tblsp flour
1 (3 lb) smoked, boneless pork shoulder butt
1 (27 oz) can Libby's sauerkraut, drained
1/4 cups brown sugar, firmly packed

1 medium apple, pared and diced
1/2 to 3/4 tsp caraway seed
1/4 tsp pepper

Place flour in 14" x 20" cooking bag; shake to coat inside. Place pork in bag; close with twist tie. Place bag in 9" x 13" x 2" baking pan. Puncture 6 small slits in top of bag. Bake at 350° for 2 hours. Remove from oven; open bag. Combine remaining ingredients; mix well. Spoon over and around pork. Re-tie bag. Bake for 40 minutes longer.

Toutiere (French-Canadian Pork Pie)

1 lb lean ground pork
1/4 cup chopped onion
1/2 tsp salt
1 clove garlic, minced
Dash pepper
Dash ground cloves and poultry seasoning

1 small bay leaf
1/2 cup boiling water
1/4 cup dry bread crumbs
Pastry for a 2-crust pie
1 egg, beaten

Mix pork, onion, seasonings, bay leaf and water in a saucepan. Simmer, uncovered, for 20 to 30 minutes. Discard bay leaf. Drain meat, stir in bread crumbs and cool.

Line pie pan with pastry. Fill with meat. Cover with pastry, sealing edges. Make slits on top for steam vents. Brush with beaten egg. Bake at 425° for 30 minutes or until golden brown.

Editor's note: May be frozen up to 6 weeks. Bake frozen pie for 25 minutes at 425°. Good hot or cold.

Sausage Stroganoff

1 garlic clove
2 lbs hot sausage
3 tblsps flour
2 cups milk
2 onions, diced

1 cup sliced mushrooms
2 tblsps margarine
2 tsps soy sauce
2 tblsps Worcestershire sauce
2 cups sour cream

Rub a large skillet with garlic clove. In the pan, brown crumbled sausage, cooking it thoroughly. Pour off all grease. Mix sausage with flour, add milk and simmer until slightly thickened. In another pan, sauté onions and mushrooms in margarine. Add soy sauce and Worcestershire sauce. Fold into sausage mixture and cook until it bubbles. Just before serving, add sour cream (do not let it boil) and pile high on biscuits, rice or noodles.

Olive Soufflé Casserole

1/2 lb Spanish or sweet Italian sausage, parboiled and sliced
1 cup sliced onion
1/4 cup olive or salad oil
4 medium potatoes, cooked, peeled and diced

1/2 cup sliced pimiento-stuffed green olives (to taste)
1 (16 oz) can stewed tomatoes
6 egg yolks, beaten
6 egg whites, stiffly beaten

Sauté sausage and onion in 1 tblsp oil in large skillet until lightly browned. Remove to shallow 2 1/2-quart casserole. Heat remaining oil in skillet. Add potatoes. Sauté for 3 minutes. Add olives and tomatoes; mix well. Pour over sausage mixture. Bake at 400° for 15 minutes. Fold egg yolks into whites. Stir potato mixture; pour eggs over top. Bake 17 minutes longer or until eggs test done when wooden pick is inserted into center.

Seafood

*Main entry
foyer to
Education
Center*

Beer Batter for Fish

1 tblsp melted butter
1 cup flour
1/2 tsp salt

1 tsp paprika (or a few dashes or cayenne pepper or a few dashes of Tabasco® sauce)
2/3 can beer
2 eggs

Mix butter, flour, salt, paprika and/or hot pepper/Tabasco® and beer together and put in a warm place for 3 hours. Separate eggs, beat yolks and add to batter. Beat the whites until they form stiff peaks and fold into batter. Dip fish into batter and cook in hot oil (400°) until golden brown.

Fish Batter for Deep Frying

1 cup corn starch
1 cup all-purpose flour
1 tsp baking powder
1 tsp baking soda

1 tsp salt
2 dashes of garlic powder
2 dashes of onion powder

Mix all ingredients well. Coat filet or large pieces of fish in batter, set aside a few minutes. Deep fry a few pieces at a time, turning to brown all over. When done, place on brown bag to absorb drippings. Serve with Pipeline Hush Puppies (see Breakfast, Brunch & Lunch) and coleslaw.

Editor's note: Recipe also good for batter fried vegetables.

Basic Baked Fish

1 onion (medium or large, depending on the size of the fish
1 to 1 1/2 cups white wine, depending on the size of the fish

1 baking size fish

Peel onion and slice thinly. Put wine in the bottom of a roaster large enough to hold the fish. Put the fish in the pot. Top the fish with sliced onions. Cover with the roaster lid and bake at 350°. When the fish flakes when tested with a fork, it is done. Do not overcook.

An old rule of thumb: Cook large fish or thick slices of fish 10 minutes for each inch of thickness at the thickest part of the fish.

Quick and Easy Fried Fish

1/2 lb dressed fish, or 1/3 lb fish fillets per person
Salt for sprinkling
Lemon and pepper seasoning for sprinkling

1 to 2 cups dry pancake mix
Fat or oil for frying

Wash and dry fish. Dip fish into clean, cool water and sprinkle with salt, lemon and pepper seasoning; then coat lightly with pancake mix.

Fry in deep fat at 350° for 4 to 5 minutes or fry in 1 1/2" hot fat in fry pan, 4 to 5 minutes on each side. Fish is done when brown on both sides and flakes easily when tested with a fork. **Be careful not to over cook.**

Remove fish from pan and drain on paper towels. Serve with cocktail or tartar sauce.

Editor's note: If desired, fish may be pan-fried over medium to low heat, in just enough fat or oil to keep from sticking, until done as described above.

Baked Stuffed Fish

1 fish (4 to 5 lbs), dressed
Salt and pepper
1 tblsp lemon juice

Melted fat or oil for basting
2 cups stuffing (your own favorite or packaged, prepared as directed)

Wash and dry fish thoroughly. Sprinkle inside of cavity with salt, pepper and lemon juice. Put in shallow, foil lined baking pan. Stuff cavity of fish loosely with stuffing and secure edges (small skewers are good for this). Baste liberally with fat or oil. Bake at 350°, basting frequently, until fish flakes easily when tested with a fork, 45 to 60 minutes suggested. **Do not over cook.**

Creole Baked Fish

Prepared Creole sauce in a jar, or make your own with canned tomatoes, olive oil, minced onion, minced green pepper, garlic to taste and salt, all put together and simmered until thick.

1 baking size fish

Cover fish in roaster with Creole sauce. Bake at 350° until it flakes when tested with a fork. **Do not over cook.**

Seaside Poached Fish

2 lbs fish fillets
1 medium onion, sliced
2 stalks celery, including tops, cut in strips
2 carrots, cut in strips

2 tsps salt
1/4 tsp pepper
Water, just barely to cover

Put fish in single layer in wide shallow pan (such as large fry pan). Add vegetables and seasonings. Add water to just barely cover. Bring to a boil, cover and simmer slowly, just until fish flakes easily when tested with a fork, 5 to 10 minutes. **Do not over cook.** Remove fish from pan and use as desired. Makes 6 servings as an entree. Makes almost 4 cups cut-up fish for use in a salad.

Fish Salad Supreme

2 lbs poached fish
2 tblsps finely chopped onion
2 tblsps finely chopped green pepper
1/2 cup salad oil
1/4 cup wine vinegar

1/8 tsp garlic powder
1/4 tsp oregano
2 tsps parsley flakes (or fresh parsley, minced)
Salt and pepper to taste
1/4 cup sour cream

Cut fish into very small pieces. Put in a bowl and add all other ingredients except sour cream. Toss gently. Refrigerate until thoroughly chilled. Just before serving, stir in sour cream. Makes 4 cups salad.

Tuna Fish Casserole I

3 tblsps margarine
2 tblsps flour
1/2 tsp salt
1/8 tsp pepper
1 cup milk

1 (7 oz) can white tuna fish
1/2 cup chopped walnuts
1 tblsp margarine
1 cup soft bread crumbs

Melt margarine, add flour and salt; cook until smooth. Add milk slowly and cook, stirring constantly, until thickened.

Blend 1 tblsp margarine with soft bread crumbs. Mix tuna and walnuts into cream sauce and put in a 9" pie plate. Sprinkle with crumbs. Bake in a 275° oven for 15 minutes until crumbs are browned. Makes 4 servings.

Tuna Casserole II

1 can grated tuna (about 7 oz)
1/4 cup lemon juice
1 onion, chopped
1 can cream of mushroom soup

1 cup milk
1/8 tsp pepper
3 cups crushed potato chips

Put tuna in bowl and pour lemon juice over it. Sauté onion, add mushroom soup, milk and pepper. Heat until warm and mixed. Add to bowl along with chips. Mix. Bake uncovered 350° for 25 minutes. Freezes well (reheat with lid). Makes 5 to 6 servings.

Tuna Fish Casserole III, Overnight (Microwave Oven)

1 (10 3/4 oz) can condensed cream of celery soup
1 cup milk
1 (6 1/2 oz) can water-packed tuna, drained and flaked with a fork

1 cup uncooked elbow macaroni
1 cup frozen green peas
1 cup coarsely shredded cheddar cheese (reserve 1/4 cup)

Whisk soup and milk in a 2-quart microwave safe bowl until well blended. Stir in remaining ingredients except reserved 1/4 cup cheese. Cover and refrigerate at least 12 hours or overnight.

Cover with lid or vented plastic wrap. Microwave on high 15 to 17 minutes or until bubbly. Sprinkle with reserved cheese. Let stand uncovered 5 to 7 minutes until cheese melts. Makes 4 to 6 servings.

Tuna Turnover

Pastry for single-crust 9" pie
2 tblsps soft butter or margarine
1 (6 1/2 oz) can chunk-style tuna, well drained
1/3 cup thinly sliced green onion
1/3 cup thinly sliced celery
1/3 cup sour cream

1/3 cup chopped dry roasted peanuts
1 tsp lemon juice
1/2 tsp dill weed
1 red or green bell pepper, seeded and cut in rings
Dill pickle slices

Prepare pastry and roll out dough on a lightly floured board into a 12" circle. Spread evenly with soft butter or margarine. Combine tuna, green onion, celery, sour cream, peanuts, lemon juice and dill; spread over half the dough to about 1" from edge. Fold unfilled half over top and crimp edges with the tines of a fork to seal in filling. Transfer to an ungreased baking sheet; slash top in 2 or 3 places. Bake in a 425° oven for about 20 minutes or until golden brown. Garnish with pepper rings and dill pickles. Serve at once. Makes 2 to 3 servings.

Tuna Macaroni Casserole

2 tblsps chopped celery
1/4 cup chopped onion
2 tblsps chopped green pepper
1 tblsp oil or water
1 tblsp flour
1/2 tsp salt
1/4 tsp pepper
1 cup skim milk

1/2 cup no-fat cheese, cubed
1 cup cooked elbow macaroni
2 fresh tomatoes, chopped
1 (6 1/2 oz) can water packed tuna, drained
2 tblsps chopped fresh parsley
1 tblsp lemon juice
Paprika

Preheat oven to 375°. Sauté celery, onion and green pepper in oil or water until tender. Stir in flour, salt and pepper until smooth. Gradually stir in milk. Cook, stirring constantly, until thickened. Add cheese and stir until melted. Add macaroni, tomatoes, tuna, parsley and lemon juice. Pour into casserole and sprinkle paprika over top. Bake 30 to 35 minutes.

Imperial Crab

1 lb backfin lump crab meat
1 green pepper, chopped
1 tblsp butter
3 tblsps thick cream sauce
1 tblsp Worcestershire sauce

1 small jar pimientos, chopped
1 tsp salt
1/4 tsp dry mustard
Mayonnaise

Cook crab meat and green pepper in butter for one minute. Cool.
Add thick cream sauce, Worcestershire sauce, pimientos, salt and dry mustard. Fill cleaned crab shells or ramekins. Cover lightly with mayonnaise. Bake in moderate 350° oven until brown. Makes 4 servings.
Editor's note: For cream sauce, see The Ditty Bag.

Crab Fritters

1/4 cup instant minced onion
1/4 cup water
12 ozs crab meat
1 large egg, beaten
2 tblsps dried parsley

1 1/2 tsps dry mustard
1/4 tsp pepper
1/2 cup dry bread crumbs
Oil for frying
Cucumber slices

Mix onion and water and let stand 10 minutes. Add all ingredients to onion. Shape into 1" balls, about 4 dozen. Heat 2" oil to 375° and fry a few at a time, about 1 minute. Drain. Serve with cucumber slices.

Soft Shell Crabs I

Soft shell crabs
Flour

Butter
Tartar sauce

Place the required number of crabs on their backs. Remove the aprons and clean the crabs. Rinse and pat dry. Place about 3 tblsps butter or margarine in a frying pan. More may be used if desired. Dust the crabs lightly with flour on both sides. Place in the pan and cook over moderate heat until done. The length of time will depend on the size of the crabs. Serve with tartar sauce.
Tartar sauce: Mix 1 cup mayonnaise with 1/4 cup of chopped sweet pickle relish or 1/4 cup chopped dill pickles.

Soft Shell Crabs II

8 to 12 medium to large cleaned soft shell crabs

Marinade

Mix the following in a bowl:

1/2 cup virgin olive oil
Juice of 1 fresh lemon
1/4 cup lemon juice
1 medium clove garlic, chopped
2 to 3 tblsps Baltimore Spice Old Bay Seasoning

2 to 3 sprigs fresh rosemary
1/4 cup fresh chopped parsley
Dash of Worcestershire sauce
Dash of Tabasco® sauce

Rinse and pat crabs dry. Arrange crabs in rows, bottom down in a non-reactive pan. Cover with mixed marinade for 1 hour. Marinade should almost cover tops of crabs. Turn crabs over after 1/2 hour, if there is not enough liquid to cover.

When charcoal is ready, arrange crabs, bottom down over grill. Cook 5 to 7 minutes on each side, turning with spatula. Continue to brush crabs with marinade if they appear dry. Cooking time will vary based on size of crabs and temperature of charcoal. Color will change to deep red and shell should be slightly crispy when done.

Crab Rice Casserole

1/4 lb butter
1 cup onion, chopped
1 bell green pepper, chopped
1 small garlic pod, minced
2 stalks of celery, chopped
1 can cream of mushroom soup

1/4 cup pimiento, chopped
3 parsley sprigs
2 cups crab meat
3 cups cooked rice
1 cup bread crumbs
4 tblsps butter

Sauté in butter onion, bell pepper, garlic and celery until wilted. Add mushroom soup, pimiento, parsley sprigs and crab meat. Cook 5 minutes; add cooked rice, seasoned to taste. Pour into 2-quart casserole dish. Sprinkle with bread crumbs and dot with the butter. Bake 1/2 hour at 375°, covered. Then uncover and bake for 5 minutes more. Makes 6 servings.

Maryland Crab Cakes

1 lb backfin lump crab meat
2 slices day old bread
1 scant tsp salt
1/2 tsp pepper
1/2 tsp prepared mustard

2 sprigs parsley
1 egg
3 tblsps Hellmann's® mayonnaise
Butter

Make sure all shell has been removed from crab meat. Break up slices of bread very finely. Stir together all ingredients in one large bowl. Make into 10 medium patties. Cover and chill in refrigerator for about 3 hours to improve the flavor. Fry in pan with butter 1/8" deep.

Editor's note: Claw meat will make very good cakes. Be sure to pick over carefully.

Shrimp Tempura

1 cup flour
1/4 tsp salt
1 tsp ajinomoto (optional)
1 egg, lightly beaten

3/4 cup milk
1 lb shrimp, cleaned and deveined, with tails on
Peanut oil for deep frying

Sauce

1/2 cup chili sauce

1 1/2 tsps Worcestershire sauce

Sift together the dry ingredients into a bowl. Add the egg and milk, making a medium-thick batter.

Heat about 2" of oil to 375°. Dip shrimp in batter and drop into the oil, holding by the tail with tongs. Cook until golden. Drain on paper towels. Mix together the remaining ingredients and use as a dipping sauce. Makes 6 servings.

Editor's note: For vegetable tempura, use assorted vegetable slices about 1/4" thick on the diagonal. Suggestions include mushrooms, carrots and yams. Leave string beans whole. Slice green bell peppers into strips.

Shrimp Supreme

3 tblsps margarine
1 small onion, chopped fine
3 tblsps green pepper, chopped fine
1 bud garlic, chopped
1 can cream of mushroom soup (not golden mushroom soup)
1 cup tomato juice
1 tsp prepared mustard

1 tsp Worcestershire sauce
1 tsp salt (optional)
Dash of Tabasco® or cayenne pepper
Dash of vinegar
1 bay leaf
1 tsp lemon juice
1 1/2 cups grated sharp cheese
1 lb cleaned shrimp, fresh or frozen

In a large skillet, lightly brown onion, green pepper and garlic in the margarine. Set aside.

In a separate pan, combine all ingredients from soup through bay leaf. Combine with first mixture in the skillet. Add lemon juice, cheese and shrimp. Simmer and stir constantly until cheese is melted. If too thick, add more tomato juice. Simmer until all ingredients are done. Remove the bay leaf. Serve over steamed rice. This dish will keep for several days if kept well chilled.

Editor's note: Sauce without the shrimp may be used on chicken, vegetables, toast or as a dip.

Shrimp or Crayfish Fettucine

3 sticks butter
3 medium to large onions, chopped
3 medium green bell peppers, chopped
3 stalks celery, chopped
4 cloves garlic
4 tblsps dried parsley

3 lbs crayfish tails or shrimp, shelled
1/4 cup flour
1 pint half and half
1 lb (3 rolls) Kraft® Jalapeño Pepper Cheese
1 lb flat regular egg noodles
Grated American and Parmesan cheese, or mozzarella cheese

Melt butter; sauté onions, bell peppers and celery. Add garlic, parsley and crayfish (or shrimp). Cook 10 minutes. After 10 minutes, add flour, half and half and Jalapeño cheese. After this has cooked, simmer 25 to 30 minutes. Cook noodles and mix together. Put into casserole dish (3-quart dish, or can be divided into smaller casserole dishes) and top with grated cheeses. Bake at 350° for 20 minutes. Makes 20 average servings.

Shrimp De Jonghe

1 large clove of garlic, mashed
1 cup butter or margarine, softened
1/4 tsp dried tarragon
1/4 tsp dried marjoram

3 cups fine dry bread crumbs
Juice of 1 lemon
2 lbs cooked shrimp, peeled and deveined
Chopped parsley

Combine garlic, butter, tarragon and marjoram; cream until blended well. Add bread crumbs and lemon juice; mix well. Alternate layers of shrimp and bread crumb mixture in buttered baking dish or 6 to 8 ramekins, sprinkling parsley over each layer. Bake at 375° for 20 minutes or until heated through. Serve immediately.

Shrimp Elegant

1 chicken bouillon cube
1 1/2 cups of water
1 tblsp Worcestershire sauce
1/2 cup green onions and stems, chopped
2 tblsps corn starch

1 1/2 lbs large shrimp
1 (7 oz) pkg snow peas
2 cups fresh tomatoes, quartered
Rice with parsley

Dissolve bouillon cube in boiling water. Add Worcestershire sauce and green onions plus stems. Cool 5 minutes. Add corn starch and stir until sauce begins to thicken. Add shrimp and cook until pink (**don't over cook**). Add snow peas and tomatoes. Heat thoroughly. Serve over parsley rice.
Editor's note: For variety, add scallops and almonds.

Shrimp Salad

1/4 cup raw white rice, washed
1 cup (3/4 lb) canned or cooked shrimp
3/4 tsp salt
1 tblsp lemon juice
1 tblsp chopped scallions
2 tblsps French dressing

1 tblsp chopped stuffed olives
1/4 cup slivered green pepper
3/4 cup diced raw cauliflower
Speck of pepper
1/3 cup mayonnaise
1/2 small head lettuce, finely shredded

Cook rice in 2 1/2 cups boiling water until tender, 15 to 20 minutes. Drain and chill. Clean shrimp and cut in 1/2" pieces. Combine with remaining ingredients. Serve on lettuce. Makes 4 servings.

Seafood Casserole

1 cup chopped celery
1/2 cup chopped green pepper
2 cups chopped sweet onion
2 tblsps margarine
12 ozs chopped pimientos
1 can cream of celery soup
1 (8 oz) pkg cream cheese

1/2 cup milk
1 cup cooked rice
4 1/2 ozs canned shrimp
4 1/2 ozs canned white crab meat (backfin lump)
Crushed Ritz crackers
Melted margarine

Sauté celery, pepper and onion in margarine. Add pimentos, soup, cream cheese and milk. Heat slowly. Add rice, shrimp and crab meat. Pour into 10" x 13" pan and bake 30 minutes at 350°. Cover with crackers and drizzle with margarine. Bake 10 minutes longer.

Hawaiian Seafood Stir Fry

4 tblsps soy sauce
2 tblsps corn starch
1/2 lb medium shrimp
1/2 lb scallops
1 can pineapple chunks, reserve juice

1/2 can chicken broth
2 tblsps vegetable oil
1 green pepper, chopped
1 small onion, chopped
1 tblsp minced fresh ginger or 1 tsp dry

Combine 1 tblsp soy sauce and 1 tblsp corn starch; add shrimp and scallops and mix well. Drain pineapple; to juice add broth, 3 tblsp soy sauce and 1 tblsp corn starch. Heat 1 tblsp oil in heavy skillet and stir fry shrimp and scallops for 2 minutes. Remove. Add to pan 1 tblsp oil, heat, and stir fry pepper, onion and ginger for 3 minutes. Add shrimps, scallops, pineapple and sauce and cook until it boils. Serve with rice.

Clams Casino

12 cherrystone clams in shell
1 to 2 drops Worcestershire sauce for each clam
1 to 2 drops hot sauce for each clam

3 strips partially cooked bacon, cut in quarters
Seasoned bread crumbs for topping

Open shells, letting clam remain on one half. Discard the other half. Arrange clams in shallow baking pan. On each clam, put Worcestershire sauce, hot sauce, 1/4 strip bacon and bread crumbs. Broil 4" from source of heat until edges of clams curl and bacon is done (2 to 3 minutes).

Party Clam Cakes

1 cup sifted flour
1/2 tsp salt
1 tsp baking powder
2 eggs

1/2 cup milk
1 tblsp melted butter
1 can minced clams

Sift dry ingredients. Add unbeaten eggs, milk and butter. Stir well. Add clams and stir. Drop by teaspoonfuls into hot fat at 375°. Cook until golden brown.
Editor's note: Apples, corn or bananas in 1/2 cup amounts may be substituted for the clams.

Fried Soft Clams

4 cups dry pancake mix (any type)
1 qt freshly shucked soft shell clams, drained

Fat or oil for frying
Salt

Put pancake mix in large shallow bowl. Add clams, a few at a time and toss lightly until well coated. Shake off excess breading in wire basket. Fry in deep fat at 375° until golden brown, 1 1/2 to 2 minutes. Drain on paper towels. Repeat process until all clams are cooked. Salt lightly and serve at once with cocktail or tartar sauce.
Editor's note: Equal results may be obtained by frying clams in 1" to 2" hot fat or oil in large fry pan. Keep turning clams until browned. Drain on paper towels.

Quick and Easy Fried Oysters

1 to 2 cups dry pancake mix (any type)
1 pt shucked standard oysters, drained

Fat or oil for frying
Salt

Put pancake mix into large shallow bowl. Add oysters, a few at a time and toss lightly until well-coated. Shake off excess breading in wire basket. Fry in deep fat at 350° until golden brown, 1 1/2 to 2 minutes. Drain on paper towels.

Equal results can be obtained by frying oysters in 1" hot fat or oil in large frying pan. Keep turning oysters until browned. Drain on paper towels. Makes 4 servings.

Oyster Fritters

1 pt shucked standard oysters
1/2 cup evaporated milk
1 cup dry pancake mix (any type)
2 tblsps corn meal

1 tsp salt
1/4 tsp black pepper
3/4 cup oil

Drain oysters, reserving liquid. In a bowl, mix milk, pancake mix, corn meal, salt and pepper. Gently fold in oysters. Batter will be thick. Drop batter into hot oil by tablespoons, making sure to include 2 oysters in each portion. Cook until brown on one side, 1 to 2 minutes. Turn carefully and brown other side. Makes about 18 fritters.

Editor's note: If batter becomes too thick from standing, thin with oyster liquor. If more oil is needed, make sure it is hot before continuing.

Scalloped Oysters

1 qt shucked standard oysters with liquor
2 to 3 cups coarsely crushed fresh crackers
1 stick margarine or butter

1 to 2 cups milk
Salt and pepper as desired

In a greased 2-quart casserole, place alternate layers of oysters and crackers, dotting each layer with margarine or butter and sprinkling with salt and pepper. End with layer of crumbs. Add milk until liquid almost reaches top of casserole. Dot with remaining margarine or butter. Bake in a preheated oven at 350° until browned, 45 to 60 minutes. Makes 6 generous servings.

Traditional Oyster Stew

1 pt shucked standard oysters with liquor
1 qt milk

1/2 cup margarine or butter
Salt and pepper to taste

Cook oysters in their liquor until edges just begin to curl. Add milk, margarine or butter, salt and pepper. Heat slowly; do not boil. Serve immediately. Makes about 6 cups of stew.

Salmon Loaf I (very moist)

1 cup milk, scalded
1/2 cup cracker crumbs or rice, cooked
1 tblsp onion, grated
1/4 tsp salt (if desired)
1/2 tsp black pepper

1/4 tsp sugar
1 tblsp lemon juice
7 3/4 ozs salmon (canned or cooked)
1 egg
1/4 cup melted butter

Combine milk, cracker crumbs, onion, salt, pepper, sugar, lemon juice and salmon in a bowl. Mix well. Beat the egg well and add to the mixture, stirring thoroughly. Pour into a buttered casserole. Bake at 350° until firm and brown on top. Pour the melted butter on top. Serve hot or cold.

Salmon Loaf II

1 (15 oz) can salmon
3 tblsps salmon liquid
1 1/2 cups bread crumbs
1 egg

2 tsps grated onion
1/3 cup evaporated milk
Salt and pepper

Combine all ingredients. Pack into greased and floured 8 1/2" x 4 1/2" x 2 5/8" loaf pan. Bake at 350° for 40 to 45 minutes. Serve with lemon-butter sauce.

Salmon Casserole

4 cups bread cubes
1 (1 lb) can salmon
1/2 to 1 cup onion, chopped
1/2 to 1 cup celery, diced
2/3 green pepper, chopped

1/2 cup mayonnaise
4 eggs
2 cups milk
1 cup cream of mushroom soup
3/4 cup sharp cheddar cheese

Place half of bread cubes in bottom of buttered dish. Top with salmon mixed with onion, celery, pepper and mayonnaise. Top with rest of bread cubes. Beat eggs and blend with milk and undiluted soup. Pour over salmon and cubes. Cover and refrigerate over night. Top with grated cheese and bake at 350° for 1 1/4 hours. Can be made a day ahead.

Lobster Noodle Casserole

4 tblsps melted butter
4 tblsps sauce flour
2 cups milk
1/2 tsp dry mustard
1/4 tsp Worcestershire sauce
1 tsp onion salt

Tabasco® to taste
3 tblsps dry white wine
3/4 lb cooked, chopped lobster meat
4 ozs thin noodles (half 8 oz pkg), cooked and drained
1/4 lb grated cheese

Add flour to melted butter over low heat and stir until smooth. Add milk slowly, stirring constantly until sauce is thickened and smooth. Add seasonings, including wine, and mix well. Fold in lobster meat and noodles. Spoon half the mixture into a greased casserole. Add half the grated cheese. Spoon in remaining lobster/noodle mixture and top with rest of cheese. Bake 20 minutes in a 375° oven. Makes 4 servings.

Creamed Lobster in Patty Shells

1 clove garlic, cut
2 tblsps butter or margarine
2 tblsps sauce flour
1/4 tsp salt
1/2 tsp paprika
Dash cayenne pepper
1 1/4 cups rich milk

1 tsp lemon juice
1 egg yolk, beaten with a little milk
1 3/4 cups lobster meat, chopped
Pepperidge Farm® Patty Shells (baked according to directions)
Minced fresh parsley

Rub saucepan with cut garlic clove and discard garlic. Melt butter in pan, stir in flour, salt, paprika and cayenne pepper Add milk slowly stirring constantly until sauce is smooth and thick. Add lemon juice. Stir a bit of the hot sauce into the beaten egg yolk and then add that mixture to sauce in pan, stirring well. Add lobster meat and heat thoroughly. Spoon into patty shells, <u>just before serving</u>. Spoon in generously enough to let a little bit overflow. Garnish with parsley. It is important not to fill shells ahead of time. They get mushy.

Editor's note: Lobster recipes are mainly for people who live in regions where they don't have to mortgage the house to buy lobster meat.

Lobster Supreme

3 cups cooked lobster meat
6 tblsps margarine or butter
6 tblsps sauce flour
1 1/2 cups milk
1/2 cup dry sherry
8 drops Worcestershire sauce

1/2 tsp lemon and pepper seasoning
Salt to taste
3 green onions, minced (about 1/4 cup)
2 (4 oz) cans sliced mushrooms, drained
2 tblsps margarine or butter
Paprika for sprinkling

Cut lobster meat into bite-size pieces. In a 3 quart saucepan, melt 6 tblsps margarine or butter; mix in flour. Slowly add milk. stirring constantly to keep mixture smooth and free from lumps. Cook, stirring over medium heat until mixture comes to a boil and thickens. Add sherry, Worcestershire sauce, lemon and pepper seasoning and salt. Simmer 2 minutes.

In another pan, sauté green onions and mushrooms in 2 tblsps margarine or butter until green onions are tender. Add to sauce mixture. Gently stir lobster meat into sauce mixture. Put into ramekins or greased 2-quart casserole. Sprinkle paprika over top. Bake at 450° until hot and bubbly and lightly browned on top, 10 to 15 minutes. Makes 6 servings.

Lobster Newburgh

2 cups boiled lobster meat
2 tblsps butter
1 cup light cream
3 egg yolks, well-beaten

1/2 cup dry sherry
Salt and cayenne pepper
Pepperidge Farm® Patty Shells or a plate of hot buttered toast

Bake shells according to recipe on box.

Cut the lobster meat into good sized pieces. Melt the butter in a saucepan and add the cream. Let boil gently for 30 seconds and add the lobster. When the cream/lobster mixture has again reached the boil, pour a little into the egg yolks and mix. Add the sherry to the egg yolks, and add the egg yolks to the cream/lobster mixture. Season to taste with salt and cayenne and let thicken a minute or two, stirring constantly. Pour into patty shells or onto toast.

Editor's note: Real cream and butter are obligatory in this dish because of the flavor. Never fill shells or top toast until ready to serve. This can be made at the table in a chafing dish if desired.

Cod Fish Cakes

1 can Gorton's Cod Fish Cakes
2 eggs, beaten

1 tsp minced onion or 1 tsp dried onion
Fat for frying

Mix cod fish cakes, eggs and onion. Make into 4 to 6 cakes. Fry in fat until brown on both sides. Vegetable oil may be used, but for better flavor, fry 4 strips of bacon until crisp. Fry cakes in bacon fat. Crumble bacon over cakes.

Haddock with Crumb Topping

1 to 1 1/2 lbs haddock fillets
1 tsp salt
1 tblsp lemon juice
2 tblsps minced onion
1/3 cup mayonnaise

1/2 cup fresh bread crumbs
1/2 tsp paprika
1/4 cup finely grated sharp cheddar cheese
Lemon wedges

Put fish in flat buttered casserole (just to fit). Sprinkle with salt and lemon juice. Let stand 30 minutes. Meanwhile, mix mayonnaise with minced onion. After 30 minutes, spread mayonnaise mix over entire top surface of fish. Mix crumbs, cheese and paprika and sprinkle on top. Bake in 450° oven for 25 minutes until well browned. Serve with lemon wedges.

Scallop Casserole

1/4 cup flour
1 lb scallops
Margarine
3 tblsps minced green onion
1/4 tsp garlic powder

Salt and pepper to taste
1/2 cup dry white wine
1/2 cup mushroom caps
1/2 cup grated cheddar cheese
1/4 cup melted butter

Sauté floured scallops in margarine. Add green onions, garlic powder, salt, pepper, wine, mushrooms and simmer covered for 3 to 4 minutes, then uncovered until the sauce thickens. Just before serving, top with grated cheddar cheese with melted butter. Broil in Pyrex® dish until brown.

Vegetables

Asparagus Casserole

1 large can asparagus
2 hard cooked eggs, sliced
1 can cream of celery soup

Toasted bread crumbs
1/4 lb cheese, grated

Arrange alternating layers of asparagus and eggs in casserole. Cover with soup. Sprinkle with crumbs and cheese. Bake at 350° for 20 minutes. Makes 6 servings.

Sweet and Sour Brussels Sprouts

1 (8 oz) pkg sliced bacon (diced)
6 (10 oz) pkgs frozen Brussels sprouts
1 medium onion (minced)
1/3 cup cider vinegar

3 tblsps sugar
1 1/2 tsps salt
1/2 tsp dry mustard
1/4 tsp pepper

About 30 minutes before serving, in 6-quart Dutch oven or sauce pan over low heat, cook bacon until browned. With slotted spoon, remove bacon to drain on paper towels. In bacon drippings, cook Brussels sprouts with remaining ingredients until tender and crisp, about 10 minutes, stirring constantly. Stir in bacon. Makes 18 servings.

Celery Casserole

3 cups celery, sliced thin
2 cans cream of celery soup

1/2+ cup grated cheddar cheese
Slivered almonds

Bring sliced celery to a boil, drain. Layer in baking dish celery and grated cheese in 2 or 3 layers. Pour celery soup over and stir gently. Top with slivered almonds. Bake at 350° about 45 minutes or until bubbly.

Cucumber Au Gratin

2 cucumbers
Salted water
1 1/2 cups Gruyere cheese, grated

Salt and black pepper
Butter or margarine

Peel the cucumbers and cut them into 3" pieces. Slice each in half, lengthwise, and remove the seeds. Cook the cucumbers in boiling salted water for 10 minutes, then drain and dry. Arrange a layer of cucumbers in the base of a buttered, oven proof dish. Sprinkle with 1/3 of the cheese. Season with salt and freshly ground pepper. Repeat the layers, finishing with cheese. Dot the top with butter. Bake the cucumbers in the center of a preheated oven at 400° for 30 minutes.

Green Peas French Style

Lettuce leaves
1 pkg frozen green peas
1 tblsp minced onion

1 tblsps butter or margarine
1/2 tsp salt or to taste
2 tblsps water

Line a heavy sauce pan with wet outer leaves of lettuce. Put in peas, minced onion, butter and salt. Add water. Cover with more lettuce leaves and cook gently until peas are tender. Discard lettuce leaves and serve with sauce from the pan.

Macaroni and Cheese

1/2 lb macaroni
1 tsp butter
1 egg, beaten
1 tsp salt

1 tsp dry mustard
1 tblsp hot water
1 cup milk
3 cups grated sharp cheese

Boil macaroni in water until tender and drain thoroughly. Stir in butter and egg. Mix salt and mustard with hot water and add to milk and cheese, reserving enough to sprinkle on top. Pour macaroni into buttered casserole, stir in milk, sprinkle with cheese. Bake at 350° for 45 minutes or until custard is set and top is crusty.

Santa Fe Soufflé

1 1/4 cups grits (uncooked)
1 tsp Tabasco® sauce
1 tsp salt
6 cups water (or according to recipe on grits package)
1 lb Velveeta cheese, chopped

1 stick margarine
3 eggs, beaten
2 small cans diced green chilies
1/2 tsp cayenne pepper

Boil together first four ingredients until water is absorbed, stirring occasionally. Stir in cheese and butter, and melt. Remove from heat and add other ingredients. Pour into large (it puffs up) well buttered baking dish. Bake at 350° about 45 minutes to one hour or until puffy and brown.

Soul Food Arabe

In this dish, kale, mustard greens or collards may be substituted for chard.

2 large bunches of chard
1/2 cup fine cracked bulgar wheat
1/4 cup vegetable oil

1/2 cup medium onion, chopped
1 (15 oz) can of "dry" black-eyed peas (no meat added)
Salt and pepper

Wash, drain and chop the chard. Fill a 2-quart kettle about 1/3 full of water and bring it to a rolling boil. Add the chard, return to a boil, then lower the heat. Cook uncovered for about 5 minutes, stirring occasionally. Midway in this process, add the cracked wheat and stir to keep the kernels separated. Pour gently into a sieve or colander.

Using the same kettle, sauté the onion in the oil for a few minutes. Add the chard mixture and the black eyed peas; season to taste with the salt and pepper and stir-fry over medium heat for five minutes. Serves 4.

Beets with Orange

1 lb cooked beets
2 tblsps unsalted butter or margarine

1 tsp orange marmalade
Juice of 1/2 orange

Peel and dice the cooked beets. Put the butter, marmalade and orange juice into a sauce pan and heat until the butter melts. Add the beets. Simmer gently, stirring occasionally for about 10 minutes until the liquid has evaporated and the beets are evenly glazed. Put the beets in a hot serving dish.

Editor's note: For most beet dishes, canned beets are perfectly acceptable.

Spiced Beets

1 to 1 1/2 pints canned beets, sliced
1/4 cup vinegar
1/2 cup sugar
1/2 cup water

1 tsp ground cinnamon
1/4 tsp ground allspice
1/2 tsp lemon juice

Mix all ingredients for dressing and bring to a boil. Add beets and simmer about 4 minutes. Serve either hot or cold.

Harvard Beets

1 lb can diced red beets
2 tblsps sugar
1 tblsp corn starch

1/4 tsp salt
1/4 cup cider vinegar
2 tblsps butter

Drain beets and reserve 1/3 cup liquid. In a sauce pan, combine the sugar, salt, corn starch; stir in reserved liquid, vinegar and butter; cook and stir until thick and bubbly. Add drained beets and heat until beets are hot. Serves 4 to 6.

Green Beans

3 cups fresh green beans
2 to 3 tblsps butter
1/2 cup chopped onion (fine)
1/4 cup chopped celery (fine)

Garlic
1/2 tsp rosemary
1/2 tsp basil
Salt and pepper

Cook the green beans; drain. Add the rest of the ingredients; cook, covered, 10 minutes more.

Green Bean Bundles

2 cans whole green beans
1/2 lb bacon, cut in half
1/2 stick butter (1/4 cup)

1/2 cup brown sugar
Garlic powder

Drain beans; wrap 6 or 8 beans in a slice of bacon. Place bundles in a shallow baking pan. Melt butter, stir in brown sugar. Pour over bundles. Sprinkle with garlic powder. Bake in a preheated 350° oven, uncovered, for 30 minutes. Serves 4.

Swiss Green Beans

1 onion, chopped
2 tblsps butter
1 tblsp sugar
2 tblsps flour
Salt and pepper

1 cup sour cream
1/2 lb Swiss cheese, grated
2 cans (4 cups) French style green beans, drained
Dry bread crumbs

Sauté onion in butter. Stir in sugar, flour, salt and pepper. Then stir in sour cream and half the cheese. Stir until thick and creamy. (It may be thinned with a little milk.) Stir in beans and the rest of the cheese. Place in a casserole. Sprinkle with bread crumbs. Bake at 350° for 45 to 60 minutes.

Green Beans with Sauce Vinaigrette

1 lb green beans
Salted water
6 tblsps vegetable oil

2 tblsps wine vinegar
2 tsps chives, finely chopped
Salt and black pepper

Trim and wash the beans but leave whole. Boil in salted water 5 to 10 minutes or until the beans are tender. Drain well.

Put the oil and vinegar in a bowl or a screw-type jar. Beat with a fork, or shake vigorously before seasoning to taste with chives, salt and pepper. Add to the beans, reheat slowly and serve immediately.

String Bean Casserole

2 medium cans string beans
1 medium can Chinese vegetables
1 can condensed cream of celery soup

1 medium can French fried onion rings
1 cup grated cheddar cheese
Salt and pepper

Drain beans and vegetables. Add condensed soup, as it comes from can (do not add water). Top with fried onion rings. Bake for 25 minutes at 325°. Sprinkle cheese over top and bake an additional 5 minutes. Add salt and pepper to taste.

Green Bean Casserole

2 (9 oz) pkgs frozen cut green beans
3/4 cup milk
1 can cream of mushroom soup

1/8 tsp black pepper
1 can French fried onions

Cook beans and drain. Combine beans, milk, soup, pepper and 1/2 can onions. Pour into 1 1/2-quart casserole. Bake, uncovered, at 350° for 30 minutes. Top with the remaining onions. Bake 5 minutes longer.

Harvest Bounty Casserole

3 cups green beans, cooked, drained and cut up
2 medium green peppers, chopped
6 medium tomatoes, chopped
3 cups (10 oz) cheddar cheese, grated
1 cup Bisquick® baking mix

2 tsp salt
1 tsp cayenne pepper
1 cup milk
6 eggs

Heat oven to 350°. Grease a 13" x 9" baking dish. Spread beans and peppers in dish; sprinkle with tomatoes and cheese. Beat remaining ingredients with hand beater until smooth. Pour over vegetables and cheese. Bake uncovered at 350° until golden brown, 45 to 50 minutes. Let stand 10 minutes before serving.

Vegetable Casserole Rancheros

2 cans French style green beans (drained)
1 can Ortega® green chili salsa

10 strips bacon
Salt and pepper to taste

Fry bacon until crisp and break into small pieces. Mix all ingredients and heat either on top of stove in a pan or in oven as casserole at 350°. Serves 8.

Crock O' Beans 'N Franks

1 tblsp shortening
1/2 cup chopped onion
3/4 cup firmly packed brown sugar
1/2 cup catsup
2 tsps vinegar
1 tsp salt
1 tsp dry mustard

1/8 tsp pepper
2 (1 lb) pkgs beef franks*
1 (1 lb) can lima beans, drained
1 (15 oz) can kidney beans, drained
1 (1 lb) can pork and beans in tomato sauce

*1 lb turkey sausage and 1 lb turkey hot dogs may be used

Preheat oven to 350°. Melt shortening in a 2 1/2-quart stew pot. Add onion and cook until tender. Add next 6 ingredients. Cut franks into bit-sized pieces. Add frank pieces, lima beans, kidney beans, and pork and beans to pot; mix well. Bake 45-50 minutes or cook over medium heat, stirring often, for 15 minutes. Makes approximately 10 servings.

New England Baked Beans

1 lb dry beans (navy or red kidney)
Boiling water
1 medium onion
1 tblsp salt
1/2 cup brown sugar

1 tblsp dry mustard
1/4 cup molasses
3 tblsps canola oil
Boiling water

Wash and soak beans over night in tap water, using large pot to allow for swelling. In the morning, drain and rinse. Cover with boiling water and parboil slowly for 20 minutes. Drain beans well and put in bean pot.

Add remaining ingredients. Cover with boiling water and bake at 325° for 8 hours. Add water as needed until 2 hours prior to finish.

Baked Bean Casserole

1/4 lb bacon
1 lb ground beef
1 onion, chopped
1/2 cup brown sugar
1/2 cup catsup
1 tblsp vinegar

1 tblsp mustard
1 tsp salt
1 (16 oz) can green lima beans
2 (16 oz) cans pork and beans
1 (16 oz) can kidney beans

Mix and brown bacon, ground beef and onion. Drain. Add brown sugar, catsup, vinegar, mustard and salt. Add all the beans and bake for 1 hour at 350°.
Can be cooked in crock pot also. Can be cooked in advance and reheated.

Boston Baked Beans Casserole

1 can (16 oz) Boston baked beans
1 can (11 oz) mandarin oranges (drained if preferred)

1/3 cup white onion, chopped (sautéed if preferred)

Combine all ingredients and pour into a buttered 1-quart casserole. (May also be combined right in the casserole.) Bake, uncovered, in 350° oven for 30 minutes. If juice is left in from oranges, baking may be extended to an hour. Makes 4 servings.

Hawaiian Baked Beans

1 cup (16 oz) pork and beans
1 cup (15 oz) three bean salad, drained
1 cup (8 oz) crushed pineapple (juice pack)

1/3 cup bottled barbecue sauce
1 tblsp Worcestershire sauce

In 2-quart microwave safe casserole, combine pork and beans, three bean salad, crushed pineapple, barbecue sauce and Worcestershire sauce. Cook, covered, on high 11 to 13 minutes or until heated through, stirring twice. Stir before serving. Makes 6 servings. Good cold.

Bean Casserole

1/4 lb bacon
2 tblsps Crisco
2 lbs ground beef
1/2 cup onion, chopped
1/2 cup celery, chopped
1/4 cup green pepper, chopped
1 tsp salt
1/8 tsp black pepper
1 cup ketchup

2 tsps dry mustard
6 tblsps brown sugar
1 tblsp Worcestershire sauce
1 cup tomato juice or 1 can sloppy joe sauce
1 can pork and beans
1 can lima beans, drained
1 can butter beans, drained
1 can kidney beans, drained

Fry bacon, set aside. When cool, cut it up in small pieces. In Crisco, fry ground beef until brown, add onion, celery, and green pepper. Fry until soft. Drain grease. Put in big casserole, add the salt, black pepper, ketchup, dry mustard, brown sugar, Worcestershire sauce, tomato juice, and bacon. Fold in pork and beans, lima beans, butter beans and kidney beans. Put in 350° oven for about 1 hour.

Hearty Bean and Pasta Stew

1 cup coarsely chopped tomato (about 1 large)
3/4 cup uncooked macaroni shells
1/4 cup chopped onion (about 1 small)
1/4 cup chopped green bell pepper
1 tblsp chopped fresh or 1 tsp dried basil

1 tsp Worcestershire sauce
1 clove garlic, finely chopped
1 can (16 oz) kidney beans, drained
1 can (14 1/2 oz) chicken broth
1 can (8 oz) garbanzo beans, drained

Mix all ingredients in 2-quart sauce pan. Heat to boiling, stirring occasionally; reduce heat. Cover and simmer about 15 minutes, stirring occasionally, until macaroni is tender. Makes 4 servings (about 1 cup each).

Mexican Chili Beans, Arizona Style

2 (1 lb) pkgs pinto beans, picked over and rinsed in hot water
Large container of hot water
4 qts water
2 ham hocks (smoked)
3 lbs hamburger meat, scrambled and drained

6 cloves garlic, diced
1 cup diced onion, sautéed and drained
6 pickled hot peppers, seeded and chopped
2 or 3 tblsps sugar
Seasoned salt to taste
Black pepper to taste

Pick pinto beans carefully to remove bits of rock. Rinse thoroughly in hot water. Place beans in large container of water and soak overnight. Drain and rinse well. Return beans to container, add about 4 quarts of water and ham hocks, bring to a boil and simmer until beans are done. Remove ham hocks from beans, remove skin and bones, chop meat and return meat to beans. Add the scrambled hamburger meat, sautéed onions and chopped hot peppers to beans and mix well. Add seasoned salt, black pepper and sugar. Simmer slowly for about 30 to 45 minutes. If additional hot seasoning is needed, use crushed hot peppers.

Broccoli Viennese

1 1/2 lbs fresh broccoli

2 cups salted water

Sauce

1 cup sour cream
3 tblsps onion, finely chopped
1/2 tsp celery seed
1/4 tsp salt

1 tsp sugar
2 tsps vinegar
1 tsp horseradish

Wash and trim broccoli. Cook in salted water, covered, 10 to 12 minutes until tender, crisp. Drain. Place on a serving platter. Mix all sauce ingredients together. Cover broccoli with sauce. Serve hot or cold.

Broccoli and Rice

1/2 to 1 stick margarine
8 ozs Cheez Whiz®
1 can cream of chicken soup
1 pkg chopped broccoli

1 can water chestnuts, sliced
1 cup Minute® Rice, uncooked
1/2 cup celery, chopped
1/4 cup (or less) onion, chopped

Melt butter, cheese and soup together. Add all other ingredients. Bake at 375° for 20 to 25 minutes.

Broccoli Casserole

2 pkgs frozen chopped broccoli
1 can cream of mushroom soup
2 cups grated cheddar cheese
2 eggs, beaten

1 cup mayonnaise
2 tblsps grated onion
1 cup cheese crackers, crumbed
Salt and pepper

Cook broccoli 5 minutes; drain. Combine with other ingredients except cracker crumbs. Pour into greased casserole. Sprinkle top with cracker crumbs. Bake at 400° for 20 minutes.

Broccoli-Corn Casserole

Boiling water
1 (10 oz) pkg frozen broccoli
1 egg, slightly beaten
1 (17 oz) can cream-style corn

1 tblsp finely chopped onion
1/2 tsp salt
1/8 tsp pepper
3 ozs grated cheddar cheese

Topping

1 tblsp margarine, melted

1/4 cup herbed seasoned stuffing crumbs

Pour boiling water over broccoli. Drain. Cut into pieces; place in bottom of greased baking dish.

Mix corn, egg, onion and seasonings. Pour corn mixture over broccoli. Top with cheese.

Mix melted margarine and stuffing crumbs; sprinkle over cheese. Bake uncovered in 350° oven for about 45 minutes. Serves 5 to 6. To double the recipe, put in a 9" x 13" baking pan.

Broccoli Salad Casserole

2 pkgs frozen chopped broccoli
1 cup Minute® Rice
1/4 cup water
1/4 cup milk
1 medium onion, chopped

1 stick margarine
1/4 lb pkg American cheese slices
1 can cream of celery soup
1/4 can water
2 cans French fried onion rings

Butter a 9" x 14" oven-proof dish lightly. Spread broccoli on bottom of the dish. Pour rice over broccoli. Pour 1/4 cup water over rice. Pour 1/4 cup milk over rice. Sauté onion in margarine. Pour over rice. Lay cheese slices over rice. Dilute soup with 1/4 cup can water and pour over cheeses. Cover with foil and bake 40 minutes at 350°. Remove foil and sprinkle top with onion rings. Put uncovered in oven for about 3 minutes to heat onion rings.

Broccoli "Lasagna"

1 large bunch broccoli
1/4 tsp salt (optional)
1 (16 oz) container 1% low-fat cottage cheese
2 egg whites
1/4 cup grated Parmesan cheese

3 tblsps all-purpose flour
1/2 tsp Italian herb seasoning
Vegetable cooking spray
1/2 (15 to 15 1/2 oz) jar spaghetti sauce (about 3/4 cup)
1/2 (8 oz) pkg part-skim mozzarella cheese, shredded

About 1 1/2 hours before serving:

With sharp knife, slice broccoli lengthwise into 1/4" thick slices. In 10" skillet over medium heat, heat 2 cups water, and salt if desired, to boiling; add broccoli; heat to boiling. Reduce heat to low; cover and simmer 5 minutes; drain.

Preheat oven to 375°. In food processor with knife blade attached, or blender, blend cottage cheese, egg whites, Parmesan cheese, flour and Italian herb seasoning until smooth.

Spray 12" x 8" baking dish with vegetable cooking spray. In baking dish, arrange half of broccoli in single layer; top with cottage cheese mixture, then layer with remaining broccoli. Spoon spaghetti sauce over broccoli and sprinkle with mozzarella cheese. Bake, uncovered, 35 minutes or until hot and bubbly in center. Let stand 5 minutes for easier serving. Makes 6 servings.

Baked Cabbage

1 medium sized head of cabbage
1 tblsp sugar
2 tblsps flour

1 cup cream or undiluted evaporated milk
Salt and pepper to taste
Sliced bacon to cover

Shred cabbage and place in casserole. Mix sugar, flour and cream thoroughly. Pour over cabbage. Place slices of bacon on top, cover and bake 50 minutes in moderate oven. Remove the cover a few minutes before taking from the oven so bacon will be crisp.

Sweet and Sour Red Cabbage

1 medium onion, finely chopped
3 tblsps butter or margarine
9 cups shredded red cabbage
1 large tart apple, diced
3 tblsps cider vinegar
1 cup water

3 tblsps brown sugar
1 tblsp caraway seed, crushed (optional)
1 1/4 tsps salt
1/4 tsp pepper
1/2 cup seedless raisins

Cook onion in butter in large pot about 5 minutes. Add cabbage and 1/2 of the water. Toss, cover and cook about 5 minutes more. Add remaining ingredients. Mix well. Cover and simmer 15 minutes until crispy and lightly tender. Serve warm. Makes 6 to 8 servings. Can be frozen and reheated when needed.

Noodles and Cabbage

1/4 cup butter or margarine
1/2 cup chopped onion
4 cups chopped or sliced cabbage
1 tsp caraway seed

1/2 tsp salt
1/8 tsp pepper
1 (8 oz) pkg egg noodles
1/2 cup sour cream (optional)

Melt butter in large skillet. Add onion and sauté until soft. Add cabbage. Sauté 5 minutes. Stir in salt, pepper and caraway seed. Cook noodles in salted boiling water. Drain well. Add to cabbage. Add sour cream. Cook 5 minutes, stirring frequently.

Fried Cabbage and Vegetables

1/2 medium onion, thinly sliced
1 to 2 cloves garlic, crushed
1/2 cabbage, thinly sliced
1 large carrot, shredded
1/4 cup celery, thinly sliced
3 to 4 radishes, thinly sliced
1/4 cup green peppers, sliced

1/4 cup red peppers, sliced
1/2 cup mushrooms, thinly sliced
1/2 tsp ground ginger
1 tsp sugar
Dash liquid smoke
1 tblsp soy sauce or teriyaki sauce
Oil for frying

Prepare the vegetables. Heat enough oil to coat the bottom of a wok or frying pan. Sauté the onion and garlic. When the onion is transparent, add the remaining vegetables. Add ginger and sugar. Stir fry, adding liquid smoke and soy sauce. Sauté over medium-high heat until the vegetables are limp and the liquid is absorbed. If more heat is desired, sprinkle with crushed red peppers before removing from the pan.

Cabbage Casserole

1/2 sweet green cabbage
2 or 3 carrots
1/2 large white sweet onion
1 can cream of celery soup

1/2 stick (about 1/2 lb) cheddar cheese
Several dashes of coarsely ground pepper over last layer
before saltines (optional)
Crushed saltines

Slice cabbage in no larger than 1/2" slices. Slice carrots and onion. Place all in covered pan in just enough water to steam vegetables until they are crisp, but tender.

In casserole, put 1/2 can of soup, then 1/2 vegetables. Slice half the cheese to top this. Repeat layering and top all with thick layer of crushed saltines. Place in reheated 350° oven about 1/2 hour or until begins to bubble. Do not over cook. Serve hot. Serves 8.

Sweet Carrots

1 lb bag of carrots, peeled and sliced
1/2 stick butter
1/2 cup sugar

Sprinkle of cinnamon
Dash of cloves
Dash of nutmeg

Place cut-up carrots in sauce pan. Add other ingredients and cook over medium to low heat until crisply done.

Carrots Elegante

1 lb carrots, sliced thinly
1/4 cup golden raisins
1/4 cup margarine
3 tblsps honey

1 tblsp lemon juice
1/4 tsp ground ginger
1/4 cup sliced, unpeeled almonds

Cook carrots, covered in 1/2" boiling water 8 minutes; drain. Turn carrots into a 1-quart baking dish. Stir in raisins, margarine, honey, lemon juice and ginger. Bake, uncovered, in a preheated 375° oven 35 minutes; stir occasionally. Spoon into serving bowl. Sprinkle with almonds. Serves 4.

Carrot Cutlets

2 eggs, beaten
2 cups day-old coarse bread crumbs
1/2 tsp celery salt
1/2 tsp salt
2 cups grated raw carrots
1/2 cup (2 oz) grated cheese

3/4 cup rolled corn flakes
1/4 cup shortening
1 1/2 cups medium white sauce*
2 tblsps green onions, finely sliced
2 tblsps parsley, chopped

Combine the first six ingredients and mix well. Divide mixture into cutlets by packing it firmly into a 1/4 cup measure and dropping out onto the rolled corn flakes. Pat into a flat shape, lightly cover with the flakes. Pan fry over low heat to form a golden brown crust on each side of the cutlets. Turn once during frying. Serve with 1 1/2 cups medium white sauce* seasoned with 2 tblsps each finely sliced green onions and chopped parsley. 4 servings.

*See The Ditty Bag for cream or white sauce.

Parsleyed Carrots

8 medium carrots
2 tblsps water
2 tblsps margarine
1 tsp sugar

1/4 tsp salt
Pepper
2 tsps snipped parsley

Pare carrots, slice about 1/4" thick. Place in baking dish. Add water, margarine, sugar, salt and pepper. Cover tightly. Bake in 350° oven for about 40 minutes or until tender. To serve, sprinkle with parsley. Makes 4 to 6 servings.

Dilly Carrots and Beans

3/4 cup water
1 tsp sugar
1/2 tsp salt
1/2 tsp dill seed

1/2 lb fresh green snap beans
4 medium carrots
1/4 cup Italian dressing

Combine water, sugar, salt and dill seed in a sauce pan and bring to boiling. Simmer 5 minutes. Add beans. Cut carrots into thin strips 2" to 3" long. Add to beans. Boil until both vegetables are tender and liquid is almost evaporated, about 10 minutes. Add Italian dressing and toss to mix well. Serve hot or chilled and use in tossed vegetable salads.

Company Carrot Casserole

1 small onion, minced
1/4 cup melted butter
1/4 cup flour
1 tsp salt
1/4 tsp pepper

2 cups milk
4 cups sliced cooked carrots
6 slices American cheese
2 cups buttered fresh bread crumbs

Sauté onion in melted butter. Stir in flour, salt and pepper. Gradually add milk, stirring constantly. Arrange a layer of carrots in a 2 quart casserole. Place 3 slices of cheese over carrots. Repeat layers. Pour sauce over carrots. Top with bread crumbs. Bake at 350°, uncovered, 25 minutes. Serves 8. May be made day before; refrigerate and bake.

Marinated Carrots

2 lbs carrots, cut into 1/2" slices
Salt
1 medium onion, sliced
1 green pepper, cut into rings
1 (10 3/4 oz) can condensed tomato soup
3/4 cup sugar

3/4 cup white vinegar
1/2 cup vegetable oil
1 tsp salt
1 tsp dried dill weed
1 tsp Worcestershire sauce
1/4 tsp pepper

Cook carrots in 1" boiling salted water (1/2 tsp salt to 1 cup water) just until crisp and tender, 8 to 9 minutes. Layer carrots, onion and green pepper in large bowl. Heat remaining ingredients to boiling, stirring occasionally. Cool slightly; pour over vegetables. Cover and refrigerate at least 8 hours but no longer than 1 week.

Cauliflower with Cheese Sauce

1 cauliflower

1 can cheddar cheese soup

Cut flowerets off cauliflower and cook in lightly salted water until tender. Dilute desired amount of cheddar cheese soup with a little water and add a dash of cayenne pepper. Heat until boiling and pour over cauliflower. The amount of cheese sauce depends on the size of the cauliflower.

Cauliflower Polonaise

1 cauliflower

Buttered toasted bread crumbs

Peel off the leaves of the cauliflower and cut off the tough stem but leave the cauliflower whole. Cook, covered in lightly salted water until it is tender but not mushy. Test it with a sharp fork. Drain it well and place it in a warm bowl. Sprinkle heavily with crumbs.

Cauliflower Italian

1 cauliflower
Prepared spaghetti sauce

Parmesan cheese, grated

Cut flowerets off cauliflower and cook until tender in lightly salted water. Heat desired amount of spaghetti sauce until very hot. Drain cauliflower well, put it in a bowl and pour sauce over. Sprinkle with cheese.

Spanish-Style Cauliflower

1 head cauliflower
1/4 cup melted butter or margarine
1 tblsp sugar
1/2 tsp salt
1/2 tsp pepper

3/4 cup cracker crumbs
1/2 cup diced green pepper
1 (16 oz) can tomatoes
1 medium onion, chopped
1 1/2 cups shredded cheddar cheese, divided

Wash cauliflower and remove green leaves. Break into flowerets. Cover and cook in a small amount of boiling salted water 5 minutes; drain.

Combine butter, sugar, salt, pepper and cracker crumbs. Stir in green pepper, tomatoes, onion, 1 1/4 cups cheese and cauliflower. Pour into a 2-quart casserole; sprinkle remaining cheese on top. Bake at 350° for 1 hour. Makes 6 to 8 servings.

Corn Casserole

1 (8 oz) corn meal muffin mix
2 eggs
1 cup cream-style corn
1 cup whole kernel corn

1/2 cup melted butter
1 cup sour cream
1 cup grated Swiss cheese

Mix all together except cheese. Pour into 8" x 8" pan. Bake at 350° for 35 minutes. Take from oven. Sprinkle with cheese. Bake 10 minutes longer.

Bar-B-Q Corn (Baked)

Preheat oven to 375°.

1 can whole kernel corn
1 can cream corn
2 medium onions, chopped
1/2 medium green bell pepper, chopped
1/2 medium red bell pepper, chopped

2 tblsps sugar
2 tblsps bacon drippings
2 tblsps chili powder
3 tblsps yellow corn meal

Mix all ingredients except corn meal. Bake at 375° until it starts to bubble. Remove from oven. Reduce heat to 350°. Add corn meal and mix well. Return to oven and bake an additional 45 minutes.

Kansas Corn Scallop

1 (12 or 16 oz) can whole kernel corn
2 eggs
1 (1 lb) can cream-style corn
1 small can evaporated milk (2/3 cup)
4 tblsps (1/2 stick) butter or margarine, melted

2 tblsps instant minced onion
1/2 tsp salt
1/4 tsp pepper
2 cups coarsely crushed saltines
1 (12 oz) pkg processed Swiss cheese, diced

Drain liquid from whole kernel corn into cup. Beat eggs slightly in a large bowl; stir in corn and 1/4 cup of the liquid, cream-style corn, evaporated milk, melted butter or margarine, onion, salt and pepper. Fold in saltines and diced cheese. Spoon into a greased 8-cup baking dish. Bake at 325° for 1 hour or until set. Let stand 5 minutes before serving. Serves 8 to 10.

Shoe Peg Corn Casserole

1/2 cup chopped onion
1/2 cup chopped celery
1/4 cup chopped bell pepper
1 can cream of celery soup
1/2 pint sour cream
Salt and pepper to taste

1/2 cup grated sharp cheddar cheese
1 can Green Giant® shoe peg corn
1 can French cut string beans, drained
1 stack Ritz crackers, crushed
1 stick margarine, melted

Mix all together except crackers and margarine. Spread in 9" x 13" pan. Melt margarine and stir in crackers. Spread over casserole. Bake about 45 minutes in 350° oven.

Corn Pudding

1 (12 oz) can whole kernel corn
2 (17 oz) cans cream-style corn
5 lightly beaten eggs
4 tblsps corn starch
1/2 tsp dry mustard

1/2 cup milk
1/2 cup sugar
1 1/2 tsps seasoned salt
1 tsp instant minced onion
1/2 cup melted butter

Mix together all ingredients. Pour into greased 3-quart casserole and bake at 400° for 1 hour.

Fried Eggplant (A Mid-East Recipe)

Eggplant
Flour
Milk

Salt
Olive Oil

Peel the eggplant, slice and leave the slices to soak in milk with a little salt added for several hours. The eggplant, having soaked in milk, will not soak up oil when frying. Remove the slices from the milk, letting the excess run off; dip slices in flour and fry in virgin olive oil until crisp.

Editor's note: It is not really necessary to use olive oil. A good vegetable oil will suffice.

Eggplant Casserole (tastes like oyster dressing)

1 large eggplant, peeled and cut into pieces, boiled until tender and drained
1/4 lb crackers, rolled into crumbs

1/2 stick margarine
4 large eggs, separated
Salt and pepper

Mix eggplant, crackers, margarine and egg yolks. Beat egg whites until stiff, fold into eggplant mixture. Add salt and pepper to taste. Pour into well greased casserole. Bake in a 350° oven for about 30 minutes or until firm and lightly browned.

Guinea Squash Pie (Eggplant)

1 medium eggplant
Salted water
3 slices toasted bread
Water
2 eggs, slightly beaten

1 onion, chopped
3 tblsps melted butter
1 tsp salt
Pepper to taste
2 tblsps cream

Peel and cube the eggplant. Boil the cubes in salted water. Drain and mash. Soak the bread in water until it is soft. Mix with the eggplant. Mix in the eggs. Blend the onion, melted butter, salt and pepper in with the eggplant. Put in a buttered casserole. Put cream on top. Bake at 350° until golden, about 25 minutes.

Eggplant, Zucchini, Mixed Vegetable Casserole

1 medium eggplant, sliced
Salt
1/4 lb fresh mushrooms, sliced
8 ozs cream cheese, cubed
4 to 5 strips green pepper, chopped

4 to 5 strips red pepper, chopped
2 medium zucchini sliced
2 to 3 cups spaghetti sauce
Bread crumbs

Sprinkle eggplant lightly with salt and let stand 1/2 hour. Rinse and pat dry. In a 9" x 13" pan, layer eggplant, mushrooms, cream cheese and peppers. Cover with zucchini. Pour spaghetti sauce over the mixture.

There are two methods of cooking:

1. Microwave on high for 10 minutes. Remove, cover with crumbs already toasted or run under broiler for a few minutes until crumbs are lightly toasted.

2. Bake in the oven until completely tender.

Editor's note: If only the oven is used, it might be wise to add the crumbs toward the end of the baking.

Eggplant Parmesan

1 (1 lb) eggplant
2/3 cup unbleached flour
1/2 tsp salt
3 cups whole-wheat cracker crumbs
2/3 cup freshly grated Parmesan cheese

1/2 tsp leaf oregano
1/2 tsp basil
2 large tomatoes, cored, thinly sliced
2 cups shredded mozzarella cheese

Remove stem end and slice eggplant into 1/4" thick rounds. Mix flour with salt in a shallow dish. Combine crumbs, Parmesan cheese, oregano and basil in another bowl. Oil a 9" x 13" baking dish. Dip eggplant slices first in flour, then in crumb mixture, coating each side well. Overlap slices in the baking dish and cover with tomato slices. Cover with foil and bake in a preheated 350° oven for 30 to 35 minutes, or until eggplant is tender. Remove cover and sprinkle with cheese; bake until cheese melts and bubbles. Serves 5 to 6.

Eggplant-Cheese Casserole

3 small eggplants (about 3 lbs total) stemmed
1 large (about 10 oz) onion, chopped
1 large (about 1/2 lb) green bell pepper, stemmed, seeded and chopped
3/4 cup fine dried bread crumbs

1 large (3.8 oz) can sliced ripe olives, drained
1 can (15 oz) tomato sauce
1 (1/2 lb) cup ricotta cheese
2 cups (1/2 lb) shredded sharp cheddar cheese
Salt and pepper

Cut eggplants into 3/4" cubes. In a deep 4-quart casserole, mix eggplants, onion, bell pepper, crumbs, olives, and tomato sauce; cover tightly. Bake in a 400° oven until vegetables are soft when pressed, about 1 1/2 hours; stir after 45 minutes, re-covering tightly. (If making ahead, let cool and chill, covered, up to 2 days. Re-heat covered, in a 400° oven until hot, about 30 minutes.)

Spoon ricotta in dollops onto hot vegetables, sprinkle with cheddar. Bake, uncovered, until cheddar melts, 10 to 15 minutes longer. Add salt and pepper to taste. Makes 8 servings.

Hearty Ratatouille

1/4 cup olive or vegetable oil
1 large onion, sliced or 1 scallion cut into 1" pieces
1 stalk celery, diagonally sliced into 1" pieces
1 garlic clove or 1/2 tsp garlic powder
1 green pepper, seeded and cut into 1" pieces
1 small eggplant, diced

2 small zucchini, cut into 1/4" slices
2 medium tomatoes, cut in wedges
1/2 lb sliced mushrooms
1 tsp fresh basil, shredded, or 1 tsp dried
Salt and pepper to taste

In hot oil, sauté onion, celery and garlic until vegetables are wilted. Add peppers, eggplant and zucchini. Cover and simmer 8 to 10 minutes. Add tomatoes and mushrooms and simmer another 10 minutes. Vegetables should be intact and blended, but not mushy. Add basil and salt and pepper to taste. Serve as a vegetable. Serves 4 to 6.

Bar-B-Que Onion

1 large onion
1 tsp butter
1 tblsp honey or corn syrup

Salt and pepper to taste
2 tblsps water

Peel onion and leave whole. Cut through from top about two thirds of the way down (2 or 3 times). Place on large square of aluminum foil. Add butter, salt and pepper, honey and water. Gather up edges of the foil to the top and twist to close. Bake in oven at 350° for about 30 minutes. (Can be cooked on the grill also.)

Roasted Onions

6 large Spanish onions
4 to 6 tblsps butter or margarine
Coarse salt

Paprika
Parsley sprigs

Line a deep roasting pan with aluminum foil to prevent the sugar in the onions from sticking to the pan. Cut the roots from the unpeeled onions and stand them upright in the pan. Bake in the center of the oven, preheated to 350°, for 2 hours or until the onions are tender when they are pierced with a skewer or a small knife.

Remove from the oven, carefully peel off the skins and set them on a hot serving dish. Cut a cross in the top of each onion halfway down the depth of the onion. Push a slice of butter into the cross and sprinkle with salt. Top each with a sprig of parsley and dust with paprika.

Editor's note: Use as many or as few onions as desired, even if only one or two.

Spicy Baked Onions

3 large sweet Spanish onions
6 whole cloves
3 tblsps butter or margarine
1 tblsp brown sugar

1/2 tsp salt
1/2 tsp nutmeg
Dash cayenne pepper
1/4 cup toasted, slivered blanched almonds

Peel onions and halve crosswise. Place in large saucepan with 2" of boiling salted water. Bring to a boil; cover and simmer 20 minutes, or until almost tender. Drain. Press a whole clove into each onion half. Place in casserole or oven-proof dish.

Melt butter; stir in brown sugar, salt, nutmeg and cayenne pepper. Drizzle over onions. Cover and bake at 325° for 45 minutes, or until tender, basting occasionally with glaze from bottom of baking dish. To serve, sprinkle with almonds. Serves 6.

Mashed Potatoes

6 cups mashed potatoes
1 carton (3 cups) cream-style cottage cheese
1 cup sour cream
1 1/2 tblsps grated onion

2 1/2 tsps salt
1/8 tsp white pepper (optional)
1 tblsp melted butter
Slivered almonds (optional)

Mix first 6 ingredients in order in large mixing bowl. Beat with electric beater until smooth. Turn into greased 2 1/2-quart casserole. Sprinkle top with melted butter and cover with almonds. Bake, covered, in 350° oven at least 30 minutes. Serves 6. This may be mixed ahead and frozen. Leftover mashed potatoes may be used also.

Good Old Fashioned Potatoes

1 1/2 cups diced raw potatoes
1/4 cup onion, chopped
3 tblsps butter

Dash of paprika
Salt and pepper to taste
1 to 1 1/2 cups of milk

Quickly brown potatoes and onions in butter. Add salt, pepper and paprika. Reduce heat to low. Add 1/2 cup milk. Cook about 1/2 hour, stirring occasionally. Add more milk as needed to keep small amount of liquid on potatoes. Just before serving, cook liquid down.

Herbed Potatoes

Vegetable cooking spray
4 medium baking potatoes, cut into 1/4" slices (1 1/2 lbs)
2 medium white onions, cut into 1/4" slices (12 oz)
5 plum tomatoes, sliced (1 lb)
1/2 tsp salt

1 tsp dried whole thyme
3/4 tsp dried rosemary, crushed
1 tblsp olive oil
2 tblsps fresh parsley

Coat a large baking dish with cooking spray. Layer half each of potatoes, onions, and tomatoes in dish; sprinkle with half each of salt, thyme and rosemary. Repeat layers and drizzle with olive oil. Cover and bake at 425° for 35 to 40 minutes or until tender. Sprinkle with parsley. Makes 8 servings.

Bar-B-Q Potatoes

For each serving:

1 large potato (if not peeled, scrub well)
1 tblsp minced onion (or 1 tsp dried)
Salt and pepper to taste

Garlic salt, sprinkled on
1 tblsp butter or margarine
2 tblsps water

Slice potato on individual squares of aluminum foil, add the onion, salt, pepper and garlic salt. Top each with some of butter. Gather up the edges of the foil to the top. Add 2 tblsps of water and twist foil to seal. Bake in 350° oven (or on BBQ grill) for approximately 1 hour. Peel back the foil and serve.

Green Potatoes

6 large potatoes (about 3 lbs)
3/4 cup light cream or milk
1/4 lb butter or margarine
1/2 tsp sugar
1 tsp salt

1/4 tsp pepper
2 tblsps chopped chives
1 1/2 tsps dill weed
1 (10 oz) pkg frozen spinach

Boil potatoes until done. Mash with cream or milk. Add butter, sugar, salt, pepper. Beat until light and fluffy. (More milk may be needed if potatoes are dry.) Add chives and dill weed. Fold in spinach, cooked according to directions and well-drained. Place in a greased casserole. Bake at 400° for about 20 minutes or until well heated. (This may be made ahead of time and refrigerated. If so, heat at 375° for a longer period of time.)

Hash Brown Casserole

1 (2 lb) pkg frozen hash browned potatoes
2 cans cream soup (celery, mushroom, chicken or potato)
1/4 cup onions, chopped (preferably green onions)
12 ozs sour cream

Salt and pepper to taste
1 cup shredded sharp cheese (optional)
Corn flakes for topping, if desired
Butter for topping, if desired

Defrost potatoes almost completely. Mix with soup and next 4 ingredients. Pour into buttered 9" x 13" baking pan. Cover with aluminum foil and bake two hours at 325°, uncovering the last 15 minutes. May top with mixture of crushed corn flakes with small amount of butter if desired. Serves 10 to 15.

Heaven and Earth (Potato Casserole)

4 medium potatoes, boiled, peeled and diced into 1" cubes
6 bacon strips, fried to crisp and crumbled
2 medium onions, thinly sliced and sautéed for 3 to 4 minutes
4 pears, peeled and sliced

1 tblsp sugar
1 tsp nutmeg
3/4 tsp salt
1/4 cup cider vinegar
1/4 cup minced parsley
1/2 tsp pepper

Combine all ingredients in 2-quart casserole. Bake at 375° for 20 minutes until heated.

Scalloped Potatoes

8 medium potatoes, sliced thin
1/4 cup chopped green pepper
1/4 cup chopped onion
2 tsp salt

1/8 tsp pepper
1 can cream of mushroom soup
1 cup milk

Grease the bottom and sides of a baking dish. Alternately in layers, place potatoes, green pepper and onions. Season each layer with salt and pepper. Mix the milk and soup together thoroughly. Pour over potatoes. Cover dish with aluminum foil and bake at 350° for 1 1/2 hours, remove foil and bake another 1/2 hour. Serves 8.

Carrot and Potato Gratin

2 1/4 lbs large baking potatoes, peeled and sliced thinly
1 1/4 lbs carrots, sliced thinly
1 tsp salt
Pepper

6 ozs grated Swiss cheese
1 cup chicken broth
1/4 cup unsalted butter

Cook potatoes and carrots in boiling water 5 minutes; drain. Arrange 1/4 of cooked vegetables in greased 9" x 13" x 2" baking dish. Sprinkle with 1/4 tsp salt and generous amount of pepper. Sprinkle on a quarter of the cheese.

Repeat layering with remaining vegetables, salt, pepper and cheese. Pour chicken broth over vegetables. Dot top with butter. Preheat oven to 375°. Bake, covered, 1 hour or until chicken stock is absorbed. Bake, uncovered, 10 additional minutes or until golden brown. Cool 10 minutes. Makes 8 servings.

Kugeli (A Favorite Lithuanian Dish)

2 slices bacon, diced
1 small onion, diced
5 medium russet potatoes
3 eggs, beaten

Salt and pepper, to taste
1 1/2 tblsps Cream of Wheat® or flour
1 cup milk

Fry diced bacon with onion. Grate potatoes. Add bacon and onion, eggs, salt and pepper, Cream of Wheat® (or flour) and milk. Mix well. Bake at 400° for 1/2 hour, then lower temperature to 350°. Bake another 1/2 hour until top is brown and a knife, inserted into the center, comes out clean.

Sweet Potato Casserole

3 cups mashed sweet potatoes
1 cup sugar
1/2 tsp salt
2 eggs, beaten

3 tblsps margarine
1/2 cup milk
1 tsp vanilla

Mix potatoes, sugar, salt, eggs, margarine, milk and vanilla and pour into greased 9" x 13" casserole. Bake at 400° for 20 to 30 minutes until firm.

Topping

1/2 cup light brown sugar
1/3 cup flour

1 cup chopped pecans
3 tblsps soft margarine

Mix until crumbly. Sprinkle over casserole. Bake 10 minutes at 400°.

Microwave Glazed Sweet Potatoes or Yams

1/4 cup butter
1/2 cup brown sugar

4 medium cooked sweet potatoes or yams

Melt butter and brown sugar in 1 1/2-quart glass casserole dish. Peel and cut potatoes in 1" slices. Add potatoes to casserole and toss lightly. Cover and microwave 6 minutes. Serves 6.

Yams-Apple-Mallow Bake

2 apples, sliced
1/3 cup nuts, chopped
1/2 cup brown sugar, packed
1/2 tsp cinnamon

2 (17 oz) cans of yams, drained (equal amount of fresh cooked yams may be substituted)
1/4 cup margarine
2 cups miniature marshmallows

Toss apples and nuts with combined sugar and cinnamon. Alternate layers of apples and yams in 1 1/2-quart casserole. Dot with margarine. Cover. Bake at 350° for 35 to 40 minutes. Sprinkle marshmallows over yams and apples. Broil until browned lightly. Baste with liquid during baking.

Baked Rice

Preheat oven to 350°.

1/2 stick margarine
1 (4 oz) can mushroom pieces, stems and liquid
1 (4 oz) can water
1/2 cup onions, chopped

1 can chicken gumbo soup
1 can chicken with rice soup
1 cup Uncle Ben's® Converted Rice (not instant rice)

In a 3-quart casserole, melt margarine in oven. In a sauce pan, heat mushrooms, liquid, water, onion and soups to near boiling. Remove casserole from oven and add rice, stirring slightly. When mixture in sauce pan is hot, pour into casserole over rice. Stir well and cover. Bake, covered, 30 minutes. Remove cover and bake an additional 30 minutes.

Vegetable Rice

1/4 cup onion, chopped
3 tblsps butter
1 1/2 cups mushrooms, sliced
2 cups broccoli, chopped
1 cup tomatoes, diced
2 cups water

2 cubes chicken bouillon
1 cup rice, uncooked
1/2 tsp salt
1/2 tsp oregano
1/4 cup Parmesan cheese, grated

Cook onions in butter until golden. Add mushrooms, broccoli and tomatoes and cook about 4 minutes. Add water and bouillon cubes and bring to a boil. Stir in rice, salt and oregano. Cover and cook over low heat, 20 minutes or until water is absorbed. Stir in Parmesan cheese. Serve hot or cold.

Champagne Rice Pilaf

1 1/3 sticks butter, melted
2 cups long grain white rice, cooked
1 1/3 cups fine noodles, cooked
2 2/3 cups chicken broth

1 1/3 cups champagne
1 tsp salt
3/4 cup sliced almonds, sautéed in butter until golden brown

To melted butter (or margarine), add rice and noodles and sauté until golden brown 7 to 10 minutes. Bring broth and champagne to a boil. Slowly pour over rice and noodles. Add salt and bring to a boil. Reduce heat, cover and cook 20 to 25 minutes until liquid is absorbed. Sprinkle almonds over top to serve. Freezes well. Serves 8.

Rice Romanoff

3 cups cooked rice
1/4 cup finely chopped green onion
1 1/2 cups cottage cheese
1 clove garlic, minced
1 cup sour cream

1/4 cup milk
1/4 tsp Tabasco® sauce
1/2 tsp salt
1/2 cup grated Parmesan cheese

Combine all ingredients except Parmesan cheese. Mix well and pour into greased 1 1/2-quart casserole. Sprinkle Parmesan cheese on top and bake in a 350° oven for 45 minutes.

Spanish Rice

2 cups tomatoes, chopped
2 tsps salt
1 tsp pepper
1 tsp chili powder
3 strips bacon, cut into 3" strips

1 medium onion, chopped
1 medium bell pepper, diced
1 clove garlic, minced
1 cup rice (not instant)

Heat tomatoes and seasonings in a sauce pan that has a tight-fitting lid. Fry bacon until crisp and add to tomato mixture, reserving fat. Add onion, bell pepper and garlic to bacon fat and sauté slowly until soft. Add the mixture to tomato mixture, again reserving fat. Add dry rice to bacon fat and cook until brown, stirring often to keep it from burning. Add this to the tomato mixture, stirring once to blend. Cover tightly and cook over very low heat for about 30 minutes without removing the lid.

Panned Spinach

1 lb fresh spinach
1 tblsp butter

2 tblsps olive oil
1 clove minced garlic

Wash well and remove the coarse stems from the spinach. Shake off as much water as possible. Heat in a large heavy skillet the butter and olive oil. Add the garlic, then the spinach. Cover skillet and cook over high heat until steam appears. Reduce the heat and simmer until tender, 5 to 6 minutes in all. Season to taste.
Variations: Canned spinach may be used.
To turn this into Sicilian Spinach, add 2 or more chopped anchovies.

Spinach Balls

2 (10 oz) pkgs frozen chopped spinach
6 eggs
1 (8 oz) pkg seasoned stuffing mix
1/2 tsp black pepper

1/2 tsp garlic power
1/2 tsp thyme
1/2 cup grated Parmesan cheese
1/2 cup melted margarine

Cook spinach and squeeze dry. Beat eggs. Add eggs, stuffing mix, seasonings, cheese and margarine to spinach. Blend together well. Form into small balls about the size of walnut or a little larger, if desired. Bake at 350° for 8 to 10 minutes. Serve piping hot.
Balls may be made larger (about 2") in diameter and used as a vegetable side dish. If doing this, bake at 350° for 20 to 30 minutes. Makes approximately 36 appetizers or 8 to 10 of the larger size.

Spinach Squares

2 (10 oz) pkgs frozen chopped spinach
4 tblsps butter or margarine
3 eggs, beaten
1 medium onion, grated or finely chopped
1 cup flour
3/4 cup milk

1/8 tsp white pepper
3/4 tblsp dill weed
1 tsp salt
1 tblsp baking powder
1 lb grated cheese
1/3 cup lemon juice

Thaw spinach and drain well. Mix all the other ingredients in a bowl. Add spinach and mix well. Pour in a greased baking 13" x 9" x 2" baking pan. Bake at 350° for approximately 30 minutes or until golden brown. Cool. Cut in squares. May also be frozen.

Spinach with Jalapeño Cheese

2 pkgs frozen spinach
4 tblsps margarine
2 tblsps flour
2 tblsps onions, chopped
Liquid from cooked spinach
1/2 cup milk

1/2 tsp pepper
3/4 tsp celery salt
1/2 tsp salt
1 tsp Worcestershire sauce
6 ozs Jalapeño cheese
Crumbs

Cook spinach according to directions. Drain and save liquid. Melt margarine in a pan, add flour, blend but do not brown. Add onion and cook until soft but not brown. Add spinach liquid and milk, stirring until smooth and thick. Add seasonings and cheese. Combine with spinach. May be served right away or refrigerated until the next day. Flavor improves over night. Top with crumbs and brown.

Spinach Casserole

3 tblsps butter
3 tblsps onion, grated
1 lb mushrooms, chopped
3 tblsps flour
1 tsp salt

1/4 tsp white pepper
1/4 tsp nutmeg
2 cups light cream
3 lbs fresh spinach or 2 pkgs frozen spinach, drained
3 tblsps grated Gruyere or Swiss cheese

Melt butter, sauté onions and mushrooms 5 minutes. Blend in flour, salt, pepper and nutmeg. Gradually add cream and stir to boiling point. Cook over low heat 5 minutes and taste. Spread half the spinach in a buttered baking dish and cover with half the sauce. Repeat and put cheese on top. Set in oven in a pan of hot water (not more than half way up the sides of the casserole) and bake at 325° for 40 minutes. Serves 6 to 8.

Spinach Cheese Soufflé

3 tblsps margarine
3 tblsps flour
1/4 tsp dry mustard
1 cup milk
2/3 cup grated cheese

1 to 1 1/2 cups cooked spinach, chopped
Dash of paprika
1 tsp salt, or less
2 eggs, separated (whites beaten until stiff; egg yolks beaten)

Blend margarine, flour and mustard; add milk gradually and cook, stirring constantly, until boiling. Cool slightly; add and mix in the cheese, spinach, paprika, salt (depending on the saltiness of the cheese) and beaten egg yolks. Fold in stiffly beaten egg whites. Turn into a well-oiled baking dish and bake in a moderately hot oven (350°-375°) for 25-35 minutes until perfectly set. Serve immediately.

Note: Instead of milk and grated cheese, 1 can cheddar cheese soup mix may be used.

"Easy" Spinach Lasagna

1 (10 oz) pkg frozen chopped spinach
1 (16 oz) container cottage cheese
2 cups shredded mozzarella cheese, divided
1 egg, beaten
1 tsp salt

3/4 tsp oregano, crushed
1/8 tsp pepper
1 (32 oz) jar spaghetti sauce
1 (8 oz) box lasagna noodles, uncooked
1 cup water

Thaw spinach and drain well. In large bowl, mix cottage cheese, one cup mozzarella cheese, egg, spinach, salt, oregano, and pepper. In greased 13 x 9" x 2" baking dish (non-aluminum), layer 1/2 cup sauce, 1/3 of the noodles and half the cheese mixture. Repeat. Top with remaining noodles, then remaining sauce. Sprinkle with remaining cup of mozzarella cheese. Pour water around edges. Cover tightly with foil. Bake at 350° for one hour and 15 minutes or until bubbly. Let stand 15 minutes before serving. Serves 10.
Note: For a low-fat version, use low-fat cottage cheese and skim milk mozzarella cheese.

Spinach Ring (A Swedish Recipe)

2 (8 oz) pkgs frozen chopped spinach; thaw and squeeze as much liquid out as possible
2 tblsps flour
2 tblsps soft butter or margarine
4 eggs, beaten

1 tsp salt
Dash of pepper
Small amount of McCormick® Fines Herbes and a dash of nutmeg, if desired
1 cup canned milk

Put everything but spinach in a blender, then add spinach. Put in a buttered mold or square casserole. Cover with wax paper (tie with a string). Place in a pan of water and bake at 375° for 25 minutes. Serve hot.

Summer Squash Dish

2 lbs squash (zucchini, crooked neck or combination) sliced in 1/2" slices
1/2 cup chopped onion
1 can cream of chicken soup

1 cup sour cream
1 cup shredded carrots
1/2 cup butter or margarine, melted
1 (8 oz) pkg herb stuffing

In sauce pan, cook squash and onions in boiling salted water for 5 minutes. Drain well. In the meantime, combine soup, sour cream and carrots. Fold in squash mixture. Combine melted butter and herb stuffing. Spread half the stuffing in bottom of a 12" x 7" x 2" baking dish. Spread vegetable mixture gently on top. Top with remaining half of stuffing mix. Bake at 350° for 25 to 30 minutes until it bubbles. May be prepared a day ahead or be frozen; then bake and serve.

Yellow Crooked Neck Squash Mexican Style

6 to 8 yellow squash
2 cloves garlic, minced
1 large onion, chopped
1 tblsp oil

1 large tomato, chopped
1 tsp chili powder
1 tsp cominas (if available)

Boil squash with 1 clove garlic. Drain. Sauté onions and 1 clove garlic in 1 tblsp oil. Add squash, tomato, chili powder and cominas. Simmer for 15 minutes.

Zucchini and Cheese

1 1/4 lb zucchini
1/4 cup flour
1 tsp salt
1 tsp oregano
1/4 tsp ground pepper

1/4 cup olive oil
2 sliced tomatoes
1 cup sour cream
1/2 cup Parmesan cheese

Wash and scrub zucchini well and cut into thin round pieces. Combine flour with half the salt, pepper and oregano in a bowl. Coat zucchini slices in mixture. Heat oil in a skillet and sauté zucchini until brown. Place zucchini in a greased baking dish and top with tomato. Combine sour cream and the rest of the salt, oregano and pepper and spread over tomato slices. Bake 30 minutes at 350°.

Baked Stuffed Tomatoes

4 extra-large tomatoes
1/4 cup cottage cheese
1 tblsp grated onion
1 tblsp minced parsley
1 cup canned crab, shrimp or tuna, salted to taste

2 eggs, beaten
4 tblsps bread crumbs
2 tblsps melted butter
Butter for top
1 tblsp olive oil

Scoop out centers of tomatoes. Force the pulp through a sieve, discarding the seeds. Combine the pulp with the other ingredients. Stuff the tomato shells with the mixture, sprinkle the tops with buttered bread crumbs. Dot with butter. Brush the tomato skins lightly with olive oil. Bake for 45 minutes at 375°.

Red Peppers and Tomatoes

4 red peppers, halved and seeds removed
12 to 16 cherry tomatoes, halved
Salt and pepper

1 tblsp olive oil
1 tsp honey
Oregano or basil or thyme

Lightly oil baking dish. Lay red peppers open side up in dish. Fill with cherry tomatoes. Salt and pepper. Drizzle mixture of oil and honey. Sprinkle with herb of choice. Bake at 350° for 35 to 45 minutes or microwave, covered, 15 to 20 minutes (depends on microwave power).

Peppers, Onions and Tomatoes

1 1/2 tblsps olive oil
2 medium onions, chopped
2 cloves garlic, minced
4 green peppers (seeded), cut into strips

6 large tomatoes, chopped
1/2 tsp salt
1/2 tsp black pepper
1 tsp dried basil

Heat olive oil in sauce pan. Add onions and garlic, cook over medium heat until light brown. Add pepper strips and cook until soft. Add tomatoes, salt, pepper and basil. Bring to a boil, simmer 30 minutes. Makes 4 servings.

Sour Cream and Tomatoes

1 large can tomatoes or 5 to 6 fresh tomatoes, chopped
Salt and pepper
1 tblsp onion juice

1 cup sour cream
2 tblsps flour

Simmer the tomatoes with salt and pepper 15 minutes. Add the onion juice and sour cream mixed with flour. Stir until well blended and cook 2 or 3 minutes. Serve in sauce dishes.

Editor's note: If onion juice proves difficult, substitute 1 tblsp onion, shaved and minced fine. Add to the tomatoes while they are cooking.

Tomato Soufflé

1 (1 lb) can tomatoes
2 slices bread
4 eggs, well beaten
2 tsps salt

1 tblsp sugar
1/3 cup oil
PAM®

Put tomatoes in a bowl and crush with hand until the mixture is fairly smooth. Break up bread and add to tomatoes. Crush bread into mixture with hand until it is fairly smooth. Add eggs, salt and sugar and mix well. Add oil and mix well. Spray a 1 1/2-quart casserole with PAM® and pour in mixture. Place in a preheated 400° oven and bake for 45 minutes.

This will not rise as much as an ordinary soufflé but has about the same texture.

Fried Tomatoes

4 large tomatoes
Butter for frying

Salt and pepper to taste
1/2 cup cream

Cut tomatoes in thick slices and fry in butter until brown. Turn, brown other side. Lift to flat hot dish and dust with salt and pepper. In gravy in pan, add cream and stir. Pour over tomatoes. Serve hot.

Editor's note: A suggestion: Cut a slice from the top of the tomato. With the fingers, poke out the seeds and pulp. Then slice. There will be less chance of the tomato disintegrating while being fried.

Fried Green Tomatoes

3 large green tomatoes, cored
3/4 cup unsifted self-rising flour
1 tblsp salt

1/4 tsp pepper
Vegetable oil
3 tblsps bacon grease

Cut tomatoes into 3/8" slices. On wax paper, mix flour with salt and pepper. Coat tomatoes with mixture and let sit 15 minutes.

In cast-iron skillet, heat 1/2" oil and the bacon grease over medium-high heat. Lightly recoat tomatoes with flour mixture; brown on both sides, 3 minutes in all. Serve hot.

Crockpot Vegetables

1 1/2 cups onion, sliced
2 cups celery sticks, 2" long
1 1/2 cups carrot sticks, 2" long
2 cups fresh green beans, 1 1/2" long
3/4 cup green pepper strips
2 cups canned tomatoes

2 1/2 tsps salt
1/8 tsp pepper
1 tblsp sugar
2 tblsps Minute® Tapioca
4 tblsps butter or margarine

Put in slow cooker on high for 2 hours. Turn cooker to low for 3 hours. Stir during cooking.

Fresh Vegetable Casserole

4 medium zucchini, sliced
1 tsp soy sauce, or to taste
1/4 tsp salt
1/4 to 1/2 tsp garlic salt or 1/2 tsp fresh crushed garlic
1/4 to 1/2 tsp pepper

3 tblsps margarine or butter
2 tomatoes, cut in wedges
1 medium onion, sliced
1 1/2 cups or 6 ozs shredded cheddar cheese

Put zucchini in casserole and sprinkle with 1/2 of the soy sauce and spices. Layer tomatoes and onions over zucchini. Sprinkle remaining soy sauce and spices over this. Top with cheese and margarine, chunked. Bake at 350° for 40 minutes.

Mixed Vegetable Casserole

2 cans mixed vegetables, well drained
1 can whole niblet corn
1/2 cup chopped onion
1 cup finely chopped celery

1 cup grated cheese
3/4 cup mayonnaise
Ritz crackers, crumbled
1 stick margarine

Mix well all above except crackers and margarine and place in a 3 1/2- or 4-quart baking dish. Cover with a thick layer of crumbled crackers. Melt margarine and pour over top. Bake 30 to 35 minutes at 350° until brown.

Ditty Bag
Delicacies

Banana Shakes

1 1/2 cups cold milk
1 large ripe banana

1 tblsp honey
1/4 tsp vanilla

Combine ingredients in blender and puree. Makes 1 large or 2 small servings. A scoop of ice cream may be added.

Winter Tea

15 cups water
1 tblsp whole cloves
2 1/2 cups sugar
3 or 4 whole cinnamon sticks

4 (6 oz) cans pineapple juice
1 (6 oz) can frozen lemonade
5 regular tea bags

Put broken cinnamon sticks in a tea ball or toe of an old nylon stocking. Put everything except tea bags in pot and boil 3 minutes. Throw in tea bags and let steep until it reaches desired strength.

Hot Spiced Tea (Sugarless)

1 jar (4 ozs) tea with lemon
Sugar substitute, if desired
1/2 tblsp ground allspice

1 tblsp ground cinnamon
1 tblsp ground cloves
1/2 tsp ground nutmeg

Mix ingredients and add by teaspoonful to a coffee mug of tap water (depending on serving size, one teaspoon is enough for a standard size coffee mug). Boil or heat in microwave on high for 90 seconds.

Punch

1 can pink lemonade
1 can orange juice
1 (8 oz) bottle whiskey, bourbon or rum

2 1/2 cans (size of orange juice/lemonade juice) of water
3 maraschino cherries or use Grenadine for color

Blend and put in freezer a half hour before serving.

Artillery Punch

Juice of 6 lemons
1 cup sugar
1 tsp Angostura® Bitters
1 qt claret wine
1 qt Sherry

1 qt rum
1 qt bourbon
1 qt champagne
Red food coloring, if desired

If possible, after mixing all of the ingredients except the champagne, put in freezer for about 3 days. Just before serving, add the champagne. May be diluted with some sparkling water, if desired, but not necessary. Add red food coloring, if desired, to make bright, clear red.

Pink Party Punch

1 qt size pkg strawberry unsweetened Kool-Aid®
1/2 cup sugar (more if needed)
1 qt water
1 (12 oz) can frozen orange juice
1 (16 oz) can frozen lemonade

1 (18 oz) can pineapple juice
2 qts ginger ale
1 jar maraschino cherries, optional
Mint leaves, optional

Dissolve Kool-Aid® and sugar in water. Add orange juice, lemonade and pineapple juice. Just before serving, add ginger ale, garnishing with cherries and mint leaves, if desired. Part of the punch may be frozen in a ring mold before adding the ginger ale. Float this ring in punch instead of ice.

Party Punch

1 pt lemon sherbet
1 (5 oz) can concentrated orange juice
2 cups canned pineapple juice

1 pkg frozen strawberries
2 qts ginger ale
Ice ring

Spoon sherbet into punch bowl; add concentrated orange juice and pineapple juice. Stir until concentrates and sherbet are nearly melted. Add ginger ale and thawed strawberries. Add ice ring. Makes 25 servings.

Christmas Punch

1 qt raspberry sherbet
1 qt club soda
1 qt 7Up®

1 can lemonade concentrate
1 fifth sparkling Burgundy wine

Chill the sodas. Pour all liquids over the sherbet and serve in punch bowl.

Champagne Cooler

1 bottle champagne, chilled
1 cup sherry, chilled
1/2 cup curacao, chilled

1 tblsp bar syrup or bar sugar
1 small bottle soda water, chilled
1 slice cucumber peel

Mix into bowl and then pour into pitcher. Clear glass is preferable. Do not use ice.

Champagne Cocktail and Non-alcoholic Substitute

Into each glass, put 1 cube of sugar, add 2 to 3 drops of Angostura® Bitters to each cube. Fill glass with chilled champagne.
To make a non-alcoholic drink, place the following in a blender:

6 ozs orange plus (frozen)
1 3/4 cups milk
1 3/4 cups water

3/4 cup sugar
11 ice cubes

Blend until smooth and serve.

Candy Corn

1 lb (2 1/4 cups) firmly packed brown sugar
1/2 cup water
1/2 cup light corn syrup
1/2 cup butter or margarine

1 tsp salt
1 tblsp vanilla
2 1/2 qts popped popcorn

Combine sugar, water, syrup, butter and salt in heavy saucepan and cook over medium flame, stirring until sugar is dissolved. Bring to boil and continue cooking until syrup, when dropped in cold water, separates into threads which are hard but not brittle (290° on candy thermometer), stirring frequently. Add 1 tblsp vanilla.

Spread 2 1/2 quarts popped popcorn (3/4 cup unpopped) over surface of large well-greased shallow pan. Working quickly, pour syrup in fine stream over popcorn, mixing well. Continue mixing until kernels are coated with syrup. Spread on wax paper to cool. Separate into bite-size clusters with two forks.

Divinity

3/4 cup Karo® syrup
3 cups sugar
3/4 cup water

2 egg whites
3 1/2 tblsps cherry Jell-O® (3 oz pkg) powder
1/2 tsp almond extract

Mix together the syrup and sugar and water, boil until hard ball is registered on candy thermometer. Beat egg whites until very stiff. Beat in Jell-O® powder, 1 tblsp at a time. Slowly pour sugar syrup over egg whites, beating with electric beater until very stiff. Beat in almond extract. Spoon out on wax paper. Makes about 50 pieces. Do not make a double batch.

Christmas Mints

3 tblsps boiling water
1/2 stick butter
1 lb 10X sugar

1/4 tsp peppermint flavoring
2 to 3 drops green food coloring

Pour boiling water over butter. Stir until melted. Add sugar, flavoring and coloring. Blend well. Knead until smooth. Roll into small balls and flatten with a fork. Arrange single layers on wax paper.

Maine Potato Candy

3/4 cup cold mashed potatoes (plain mashed, no butter or milk)
4 cups confectioners sugar
4 cups shredded coconut, chopped

2 tsps vanilla
1/2 tsp salt (optional)
4 squares baking chocolate

Mix potatoes and confectioners sugar. Stir in coconut and vanilla. Press into one large or two small pans so that candy will be about 1/2" thick. Melt chocolate over hot water (not boiling) to keep from getting sticky or hard. Pour chocolate on top of candy. Cool and cut into squares.

Variation: Make haystacks 1" high. Allow to stand uncovered for 20 minutes. Dip base of each cone in melted chocolate; place on wax paper until chocolate hardens. Makes about 100 small haystacks.

Pralines

1 cup real butter (2 sticks) melted in deep, heavy pan
2 cups white granulated sugar
2 cups brown sugar (light or dark)
2 to 3 tblsps white Karo® or other corn syrup
2 cups milk or heavy cream or 1 large can evaporated milk plus 4 ozs water

2 tsps vanilla and/or 1/4 to 1/2 tsp maple flavoring to suit taste
1 1/2 cups pecans or other nuts, some broken pieces and halves

Melt butter; add all the other ingredients except for vanilla and nuts. Add vanilla last before final stirring when all cooked. Cook on medium heat, stirring occasionally. Cook to a medium to firm soft ball stage. Remove from burner. Add nuts. Cool slightly; stir and when candy begins to thicken, quickly drop spoonfuls on a lightly oiled or buttered cookie sheet/pizza pan. Cool/chill and serve.

Note: Leave out the nuts for plain "penuche" spread in a pan or plain pralines.

Taffy

Boil together for 5 minutes:

1 cup sugar
1/2 cup water

1 tsp vinegar

Add:

2 tblsps molasses
1 tblsp butter

1/4 tsp salt

Cook until it makes a ball when dropped in water. Place in buttered muffin tins. Nuts may be added if desired.

White Chocolate Fantasy Fudge

2 cups sugar
3/4 cup sour cream
1/2 cup margarine
1/4 cup canned milk
1/4 cup Karo® white syrup

12 ozs white chocolate (coarsely chopped)
1 (7 oz) jar marshmallow cream
3/4 cup chopped nuts (pecans and/or walnuts)
3/4 cup maraschino cherries, candied cherries or pineapple

Combine sugar, sour cream, margarine, milk and Karo® syrup in 2 1/2- or 3-quart saucepan. Cook on low heat, go to medium heat and then bring to full rolling boil, stirring constantly. Cook to 234° soft ball stage on candy thermometer. Remove from heat, add chocolate and marshmallow cream until well blended. Add nuts and fruit. Pour into 8" or 9" square greased pan. Cool at room temperature. Makes 2 1/2 pounds. Cut into squares.

Easy Crunchy Pickles

1 qt kosher pickles
1 1/2 cups sugar

1/4 cup cider vinegar

Drain pickles; cut in chunks or slices. Return to quart jar alternating with sugar. Add vinegar. Shake several times until sugar dissolves. Refrigerate. Keeps indefinitely.

Pickle Cauliflower Medley

1 medium head cauliflower
Boiling salted water
1 cup dill pickle liquid
1 small clove of garlic, crushed

1/4 tsp liquid artificial sweetener
1/4 cup chopped onion
4 medium dill pickles, quartered
1/4 cup sliced radishes

Separate cauliflower into flowerets. Cook cauliflower in boiling salted water for 6 to 7 minutes or until tender-crisp; drain. Combine pickle liquid, garlic, sweetener, and onion in shallow dish; mix well. Add cauliflower, pickles and radishes; toss lightly to coat vegetables. Cover. Chill for 12 hours, turning occasionally. Drain before serving.

Pickled Red Beet Eggs

12 eggs
1/2 cup sugar
Salt to taste

3/4 cup vinegar
1/4 cup water
1 qt canned red beets and juice

Hard boil eggs; run under cold water and peel shells from the eggs. Mix the sugar, salt, vinegar, water and red beet juice together and heat until sugar is dissolved, stirring occasionally. Pour this mix over the hard boiled eggs; add red beets. Refrigerate at least 12 hours. Serve eggs whole or sliced in half. The white of the egg will be a pretty pink color. Makes 12.

Summer Squash Pickles

12 young squash, thinly sliced
3 large onions, sliced
1 gallon water
1 cup salt
5 cups cider vinegar

4 cups sugar
1/2 cups light brown sugar
5 tblsos mustard seed
2 tblsos celery seed
1 tsp turmeric

Choose tender squash not more than 10" long. Make brine of 1 gallon water and 1 cup salt. Place in enamel or ceramic pot (not aluminum) with sliced squash and onion. Soak overnight or up to 18 hours. Drain 1 hour but <u>do not wash</u>. Make pickling syrup of vinegar, sugar, mustard seed, celery seed and turmeric and boil 5 minutes. Add drained squash and simmer 30 minutes. Bring to a rolling boil before putting in sterilized jars; seal. Makes 5 quarts.

Pickled Black-Eyed Peas

2 (16 oz) cans black-eyed peas
1/2 to 3/4 cup vegetable oil
2 1/4 cups wine vinegar
1 clove garlic

1/4 cup thinly sliced onions
1/2 tsp salt
1/8 tsp pepper

Drain peas. Combine all ingredients, cover and chill for 24 hours. Remove garlic. Chill 2 days to 2 weeks before serving. Serves 6 to 8.

Watermelon Rind Pickles

The First Day

3 qts trimmed watermelon rind (no green or pink showing)
Boiling water to cover
7 cups granulated sugar

1/2 tsp oil of cloves
1/2 tsp oil of cinnamon
2 cups vinegar

Use rind from a firm but not over-ripe watermelon. Trim off green skin and any pink flesh; cut rind into 1" cubes. There should be about 2 1/2 to 3 quarts of rind. Place rind in a large saucepan; cover with boiling water. Boil until tender but not soft, about 10 minutes. Drain well. In another saucepan, combine sugar and next 3 ingredients; bring to boil. Pour over drained rind; cover. Let stand at room temperature overnight.

The Second Day

In the morning, drain syrup from watermelon rind; heat to boiling point and pour over rind. Cover. Let stand overnight.

The Third Day

1 small unpeeled orange, scrubbed

1 unpeeled lemon, scrubbed (optional)

Slice unpeeled orange and lemon; quarter each slice. Add orange and lemon slices to watermelon rind in syrup; heat to boiling point. Turn at once into 4 to 6 hot, sterilized 1 pint preserve jars; seal as manufacturer directs. Store in cool dry place. Flavor improves after 30 days.
Note: Oil of cloves and oil of cinnamon are obtainable from the pharmacist at most drug stores. If it is not imitation, cut amount in half.

Cheese-Stuffed Manicotti

Tomato Sauce

1 clove garlic, minced
1 tblsp olive oil or PAM®
2 (8 oz) cans tomato sauce

2 (16 oz) cans unsalted tomatoes
1 1/2 tsps oregano leaves
1 tblsp chopped parsley

Filling

2 cups low-fat cottage cheese or no-fat cottage cheese
1 cup Alpine Lace no-fat cheese, shredded
3 tblsps freshly grated Parmesan
2 egg whites

1/4 cup chopped parsley
Dash pepper
8 ozs cooked manicotti shells (15 pieces)

Preheat oven 375°. Sauté garlic in olive oil or PAM®. Add tomato sauce and tomatoes slowly. Stir in oregano and parsley. Bring to boil and simmer covered for 20 minutes to 2 hours, stirring occasionally. Makes 5 cups.
Combine filling ingredients and stuff cooked manicotti shells using small butter knife. Fill bottom of 9" by 13" casserole dish with 2 cups tomato sauce. Arrange stuffed manicotti shells in a single layer over sauce side by side. Cover shells with remaining 3 cups sauce. Cover dish with foil and bake for 50 minutes. Remove foil and bake another 10 minutes. Makes 5 to 6 servings.
Spinach Variation: To filling, add 1 (10 oz) package frozen chopped spinach (thawed and squeezed dry), 1 tblsp freshly squeezed lemon juice and 2 cloves garlic, finely minced.

No-Salt Spicy Substitute

5 tsps onion powder
1 tblsp garlic powder
1 tblsp paprika
1 tblsp dry mustard

1 tsp thyme
1/2 tsp white pepper
1/2 tsp celery seeds

Mix together.

Salt Substitute I

5 tsps onion powder
1 tblsp garlic powder
1 tblsp paprika
1 tblsp dry mustard

1 tsp thyme
1/2 tsp white pepper
1/2 tsp celery seeds

Mix well and place in shaker.

Salt Substitute II

1/2 tsp cayenne pepper
1 tblsp garlic powder
1 tsp ground basil
1 tsp ground marjoram
1 tsp ground thyme
1 tsp ground parsley

1 tsp ground savory
1 tsp ground mace
1 tsp onion powder
1 tsp ground black pepper
1 tsp ground sage

Combine all ingredients. Mix well. Put in a shaker. Use sparingly.

Spaghetti with Clam Sauce

1 or 2 boxes spaghetti
1/4 to 1/2 cup virgin olive oil
1 medium onion, chopped
1 to 2 cloves garlic, chopped
10 ripe plum tomatoes, chopped (can substitute with canned)
1 small can tomato paste

1/4 to 1/2 cup fresh basil, chopped
1/4 cup fresh chopped parsley
Dash salt
Dash fresh ground black pepper
2 dozen fresh small clams
1/2 cup each of freshly grated Parmesan and Romano cheeses

Soak clams 20 minutes in large pan of cold water or directly in sink. Vigorously scrub shells with a brush to remove all sand and mud. Rinse again in fresh water after soaking and scrubbing.

In large heavy skillet heat 1/2 of olive oil, add onion and garlic, simmer a few minutes. Begin adding tomatoes before garlic burns. Cook down tomatoes uncovered for about 10 minutes. Add tomato paste, basil, parsley, salt and pepper, continue stirring sauce uncovered for about 5 more minutes. Add cleaned clams to sauce and cover. Continue cooking over medium heat until clams open and sauce has thickened (about 20 minutes). Once clam shells have opened sauce is ready, if it appears too watery, cook uncovered a while longer.

Add spaghetti to large pan of boiling water, cook and drain into colander when done. Quickly toss remaining olive oil with spaghetti. At once, dish spaghetti into pasta bowls, cover liberally with tomato sauce and clams. Sprinkle each plate with the Parmesan and Romano cheese mixture.

Spaghetti Sauce

Sauté

2 tblsps oil (olive or other cooking oil)
2 strips bacon (lean, thin, crisp)
4" Italian sausage (sweet, chopped)

1 cup onion, minced
1 tblsp garlic, minced
1/2 to 1 cup mushrooms, sliced thin

Add

4 cans tomato sauce
1 can spicy tomato juice
1/2 tblsp oregano powder
1 bay leaf

1 tblsp basil
1 1/2 tsps salt
Black pepper, coarsely ground, to taste

Bring to boil. Cook 1 hour at low heat, stirring occasionally to prevent sticking. Serve over cooked spaghetti or as sauce on pizza.

Spaghetti Pizza Deluxe

1 (7 oz) pkg spaghetti, uncooked
1/2 cup skim milk
1/4 cup Fleischmann's® Egg Beaters
Vegetable cooking spray
1 medium onion, chopped
1 medium green pepper, chopped
2 cloves garlic, minced

1 (15 oz) can tomato sauce
1 tsp Italian seasoning
1 tsp herb seasoning
1/4 tsp salt and pepper
1 cup no-fat or low-fat cottage cheese
2 cups sliced fresh mushrooms
1 cup shredded Alpine Lace no fat mozzarella cheese

Prepare spaghetti as package directs; drain. In medium bowl, blend milk and Fleischmann's ®Egg Beaters; add spaghetti and toss to coat. Spray 15" x 10" jelly roll pan with vegetable cooking spray. Spread spaghetti mixture evenly in prepared pan. In large skillet, cook onion, green pepper and garlic until tender. Add tomato sauce and seasonings; simmer 5 minutes. Remove from heat and stir in well drained cottage cheese. Spoon mixture evenly over spaghetti. Top with mushrooms and cheese. Bake in 350° oven for 20 minutes. Let stand 5 minutes before cutting. Makes 8 servings.

Fettucine Alfredo

1 lb fettucine noodles
1 cup unsalted butter
1 cup freshly grated Parmesan cheese

1/2 cup heavy cream
Dash freshly ground pepper

Cook the fettucine in boiling salted water until "al dente" (a slight hardness in the center; test by biting into one); drain.

Heat the butter in a saucepan until barely melted. Add the noodles, remove from heat and toss. Add the cheese and toss again over low heat. When well mixed, add the cream and continue tossing until the mixture is very hot. Sprinkle with pepper and serve at once.

Note: In this dish, real butter and cream are essential. It is a very famous dish originating in Alfredo's in Rome. Mary Pickford and Douglas Fairbanks (then married) were so delighted with it that they presented Alfredo with a solid gold spoon and fork for tossing.

Brandied Cranberry Relish

1 (12 oz) pkg cranberries
1 large orange
1 medium apple
1 cup sugar (or less)

3/4 cup raisins
1 cup chopped walnuts
1 1/2 ozs brandy

Put cranberries, orange, and apple through coarse cutting plate of food grinder. Add sugar, raisins, chopped walnuts, and brandy. Mix well. Chill. May be frozen.

Cranberry Chutney

1 lb fresh cranberries
2 large pears, pared and diced

2 cups sugar
4 ozs candied ginger or lemon peel

Bring to boil. Stir constantly. Cook 5 minutes; simmer 15 minutes.

Salsa

2 large bunches green onions, finely chopped
1 (4 oz) can diced green chilies for milder flavor, or use 1 (3 1/2 oz) can diced Jalapeño peppers for hotter flavor

1 (4 1/4 oz) can chopped black olives
5 large tomatoes, diced
1 (8 oz) bottle Italian salad dressing

Mix all ingredients in a 1-quart bowl. Chill overnight. Makes 4 cups.

Spiced Nuts

1 cup sugar
1 tsp cinnamon

1/2 cup water
4 tblsps vinegar

Cook to hard ball (not crackle) stage. Keep over boiling water while dipping.

Pecans

Dip pecans in syrup and drop in the following mixture:

1/2 cup sugar
1/2 tsp cinnamon

1/2 tsp allspice
1/2 tsp cloves

Mustard

4 ozs dry mustard
1 cup cider vinegar

1 cup sugar
3 eggs

Put all ingredients in blender and blend. Transfer to top of double boiler. Water in bottom pan must not touch top pan. Cook until thick. Stir often, about 15 minutes, or cook over low heat and stir with whisk.

Sweet Mustard Sauce

2 eggs well beaten
1/2 cup sugar
1 tblsp dry mustard

1/8 cup lemon juice and 1/8 cup vinegar, or 1/4 cup vinegar
1 tblsp butter

Cook all in a double boiler until thick. Will keep well in refrigerator. Good with ham, turkey or hard pretzels.

Butter Sauce

3 tblsps butter
3 tblsps all-purpose flour
Dash salt and pepper

1 1/2 cups milk
2 egg yolks, beaten
1 tsp lemon juice

Melt butter in sauce pan. Stir in flour, salt and pepper until smooth. Add milk slowly, stirring constantly. Beat some of the hot mixture into egg yolks. Stir into remaining hot mixture. Cook 1 minute. Stir in lemon juice. Makes 2 cups; serves 4 to 6.

Cream Sauce (or White Sauce or Béchamel Sauce)

Thin Cream Sauce

1 tblsp fat
1 tblsp flour
1/4 tsp salt

Dash of pepper (optional)
1 cup milk

Medium Cream Sauce

2 tblsps fat
2 tblsps flour
1/4 tsp salt

Dash of pepper (optional)
1 cup milk

Thick Cream Sauce

3 or 4 tblsps fat
3 or 4 tblsps flour
1/4 tsp salt

Dash of pepper (optional)
1 cup milk

For all sauces: Melt fat over low heat. Add flour, salt and pepper and stir until smooth. Add milk slowly, stirring vigorously until thoroughly mixed. Boil over low heat, stirring constantly until cooked and smooth.

These recipes may be enlarged by merely multiplying all the ingredients.

Hollandaise Sauce

1 hard stick butter
3 egg yolks
Juice from 1/2 lemon

Salt
Dash of red pepper
Small cold frying pan

Place the butter in the cold frying pan. Add the egg yolks, lemon juice, salt and pepper. Cook over very low heat just until it is thick and smooth. Overcooking will result in scrambled eggs.

Mock Hollandaise Sauce

3/4 cup butter
3 tblsps flour
1/4 tsp salt
1/8 tsp pepper

1 1/2 cups milk
3 egg yolks, beaten
3 tblsps lemon juice

Melt 3 tblsps butter in a small sauce pan. Add flour and seasonings and stir until blended. Gradually add milk, stirring constantly. Remove from heat. Cook over medium heat until thick and creamy, stirring constantly. Stir in egg yolks, the remaining butter, one tablespoon at a time, and the lemon juice. Return to heat and cook and stir about 3 minutes longer. Makes 1 1/2 cups sauce.

Editor's note: Butter is obligatory in Hollandaise sauces.

Corn Bread Dressing

1 batch of corn bread made according to recipe on corn meal box omitting sugar, if called for. Crumble finely in large mixing bowl.

4 fresh Jalapeños (optional), finely processed
2 large onions, finely processed
4 stalks celery, chopped
1 tblsp sage
1/2 tsp pepper

1 tsp MSG
1 cup chopped giblets (or chicken livers), boiled 30 minutes, then medium diced
4 cups chicken bouillon (made according to directions on jar)

Mix all above items thoroughly. Adjust seasoning to taste. Pack in 3-quart casserole (or 2 smaller casseroles). Bake 1 hour at 325° in oven or microwave 10 to 12 minutes on high. Makes 12 servings.

Potato Dressing

3 or 4 potatoes, cooked and mashed
4 slices bread cubes (Italian style, not too fresh is best)
1 cup chicken broth
Butter or margarine (size of a walnut)

1 small chopped onion
1 tblsp parsley (double if fresh used)
2 eggs, beaten
Seasonings to taste

Mix all together. Can be steamed on top of stove or baked in 350° oven about 20 minutes or until set. Can be reheated and served with gravy.

Quahog Stuffing

Clams
2 pieces hard/stale bread moistened with water
15 mashed Ritz crackers
Salt and pepper
Parsley flakes

Garlic chips
3 tblsps Hunt's® Tomato Sauce
1 tblsp grated cheese
Water
Small amt of Wesson Oil®

Chop quahog into small pieces. Mix in a bowl with remaining ingredients. Brush small amount of oil over mixture. If too dry, add a little water. Fill half of each clam shell with mixture and then put shells in roasting pan. Add water to roasting pan (not enough to go over shells). Bake at 375° for 1/2 hour or until crispy looking.

Dakota Skillet Meal

2 tblsps butter or margarine
2 cups diced cooked potatoes
2 cups small bread crumbs
4 scallions, thinly sliced
1 cup diced ham or beef or pork or poultry

2 large eggs
1/4 cup cream or evaporated milk
1/2 tsp salt
1/2 tsp seasoning salt
Pepper

Melt butter or margarine in a skillet. Add potatoes, bread crumbs and scallions. Cook over medium heat, stirring often until potatoes are brown. Stir in meat or poultry. Beat eggs with cream and seasonings and pour over mixture in the skillet. Do not stir. As soon as the mixture is set, it can be folded over like an omelet and slipped onto a warm platter; or it can be served directly from the skillet. Keep in a moderate oven until serving; it will be hot and crusty.

Fruit Dip

4 tblsps Marshmallow Fluff

1 (8 oz) pkg cream cheese

Mix well. Serve as a dip for fruits such as pineapple, apples, strawberries, etc.

Non-Fat "Chocolate" Syrup

1 cup cocoa
1 1/2 cups sugar
1/8 tsp salt

1 1/4 cups boiling water
1 tsp vanilla

Combine cocoa, sugar and salt; add to boiling water and place pan directly over low heat. Boil 5 minutes. Add vanilla. Makes 2 1/2 cups. Refrigerate.

Baked Pineapple

1/2 cup butter
3/4 cup sugar
Dash salt

3 eggs, beaten
1 large can crushed pineapple
5 slices cubed bread

Cream butter and sugar. Add other ingredients. Put in 1 1/2-quart casserole. Bake 50 minutes at 400°.

Crepes

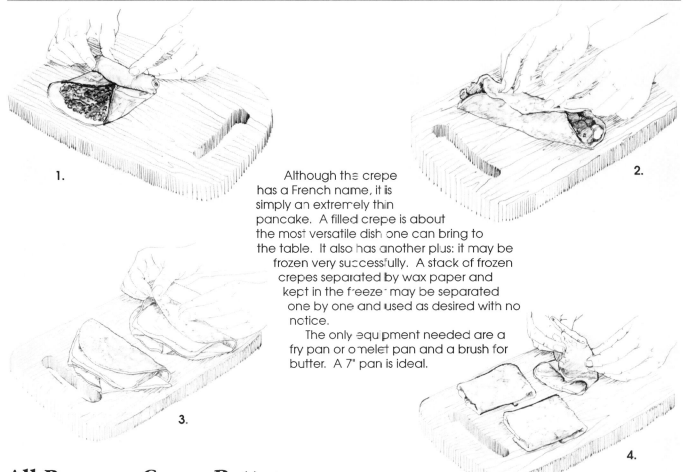

Although the crepe has a French name, it is simply an extremely thin pancake. A filled crepe is about the most versatile dish one can bring to the table. It also has another plus: it may be frozen very successfully. A stack of frozen crepes separated by wax paper and kept in the freezer may be separated one by one and used as desired with no notice.

The only equipment needed are a fry pan or omelet pan and a brush for butter. A 7" pan is ideal.

1.

2.

3.

4.

All Purpose Crepe Batter

4 eggs, beaten
1/4 tsp salt
2 cups flour

2 1/4 cups milk
1/4 cup melted butter or oil
Additional melted butter to brush on pan between crepes

Mixer or whisk method: In a medium mixing bowl, combine eggs and salt. Gradually add flour alternating with milk, beating with an electric mixer or a whisk until smooth. Beat in 1/4 cup melted butter.

Blender method: Combine ingredients in a blender jar, blend for about 1 minute. Scrape down sides of jar with a rubber spatula and blend for another 15 seconds until smooth.

Both methods: Let batter set for one hour or more. This allows the flour to expand and some of the bubbles to collapse. Brush pan with oil or butter. Heat pan over medium heat. With one hand, pour in 2 or 3 tblsps of batter (easier f using 1/4 cup measure, but not more than called for amount)

At the same time, with the other hand, lift pan above heating unit. Immediately tilt the pan in all directions so the batter covers the pan. Pour off excess (if any) back into the batter. Work quickly before the batter cooks too much to swirl. Cook crepe until the bottom is brown (that is the side that will furnish the outside of the crepe). It takes very little time. With a pancake turner, carefully turn the crepe over and cook a few seconds.

Remove from pan; stack on a plate. Repeat, stirring batter occasionally to keep mixed.

After the crepes have cooled, separate them with squares of wax paper. Pack into an air tight flat package. Freeze.

For use: Remove package from the freezer. Carefully separate as many crepes as needed. Return the rest to the package and back to the freezer.

Makes 32 to 36 crepes.

Breakfast Crepes

| Crepes | Sour cream or seasoned hot tomato sauce |
| Scrambled eggs | |

Warm crepes very slightly in a warm oven or a few seconds in a microwave oven. Put scrambled eggs on one half of the crepe and fold over. Top with sour cream or tomato sauce.

| Crepes | Frozen creamed chipped beef |

Heat chipped beef (if desired, it may be thinned a little). Place on one half crepe. Fold over and top with more chipped beef.

| Crepes | Cream of mushroom soup |
| Canned corn beef hash | |

Cook corn beef hash in a fry pan, stirring. Heat soup, dilute to sauce consistency. Put hash on one half of the crepe, fold over and top with sauce.

| Crepes | Dash cayenne pepper |
| Kraft® Cheez Whiz | Milk |

Melt Cheez Whiz, add pepper and thin with a little milk. Put a line of cheese sauce down the middle of the crepe and roll. Top with more sauce.

Chili Dog Crepes

10 cooked crepes	1 small onion, chopped
10 frankfurters	2 cups grated cheddar cheese
1 (15 oz) can chili with beans	

Cook frankfurters. Heat chili. Place one frankfurter in the center of the crepe. Top with chili and onions. Fold one half over the filing, then fold over the second half. Sprinkle with cheese. Place under the broiler until the cheese melts.

Asparagus Crepes

Crepes	Dash cayenne pepper
Frozen asparagus spears	Milk
Kraft® Cheez Whiz	

Cook asparagus according to directions. Meanwhile, heat Cheez Whiz and thin down with milk to the consistency of sauce. Add pepper. Warm crepes. Put a few spears in the middle of the crepe. Fold one side over top, then fold second side over top. Pour on cheese sauce.

Chicken Crepes (A la King)

Crepes
1 can cream of mushroom soup
1 egg, beaten

2 (5 1/2 oz) cans Swanson chicken
1 small jar chopped pimientos, drained
Dash of sherry

Heat soup and thin to the consistency of a sauce. Pour a little of the sauce into the egg, mix and return to sauce. Add chicken. Add drained pimientos. Mix all with dash of sherry and heat. Put sauce on half of the crepe, fold over and cover with sauce.

Seafood Crepes

Crepes
Canned shrimp or canned crab meat or canned drained tuna

Cream of mushroom soup or cream of shrimp soup for shrimp crepes

Heat soup and dilute to consistency of a sauce. Add seafood. Place mixture on one half of crepe and fold over. Cover with more mixture.
Variations: Add a few sliced stuffed olives to the tuna mixture. Add a dash of sherry to any of the mixtures.

Ricotta and Strawberry Crepes

2/3 lb ricotta cheese
4 tblsps granulated sugar
1 tsp vanilla

2 cups fresh strawberries, hulled and crushed
Powdered sugar

Cream the ricotta with the sugar. Add vanilla. Add berries and mix gently. Spoon the mixture down the center of a crepe and roll up. Sprinkle with powdered sugar.

Quick Crepe Suzette

1/2 cup sweet butter
1/4 cup sugar
5 tsps grated orange peel
1/2 cup orange juice

1 tsp lemon juice
10 to 12 crepes
1/4 cup orange flavored liqueur
2 tblsps apricot or peach brandy or 2 tblsps plain brandy

Cream butter, gradually add sugar. Add orange peel, orange juice and lemon juice. Heat in a skillet or chafing dish. Dip crepes in mixture. Fold crepes in half and half again. Move to the side of the pan. Heat liqueur and brandy in a small pan. Pour over crepes; ignite with a <u>long match</u>. Spoon sauce over crepes until flame dies. Serve immediately. Makes 5 or 6 servings.
Editor's note: If afraid of fire, it is not really necessary to ignite the sauce, although it makes the dish more spectacular. Just basting the crepes with the sauce is sufficient.

Crepes for Emergency Use

Crepes
Jam (strawberry or raspberry or apricot)

Reddi Wip® cream or powdered sugar

Spoon a line of jam down the middle of the crepe. Roll. Top with Reddi Wip® or just sprinkle on powdered sugar.

Crepes
Vanilla ice cream

Chocolate syrup

Put ice cream on half the crepe. Fold over and top with chocolate syrup.

Crepes
Apple sauce mixed with a dash of cinnamon

Sour cream or whipped cream

Spoon apple sauce on one side of the crepe. Fold over. Top with sour cream or whipped cream.

Dessert Crepes

Crepes
Fresh strawberries

Sugar
Whipped cream

Slice the strawberries and add sugar to taste. Let macerate until sugar is dissolved and berries are juicy. Put strawberries on one half the crepe, fold over. Top with whipped cream. Fresh ripe peaches may be used also.

Crepes
Canned mincemeat

2 dashes brandy
Instant vanilla pudding thinned to consistency of sauce

Flavor mincemeat with a dash of brandy. Fold into a package, using illustration # 4. Top with pudding to which another dash of brandy has been added.

The variety of fillings for crepes is limited only by the imagination. For anyone interested in more elaborate crepe cookery, an excellent book is:
Crepe Cookery, published by:
HP Books
PO Box 5367
Tucson, AZ 85703
(602) 888-2150
There are hard and soft cover copies, complete with color illustrations.

Desserts

Butter Cream Frosting

3 tblsps butter
2 cups sifted confectioners sugar
1/8 tsp salt

3 tblsps milk
1 tsp vanilla

Beat butter, 1 cup sugar and salt together thoroughly until light and fluffy. Use mixer at medium speed or beat by hand. Add remaining cup of sugar and milk, beating until very smooth. Add vanilla. Frosts 9" x 9" x 2" cake. For two or three layer cakes, double or triple recipe as required.

Flo's Frosting

1 small pkg instant pudding (any flavor)
1/4 cup powdered sugar

1 cup cold milk
1 small carton (8 oz) Cool Whip®

Mix instant pudding with powdered sugar. Add cold milk. When it thickens, fold in Cool Whip®. Spread on cool cake.

Topping for Angel Food Cake

1 large can pineapple chunks or tidbits, in own juice
1 pkg instant vanilla pudding, prepared according to directions

1 large carton of Cool Whip®
1 cup miniature marshmallows

To chilled pineapple, add the vanilla pudding and stir well. Add Cool Whip® and the marshmallows. (May be thinned with milk if desired.) Should be enough for 1 angel food cake, 14 to 16 slices.

Special Cake Topping

1 cup sugar
2 tblsps flour
1 tblsp corn starch
1 small can crushed pineapple

1 tsp butter
1 1/2 cups water
1 lb dates, cut fine
Pinch of salt

Cook until thick. Better if made the day before. Especially good on chocolate cake. Top with whipped cream.

Sunny Italian Dessert

1 box angel food cake mix
1 lb ricotta cheese
1 cup powdered sugar

1/2 tsp almond extract
1 pt whipping cream, whipped until thick

Whipped Cream Icing

1 pt whipping cream
1/2 tsp almond extract

1/4 cup powdered sugar

Follow directions on package for cake. Cool and slice into 3 layers. In a blender mix cheese, sugar and almond extract. Blend until smooth and creamy. Add whipped cream, blend thoroughly and use as filling between layers. Leave the top for icing. Whip cream, extract and sugar until thick and smooth. Ice cake, top and sides. Refrigerate one hour before serving.

World's Best Chocolate Cake

1 3/4 cups sugar
2 cups sifted flour
1/2 cup cocoa
1/2 tsp salt
1 tblsp baking soda

1 egg
2/3 cup sour milk* or buttermilk
1 tsp vanilla
1 cup strong coffee

Mix together in a large bowl sugar, flour, cocoa, salt and baking soda. Add egg, milk, vanilla and coffee. Mix well. Batter will be slightly lumpy. Pour into a 13" x 9" pan, which has been greased and floured. Bake at 350° for 45 minutes.

Frosting

4 tblsps butter
4 (1 oz) squares unsweetened baking chocolate
2 2/3 cups powdered sugar

1/3 tsp salt
5 tblsps milk
1 1/4 tsps vanilla

Melt butter and chocolate together. Blend in remaining ingredients; beat well. Frosting may be applied while cake is in the pan.
*To make sour milk, add 1 tsp vinegar to 1 cup milk.

Earthquake Cake

1 cup chopped pecans
1 cup coconut
1 German chocolate cake mix

8 ozs cream cheese, softened
1 box powdered sugar
1 tsp vanilla flavoring

Preheat oven to 350°.
Grease bottom of 9" x 13" pan. Mix the pecans and coconut together and spread evenly in the bottom of the pan. Prepare the German chocolate cake as directed on the box. Then pour it over the coconut and pecans. Mix together the cream cheese, powdered sugar and vanilla. Spoon over the cake batter. Bake at 350° for 45 to 50 minutes.

Chocolate Birthday Cake

9" layer pans or square layer pans or bundt pan

1/2 cup shortening
1 1/2 cups granulated sugar
2 eggs, beaten
1/2 cup sour milk* or 1/2 cup buttermilk
1 tsp baking soda

1 tsp vanilla extract
2 cups cake flour (if in high altitude, use unsifted bread flour)
2 squares unsweetened chocolate
1/2 cup water

Cream shortening with sugar. Add eggs. Dissolve soda in milk. Add liquid ingredients alternating with dry ingredients. Melt chocolate and water together. Cool. Add to batter. Grease baking pan(s) and dust with flour. Pour in batter and bake at 375° for 25 minutes or until toothpick comes out clean.

White Mountain Frosting

1 1/2 cups sugar
1/2 cup water

3 egg whites

Cook sugar and water until it forms a thread when dropped from a spoon. Beat egg whites until soft peaks form. Pour syrup gradually over egg whites, beating constantly. When thick and cool, frost cake.
*To make sour milk, add 1 tsp vinegar to 1 cup milk.

Best Ever Chocolate Cake

1 tblsp vinegar
1 cup milk, at room temperature
2 1/2 cups flour
2 tsps baking soda
1/2 tsp salt
2 cups sugar

1 cup shortening
2 eggs
1/2 cup cocoa
1 cup hot water
1 tsp vanilla

Mix vinegar and milk, set aside. Sift dry ingredients, set aside. Cream sugar and shortening. Mix in 1 egg at a time. Blend in cocoa. Add dry ingredients alternately with soured milk. Stir in hot water and vanilla. Bake in greased and floured 9" x 13' pan at 350° about 40 to 45 minutes.

Chocolate Frosting

1 cup sugar
1/4 cup margarine
1/4 cup milk

1/2 cup chocolate chips, scant
1 tsp vanilla

Bring sugar, margarine and milk to a boil. Take off stove and add scant 1/2 cup chocolate chips and 1 tsp vanilla. Beat until smooth (thickens as it gets cooler).

Chocolate Decadence (Flourless Chocolate Cake)

Spring form pan
6 ozs bitter sweet chocolate
3 ozs unsweetened chocolate
3/4 lb butter, unsalted

3/4 cup sugar
4 eggs
Dash vanilla

Preheat oven to 350°. Prepare spring form pan by sprinkling on sugar on bottom. Shake out excess sugar. Cover outside of pan with foil so dough will not slip under the bottom.

Melt chocolates and butter in double boiler; add vanilla. Whip eggs until very light (pale-colored). Add sugar and stir to dissolve; blend in well the chocolate mixture. Pour into prepared pan and set pan into larger pan half-filled with hot water, for baking. Cake will bake in 45 minutes or so, according to how many times the oven is opened. Check for doneness by inserting a toothpick or cake tester into middle of cake. When done it will have a crumb or two attached. Cake should not be left in oven until cake tester comes out clean. Texture of the cake should be light, not heavy.

Let cake sit to cool about 30 minutes before removing sides of the pan. Slice and serve with a fresh raspberry coulis (puréed raspberry sauce), fresh berries or whipped cream flavored with a dash of Chambord.

Raspberry Sauce

2 cups frozen raspberries
1/8 tsp lemon juice

Whipped cream

Thaw raspberries. Place berries and lemon juice in container of electric blender; blend until smooth. Strain mixture and discard seeds. Cover and chill. Stir before serving.

To serve: dribble sauce by spoon on individual dessert plate. Place a slice of cake 2" square in center of plate. Dribble sauce on top of cake. Top with whipped cream.

Pumpkin Cake

1 pkg yellow cake mix
1 stick melted butter
1 egg, beaten
1 small can pumpkin
3 eggs, beaten
1 tsp cinnamon

3/4 cup sugar
2/3 cup evaporated milk
1 tsp cinnamon
1 tblsp butter
1/2 cup chopped nuts

Take out 1 cup of cake mix and set aside. Mix the rest of the cake mix with the stick of melted butter and the egg. Pat the mixture into a 13" x 9" x 2" cake pan. Bake at 350° for 10 minutes. Mix the pumpkin, the eggs, sugar, evaporated milk and cinnamon together and pour over the cake. Take the extra cup of cake mix, add cinnamon, butter and chopped nuts, combine until crumbly and sprinkle over the cake. Bake at 325° for 60 minutes.

Editor's note: The cake pan should be greased and floured.

Pumpkin Pie Cake

1 recipe pumpkin pie filling
1 pkg yellow cake mix, dry
1 cup chopped nuts

1 cup melted butter or margarine
Whipped cream

Mix pumpkin pie filling and pour into a 9" x 13" greased cake pan. Sprinkle cake mix and nuts over top. Drizzle melted butter over top. Bake at 350° for 1 hour. Serve with whipped cream.

New York Cheese Cake

9" pie pan or 10" spring form pan
1 pkg graham crackers,
crushed (equals 1 2/3 cups crumbs)

1/4 cup sugar
1/4 cup melted butter

Combine and press into bottom and sides of pan.

2 lbs cream cheese
6 eggs
1 1/4 cups sugar

2 tblsps flour
2 tsps vanilla
1 pt sour cream

Beat eggs, one at a time, into the cream cheese. Add the sugar and flour, mixed together. Add the vanilla. Mix in the sour cream. Pour the mixture into the crust. Bake at 350° for 1 hour or until the cake is raised and delicately brown. Turn off the oven and leave the oven door open for 15 to 20 minutes. Refrigerate immediately, covered with wax paper. Chill.

Bake Free Heavenly Daze Cheese Cake

1 large can evaporated milk
33 crushed graham crackers
1 stick melted butter or margarine
1/2 tsp cinnamon
1 tsp powdered sugar

1 (3 oz) pkg lemon Jell-O®
3/4 cup boiling water
6 ozs cream cheese, softened
1 cup sugar
1 tsp vanilla

Pour evaporated milk into a large chilled mixing bowl and set in the freezer for approximately 1 hour.

Mix together graham crackers, butter, cinnamon and powdered sugar. Take out 1 cup and set aside for topping. Press the rest of the mixture into an ungreased 9" x 12" pan. Dissolve the lemon Jell-O® into boiling water. Set aside and cool to room temperature. Cream softened cream cheese with the sugar and vanilla. Mix Jell-O® with cream cheese mixture.

Beat evaporated milk into stiff peaks. Add Jell-O® and cheese mixture to the milk and mix well. Pour the mixture into the crumb pan. Sprinkle the remaining crumb mixture on top. Let stand in refrigerator over night. May be served with blueberries or strawberries. Serves 12.

Apple Brandy Cake

2 1/2 cups all purpose or unbleached flour
1 cup sugar
1 cup firmly packed brown sugar
2 tsps baking soda
1 tsp salt
2 tsps cinnamon

1 cup oil
1/4 cup brandy, apple cider or apple juice
2 tsps vanilla
3 eggs
3 cups chopped peeled apples
1 cup chopped nuts (optional)

Brown Butter Glaze

1/4 cup butter (do not use margarine)
1 cup powdered sugar

2 to 4 tblsps apple cider/juice or milk
Additional apple cider

Heat oven to 350°. Grease and flour 12-cup bundt or 10" tube pan. Lightly spoon flour into measuring cup; level off. In a large bowl, combine flour, sugar, brown sugar, baking soda, salt and cinnamon. Mix well. Add oil, brandy, vanilla and eggs. Stir by hand until well blended. (Mixture will be very thick.) Fold in apples and nuts. Spread in greased and floured pan.

Bake at 350° for 50 to 60 minutes or until toothpick inserted in center comes out clean. Cool cake in pan 10 minutes; invert cake onto serving plate. Cool.

In small heavy sauce pan over medium heat, brown butter until light golden brown, stirring constantly. Remove from heat. Add powdered sugar and 2 tblsps apple cider/juice or milk; blend well. Add additional apple cider until it reaches desired drizzling consistency. Spoon glaze over cake, allowing some to run down sides. Makes 16 servings.

Maine Blueberry Cake

1 3/4 cups flour
2 tsp baking powder
1/2 tsp salt (optional)
Pinch of cinnamon (optional)
1 cup sugar
1 egg

1/2 cup milk
1 tsp vanilla
1/4 cup melted butter or margarine (1/2 stick)
1 1/4 cups floured blueberries
Sugar and cinnamon for topping

Sift flour, baking powder, salt, cinnamon (if desired) together. Mix in sugar. Beat the egg with milk and add to flour mixture. Add vanilla and melted butter. Fold in floured blueberries. Place in 8" square pan which has been greased. Sprinkle top with a mixture of cinnamon and sugar. Bake for 35 to 40 minutes at 375°. This has a crusty top when eaten warm. Makes 9 to 12 squares.

Variation: Substitute 1/2 cup orange juice for the 1/2 cup milk. Add 1 1/2 tsp grated orange rind to batter. Mix 1 1/2 tsps grated orange rind with the sugar and cinnamon to be used on top.

Orange-Pineapple Cake

1 box orange cake mix
1/2 cup sour cream

2 eggs
1 can peach pie filling

Mix all the ingredients together with a fork. Pour in 11" x 13" cake pan, ungreased. Bake at 350° for 35 minutes.

Frosting

1 (8 oz) pkg cream cheese
1 (3 oz) pkg instant vanilla pudding

1 (20 oz) can undrained crushed pineapple
1 (8 oz) Cool Whip®

Mix all together and frost cake.

Swedish Applecake

4 tblsps butter
2 cups zwieback crumbs (or stale, limp Swedish rye, grated)

1 1/3 cups applesauce
Whipped cream or vanilla sauce

Melt butter in skillet, add crumbs and stir until nicely browned. Into buttered baking dish, alternate crumbs and applesauce in layers, ending with crumbs on top. Bake in 375° oven for 25 to 35 minutes. Cool before unmolding. Serve with whipped cream or a vanilla sauce.

Vanilla Sauce

1 cup cream, heated
3 yolks or 1 whole egg plus 2 whites
2 tblsps sugar

2 tsps vanilla
3/4 to 1 cup whipped cream

Beat yolks (or egg plus whites) and sugar in top of double boiler. Add heated cream and cook until thick; stir constantly. Remove from heat; add vanilla and cool, beating occasionally. Fold in whipped cream, carefully, and serve with cake.

Walnut Carrot Cake

1 1/2 cups walnuts
3 cups sifted all-purpose flour
3 tsps baking powder
1 tsp salt
2 cups brown sugar, packed
4 large eggs

1 cup oil
1 1/2 tsps cinnamon
1 tsp nutmeg
1/4 tsp powdered cloves
3 tblsps milk
3 cups grated carrots

Chop 1/2 cup walnuts fine. Grease three 9" layer cake pans well. Sprinkle each with about 2 1/2 tblsps of walnuts to coat. Chop remaining walnuts a little more coarsely; set aside. Resift flour with baking powder and salt. Combine sugar, eggs, oil and spices. Beat at high speed until light and well mixed. Add half of flour mixture; stir until well blended. Add milk, then remaining flour. Stir in carrots and chopped walnuts. Divide batter evenly in pans. Bake at 350° for 25 minutes until cakes test done. Let stand in pans on wire racks 10 minutes. Turn cakes out onto racks to cool. When completely cooled, frost with butter cream frosting (see The Ditty Bag). Decorate with walnut halves. Makes 1 large cake. 12 servings.

Loaf Cake

1/2 cup shortening
1 cup sugar
2 1/4 cups flour
1 cup milk
1 egg white beaten until stiff, or whole egg

1 tsp nutmeg
2 1/2 tsps baking powder
1/2 cup mixed dried fruit
1/4 cup raisins

Cream shortening, add sugar gradually. If whole egg is used, add (if white only is used, fold in at end). Mix dry ingredients, reserving a little flour to coat. Add fruit alternately with milk. Bake in a round pan in a 350° oven around 45 to 50 minutes. Nuts may be added with fruit, if desired.

Mincemeat Almond Holiday Cheesecake

Crust

1 1/2 cups graham crumbs
3 tblsps granulated sugar

3 tblsps melted butter

Combine all ingredients, mix well and press into a 10" spring form pan. Bake 5 minutes at 325°. Cool on rack.

Filling

3 (8 oz) pkgs light cream cheese, softened
1 cup half and half
1/2 cup granulated sugar
1 cup mincemeat in a jar with rum and brandy

1 tsp grated orange peel
1 tsp vanilla extract
4 egg whites, beaten well
1/2 cup toasted sliced almonds

Beat cream cheese until soft. Add half and half and mix well. Add 1/2 cup sugar, mincemeat, orange peel, vanilla and mix well. Fold in beaten egg whites. Fold in toasted almonds.

Turn into prepared crust. Bake at 325° for 65 minutes. Remove from oven.

Topping

1 cup sour cream
1 tblsp granulated sugar
1/2 tsp almond extract

1 cup toasted sliced almonds
Green and red Maraschino cherries for decoration

Mix all ingredients, except cherries, well. Spread over top of hot filling. Return to 325° oven for 5 minutes. Cool on rack.

Decorate: Slice red cherries in half and arrange them on top of cake with rounded tops facing up like a flower center. Slice green cherries in half and place one half to each side of red cherry, like a leaf. Press almond slices around outer edge on top of cake.

Refrigerate for 8 hours. May be frozen ahead and thawed for an hour prior to serving. (Serves 12.)

Rotation Cake

1 cup butter or margarine
2 cups sugar
5 eggs
3 cups sifted cake flour
1/2 tsp salt

3 tsps baking powder
1 cup sweet cream or milk
1 tsp lemon or other flavoring
2 tblsps liqueur (peach or apricot recommended)

Cream butter or margarine. Add sugar gradually and beat until fluffy. Add eggs one at a time and beat until light. Sift flour and measure. Add salt and baking powder. Sift again. Add dry ingredients alternately with cream or milk. Add flavoring. Add liqueur. Beat thoroughly after each addition. Pour into large greased loaf pan or tube pan. Bake at 350° for one hour. Test with toothpick to see if done. Sprinkle with 2 tblsps of liqueur.

Pig Pickin' Cake

11-oz can mandarin oranges
1 box Duncan Hines® yellow cake mix

4 eggs
3/4 cup vegetable oil

Pour can of mandarin oranges and liquid into blender and liquefy. Add to cake mix, eggs and oil in a large bowl and mix well. Pour batter into 3 greased and floured 8" pans. Bake at 350° for 20 to 25 minutes until cake tests done with a toothpick. Cool completely and then frost.

Frosting

1 large pkg instant vanilla pudding
1 large can crushed pineapple, undrained

1 (9 oz) container Cool Whip®

Mix dry pudding gradually into pineapple until all liquid is absorbed. Blend in Cool Whip®. Frost cake and store in refrigerator over night before serving. Serves 10 to 12.

Crazy Cake

3 cups flour
2 tsps baking soda
2 cups sugar

1/2 tsp salt
1/3 cup cocoa

Add

2 tblsps vinegar
1 tsp vanilla

3/4 cup salad oil
2 cups water

Beat all together until smooth. Pour into greased 9" x 13" pan; bake at 350° for 35 to 40 minutes or until toothpick comes out clean.

Topping

1 cup cocoa
1 1/2 cups water
1/2 cup sugar
1/4 tsp salt

1 tblsp corn starch dissolved in
4 tblsps water
1 1/2 tblsps margarine
1 tsp vanilla

Bring cocoa, water, sugar and salt to a boil. Add the corn starch dissolved in the water. Boil until thick and add margarine and vanilla. Spread over top of the cake after it is cooled.

Tomato Soup Cake

2 cups sifted flour
1/2 tsp baking soda
1 tblsp baking powder
1/2 tsp powdered cloves
1/2 cup shortening

1 cup sugar
2 eggs, well beaten
1 can condensed tomato soup
1/2 tsp nutmeg
1 cup seedless raisins

Sift together flour, baking soda, baking powder and cloves. Cream shortening; add sugar gradually. Add eggs, mixing well. Add flour mixture alternately with soup. Stir until smooth. Fold in nutmeg and raisins; pour into greased and floured pan. Bake at 350° about 35 minutes or until done.

Heath® Bar Cake

1 cup light brown sugar
1/2 cup sugar
2 cups sifted flour
1/4 lb margarine
4 Heath® Bars, shaved

1 tsp baking soda
1 cup buttermilk
1 tsp vanilla
1 egg, beaten

Blend together sugars, flour, soda and margarine. Remove 1/2 cup for topping. Mix 1/2 cup with Heath® Bar shavings and set aside. Add remaining ingredients, eggs, milk and vanilla. Beat well. Place in 9" x 13" pan. Sprinkle with topping mixture. Bake at 350° for 35 minutes. Serves 12.

Ice Cream Cone Cupcakes

1 pkg any flavor cake mix (18 1/4 ozs)
24 flat bottomed ice cream cones

Icing and your favorite decorations.

Prepare cake mix according to directions. Preheat oven to 400°. Fill each cone with 1/4 cup batter (about 1/2 full). If there is batter left over, bake in a small greased pan. Place each cone in a cup of muffin tin pans (mini-muffin pans work best). Bake at 400° for 15 to 18 minutes. Cool, frost with Peppermint Frosting or other favorite flavor and decorate.

Peppermint Frosting

(especially good with chocolate or white cupcakes)

1/4 cup butter or margarine, softened
3 cups powdered sugar, sifted if lumpy

3 to 5 tblsp milk
1/2 cup finely crushed red and white mints or candy canes

Place butter, sugar and milk in deep bowl. With electric mixer or by hand, beat until fluffy. Stir in peppermint. Spread on cooled cupcakes. (For stronger peppermint taste, add 3 to 4 drops of peppermint extract.)

Black Bottom Cupcakes

1 1/2 cups flour
1 cup sugar
1/4 cup cocoa
1/2 cup oil
1 tsp baking soda

1/2 tsp salt
1 cup water
1 tsp vinegar
1 tsp vanilla

Mix all ingredients together to form batter. Line cupcake pan with cupcake liners.

1 (8 oz) pkg softened cream cheese
1 egg
1/3 cup sugar

1/8 tsp salt
1 cup chocolate chips

Mix all ingredients together. Fill each lined cupcake pan about 1/2 full of batter. Add 1 tblsp of cream cheese mixture. Bake at 350° about 30 minutes. Makes 1 1/2 dozen.

Brownies I

2 cups flour
2 cups sugar
1 stick butter
1/2 cup shortening
1 cup strong brewed coffee
1/4 cup dry cocoa

1/2 cup buttermilk (substitute 2 tsps vinegar or lemon juice in 1/2 cup milk)
2 eggs, beaten
1 tsp baking soda
1 tsp vanilla
1 cup chopped nuts

In a large bowl, combine flour and sugar. In a sauce pan, combine butter, shortening, coffee and cocoa. Stir and heat to boiling. Pour over the flour and sugar mixture. Add buttermilk, eggs, baking soda, vanilla and chopped nuts. Mix well with a beater. Pour into a greased 17" x 11" jelly roll pan. Bake at 400° for 20 minutes.

Frosting

1/2 stick butter
1 tblsp cocoa
1/8 cup milk

1 3/4 cups powdered sugar
1 tsp vanilla

Mix butter, cocoa and milk in a sauce pan. Heat to boiling. Mix in powdered sugar and vanilla. Pour warm over brownies.

Brownies II

1 stick margarine
1 cup sugar
4 eggs
1 cup plus 1 tblsp flour

1 can Hershey's® chocolate syrup
Vanilla to taste
Pinch of salt
Nuts (optional)

Cream margarine and sugar. Add eggs, one at a time, beating after each addition. Add remaining ingredients and mix well. Pour into a greased brownie pan and bake at 350° for about 30 minutes.

Frosting (if desired)

1 cup sugar
6 tblsps margarine

6 tblsps milk
1/2 cup chocolate chips

Boil sugar, margarine and milk together for 1 minute. Remove from heat and add chocolate chips. Stir until spreading consistency. Spread on cooled brownies.

Congo Squares

2/3 cup shortening or butter
1 box light brown sugar
3 eggs
2 3/4 cups sifted flour

1 tsp vanilla
2 tblsps water
1 cup chopped nuts
1 pkg chocolate chips

Melt shortening, add brown sugar and stir until well mixed. Add eggs one at a time, beat well. Add remaining ingredients, mix well. Pour into a greased oblong pan. Bake at 300° for 25 to 30 minutes.

Chocolate Cream Cheese Brownies

1 pkg (4 ozs) German sweet chocolate
2 tblsps butter or margarine
2 eggs
3/4 cup sugar
1/2 cup all-purpose flour

1/2 tsp baking powder
1/4 tsp salt
1 tsp vanilla extract
1/4 tsp almond extract
1/2 cup chopped nuts

Filling

2 tblsps butter or margarine
1 (3 oz) pkg cream cheese, softened
1/4 cup sugar

1 egg
1 tblsp all-purpose flour
1/2 tsp vanilla extract

In a sauce pan, melt chocolate and butter over low heat, stirring frequently. Set aside. In a bowl, beat the eggs. Gradually add sugar, beating until thick. Combine flour, baking powder and salt, add to egg mixture. Stir in melted chocolate, extracts and nuts. Pour half of the batter into a greased 8" square baking pan, set aside.

For filling, beat butter and cream cheese in a mixing bowl until light. Gradually add sugar, beating until fluffy. Blend in egg, flour and vanilla; mix well. Spread over batter in pan. Dollop remaining batter over filling. With knife, cut through batter to create a marbled effect. Bake at 350° for 35-40 minutes or until brownies test done. Cool. Store in refrigerator. Makes about 2 dozen.

Chocolate Fudge Delight

1 1/4 cups flour
1 1/2 sticks margarine

1/2 cup chopped nuts

Cream cheese mix

8 ozs cream cheese
1 cup powdered sugar

1/2 container of Cool Whip® (12 oz size)

Topping

2 pkgs instant chocolate fudge (or any flavor) pudding mix   3 cups milk

Mix flour, margarine and nuts well and press in 9" x 13" pan. Pat down and bake at 350° for 25 to 30 minutes. Cool. Spread cream cheese mix evenly over crust. Spread topping on cream cheese mix. Spread remaining Cool Whip® and sprinkle nuts on top. Refrigerate.

Applesauce Torte

1/4 cup butter or shortening
2 cups graham cracker crumbs (about 20)
1/2 tsp cinnamon
3 eggs, separated

1 (14 oz) can sweetened condensed milk
Juice and grated rind of 1 lemon
2 cups thick applesauce

Melt butter or shortening in sauce pan and stir in the cracker crumbs and cinnamon. Pat 1/2 of the mixture in bottom of 8" spring form pan. Separate egg yolks from whites and beat yolks until light and lemon color. Stir in condensed milk, lemon juice, grated rind and thick applesauce. Beat egg whites until they hold a peak and mix them into the applesauce mixture very gently. Pour into crumb-lined pan. Spread with remaining crumbs and bake 1 hour at 325° or until cake is firm when shaken.

Note: As cake cools, it will shrink slightly.

Apple Raspberry Bavarian Tart

Ungreased 9" spring form pan

Crust

1 1/2 cups all purpose flour
1/2 cup sugar
1/2 cup butter

1 egg
1/4 tsp almond extract

Filling

1/2 cup golden or dark raisins
1/3 cup sliced almonds
2 large apples, peeled, cored, cut into 1/4" slices
2 tsps corn starch
1/4 cup milk
1 tblsp lemon juice

1/4 tsp vanilla
1/4 tsp almond extract
1 (8 oz) carton vanilla yogurt
1 egg, beaten
1/4 cup raspberry preserves, melted

Heat oven to 375°. Measure flour by leveling off. In large bowl, combine flour, sugar and butter; beat at low speed until well blended. Beat in 1 egg and 1/4 tsp almond extract to form crumbs. A hand pastry blender may be used. Press crumb mixture in bottom and 1 1/2 " up the sides of ungreased 9" spring form pan.

Sprinkle with raisins and almonds. Arrange apple slices over raisins (start from center, outward in a circle) in desired pattern.

In medium bowl, dissolve corn starch in milk. Add lemon juice, vanilla, almond extract, yogurt and 1 beaten egg; blend well. Pour over apples.

Bake at 375° for 55 to 60 minutes or until apples are tender. Cool 30 minutes; remove sides of pan. Brush preserves over apples. Garnish with whipped cream. Refrigerate any remaining tarts for future use. Makes 10 to 12 servings.

Editor's note: The raspberry preserves are more pleasant to eat if they have been put through a sieve to remove the seeds.

Butterscotch Torte

6 eggs, separated
1 1/2 cups white sugar
1 tsp baking powder
2 tsps vanilla

1 tsp almond flavoring, or to taste
2 cups graham cracker crumbs
1 cup chopped nuts
Cool Whip®

Beat egg yolks well. Slowly add sugar, baking powder and flavorings. Mix well. Beat egg whites to stiff peaks. Fold into yolk mixture. Fold in crumbs and nuts. Pour into two 9" layer pans, greased and lined with wax paper. Bake at 325° for 30 to 35 minutes. Cool and remove from pan. Frost with Cool Whip® and put Cool Whip® between layers.

Sauce

1 cup water
1/4 cup butter
1 cup brown sugar
1 tblsp flour

1 egg, well beaten
1/4 cup orange juice
1/2 tsp vanilla

Blend water, butter, sugar and flour in a sauce pan. Add egg, orange juice and vanilla. Mix well, bring to a boil and cook until thick. Cool thoroughly. Pour over top of Cool Whip® and let it drizzle over the sides of the cake.

Editor's note: Almond extract is very strong.

Three Layer Torte

Layer I

1 cup flour
1/2 cup butter

1/2 cup chopped nuts
3 tblsps confectioners sugar

Layer II

1 (8 oz) pkg cream cheese, at room temperature
1 cup confectioners sugar

9 ozs Cool Whip®

Layer III

2 pkgs instant pudding (choice of flavor)
2 1/2 cups milk

9 ozs Cool Whip®
Pecans, chopped

First layer. Blend with fork and press into a 9" x 13" pan. Bake 10 to 15 minutes at 350°.
Second layer. Beat cream cheese and sugar together until light. Fold in Cool Whip®. Pour onto cooled crust.
Third layer. Mix pudding with milk. Put on top of second layer. Spread with Cool Whip®. Sprinkle with pecans.
Note: When using banana cream instant pudding, bananas may be put on top of pudding before spreading with Cool Whip®.

Never Fail Pie Crust

3 cups flour
1 cup shortening
1 tsp salt

1 egg, well beaten
1 tblsp vinegar
5 tblsps water

Cut flour, shortening and salt together. Add egg with 5 tblsps water and 1 tblsp vinegar to moisten. Makes 4 crusts and can be re-rolled without getting tough. Can be refrigerated in covered container up to 2 weeks. Also freezes well.

Pumpkin Pie

4 eggs
2 cups pumpkin
1 1/3 cups sugar
1 tblsp flour
1 tsp ginger

1 tsp cinnamon
1/2 tsp allspice
1/4 tsp cloves
1/2 tsp salt
4 cups milk (heated)

Beat eggs. Stir in pumpkin. Mix all dry ingredients together and mix with pumpkin. Add milk to mixture and fill pies. Makes 2 pies.

Pumpkin Walnut Pie

2 cups of raw pumpkin (food processed and drained well)
1 cup brown sugar
1/2 tsp salt
1 tsp cinnamon
1 tsp ginger
1 tsp nutmeg

1 1/2 cups milk
1 tsp vanilla
1 cup chopped walnuts
3 eggs, two of them separated
2 tblsps sugar
2 pie crusts or 9" deep dish

Preheat oven to 350°. Mix pumpkin and brown sugar, salt and spices with milk and vanilla and beat well. Put in either microwave or double boiler and heat until hot. Add to mixture one egg and two yolks, well beaten. Turn into two partly cooked fluted pie crusts, then sprinkle with half of walnuts.

Bake in oven until firm (45 minutes; check using clean knife technique). When cool, beat two egg whites stiff with sugar and vanilla. Spread on pie, sprinkle on remaining nut meats and place in oven to brown.

Impossible Pecan Date Pie (Sugarless)

1 cup chopped pecans
4 eggs
1/4 cup flour
1/4 cup melted margarine

1 cup chopped dates
1 cup milk
1 tsp vanilla

Lightly grease a 9" x 9" pan; sprinkle with pecans. In a blender, mix remaining ingredients until well blended. Pour over pecans. Bake at 350° until set and golden brown, about 30 minutes.

Sunny Banana Pie

1 (9") graham cracker crust or regular baked pie shell
2 bananas
1 (8 oz) pkg cream cheese

2 cups milk
1 small pkg instant vanilla pudding mix
Toasted coconut

Slice bananas into graham cracker crust or regular baked pie shell. Gradually add 1/2 cup milk into softened cream cheese, mixing until well blended. Add pudding mix and remaining milk; beat slowly 1 minute. Pour into crust; chill. Garnish with coconut.

Sweetheart Cherry Pie

1 (8 oz) pkg cream cheese
1 (8 oz) Cool Whip®
6 tblsps powdered sugar
1/2 cup shredded coconut

1/2 tsp almond flavoring
1 can cherry pie filling
1 graham cracker crust

Cream the cream cheese until fluffy. Add Cool Whip®, powdered sugar, coconut, almond flavoring. Mix well. Fold in can of cherry pie filling. Pour into cracker crust. Refrigerate at least 3 hours.

No Cook Strawberry Pie

1 baked and cooled 9" pie crust

Glaze

2 cups fresh strawberries
Water
1 cup sugar

4 tblsps corn starch
Whole strawberries

Cup up strawberries into small pieces and fill 2 cups. Put in the water to fill up spaces. Place on stove to boil. Mix sugar and corn starch very well. When mixture in pot is all liquid, stir in sugar mixture. Keep stirring until it boils. Cook 1 1/2 minutes. Cool quickly by placing in pan of ice water until tepid.

Place 2/3 of glaze in pie crust. Pack in lots of whole strawberries, then pour rest of glaze over top of the strawberries. Cool 2 hours in refrigerator.

Out of This World Pie

1 or 2 baked and cooled pie shells
3/4 cup granulated sugar
1 tblsp corn starch
1 (20 oz) can unsweetened pineapple tidbits, undrained
1 (21 oz) can cherry pie filling
1 tsp red food color (optional)

1 (3 oz) box strawberry flavor gelatin
4 bananas, peeled and sliced
1 (10") deep dish pie shell or 2 (9") pie shells, baked and cooled
2 cups whipped cream or non-dairy whipped topping
1 cup finely chopped nuts (pecans or almonds), toasted

Measure sugar and corn starch into sauce pan; mix well. Add pineapple with its juice; mix well so no lumps form. Stir in pie filling and food color. Use a wooden spoon and stir gently to avoid mashing the cherries. Cook over medium heat until mixture comes to a boil and is well thickened, about 5 to 8 minutes. Remove from heat; stir in dry gelatin. Let cool. When mixture has cooled completely, gently stir in sliced bananas. Spoon into baked and cooled pie shell(s). Cover top(s) with whipped cream; garnish with nuts. Refrigerate until pie is set.

Tester's note: Don't panic if the filling doesn't set up quickly; it takes time for the gelatin to gel. After it does, the pie will slice neatly and easily.

Editor's note: Unbaked pie shells may be obtained in the frozen food department of the grocery store.

No-Crust Norwegian Pie

3/4 cup sugar
1/2 cup flour
1 egg, beaten
1 tsp baking powder
1/2 tsp vanilla

1/2 tsp salt (optional)
1 1/2 cups sliced apples
1/2 cup nuts
1/2 cup raisins

Mix sugar, flour, egg and baking powder. Add vanilla and salt. Stir in apples, nuts and raisins. Pour into well greased pie pan or dish and bake at 350° for 30 minutes (325° for glass).

Chocolate Pie

1 unbaked pie shell
2 eggs
1 cup sugar
1/2 cup butter, melted
1 tsp vanilla

1/4 cup corn starch
1 cup (6 ozs) chocolate chips
1 cup pecans, chopped
Whipped cream

Beat eggs, add sugar, melted butter and vanilla. Mix well. Blend in corn starch, stir in chopped pecans and chocolate chips. Pour into unbaked shell. Bake at 350° for 45 to 50 minutes. Cool 1 hour and serve with whipped cream. Freezes well. If frozen, reheat for 35 minutes at 300°.

Peanut Butter Pie

1 (12 oz) jar creamy peanut butter
1 (8 oz) pkg cream cheese
1 (8 oz) pkg powdered sugar

1 (12 oz) carton whipped topping
1 baked pie shell

Beat peanut butter, cream cheese and powdered sugar together. Add whipped topping and mix well. Pour into pie shell. Refrigerate over night. Makes 8 servings.

Oatmeal Pie

3 eggs, beaten
2/3 cup sugar
2/3 cup brown sugar
2/3 cup quick cooking oatmeal
2/3 cup coconut

3 tblsps melted butter
1 tsp vanilla
1/2 cup chopped nuts
Unbaked pie shell

Mix all ingredients and pour into an unbaked pie shell. Bake at 350° for 45 minutes. Serve with whipped cream.

Happiness Pie

9" Readymade Keebler® Graham Cracker or Chocolate Pie Crust
2 pkgs regular Jell-O® vanilla pudding
1 pkg Knox® plain gelatin
3 1/2 cups milk

3 ozs cream cheese, softened
1/2 tsp vanilla extract
Cool Whip®
Fresh strawberries or shaved chocolate

Combine pudding mix, gelatin and milk in a heavy sauce pan. Bring to a full boil over medium heat, stirring constantly.

Put cream cheese in large mixer bowl. Let pudding mixture cool for 5 minutes, stirring twice. Then pour the pudding mixture over the cream cheese and vanilla. Mix well. Pour the filling into pie crust. Refrigerate overnight. Serve with a dab of Cool Whip® and fresh strawberries, or shaved chocolate.

Shoo Fly Pie

1 (9") unbaked pie crust in pan
1 1/2 cups sifted flour
1 cup light brown sugar, firmly packed
1/4 cup margarine or butter

1/2 tsp baking soda
3/4 cup hot water
1/2 cup plus 1 tblsp Blue Label Karo® syrup

Make crumbs with flour, sugar and butter.
Dissolve baking soda in water. Combine with syrup. Pour into pie shell. Top with crumbs, spreading evenly. Bake at 350° until firm, approximately 40 minutes. Test with a toothpick.

Pinto Bean Pie

3 eggs, separated
1 1/2 cups cooked pinto beans
1 1/2 cups sugar
Pinch of salt

1 1/2 tsps cinnamon
2 tblsps flour
2 cups milk
Unbaked pie shell

Beat egg yolks, mash the beans thoroughly (or use a blender), reserve egg whites and combine all other ingredients. Pour into uncooked pie shell and bake at 350° for approximately one hour or until firm. When cool, top with meringue, using the reserved egg whites.

Ritz Cracker Pie

3 egg whites
1/2 tsp baking powder
1 cup sugar

1/2 cup walnuts
12 Ritz crackers, broken in small pieces

Beat egg whites stiff. Beat in baking powder and sugar. Fold in walnuts and crackers. Bake in greased pie plate at 325° for 1/2 hour.

White Potato Pie

5 cups mashed potatoes
1 cup sugar
1 tsp salt
1 tsp nutmeg

2 tsps lemon extract
5 eggs, separated
1/4 lb butter, melted
1 uncooked pie shell

Mix all ingredients except egg whites. Beat egg whites stiff and fold into other ingredients. Pour into uncooked pie shell. Bake at 425° for 20 minutes. Reduce heat and bake at 375° for 25 minutes. Makes 2 pies.
Notes:
1. May be served with confectioners sugar sprinkled on top and a spoonful of tart jelly on the side.
2. Use ricer to mash potatoes; they will be light and lump free.

Zuider Zee Dessert

1 pkg Holland rusk, rolled fine
1/4 cup sugar
1/2 cup butter
1 tsp cinnamon
1/4 cup sugar
2 tblsps corn starch
1/4 tsp salt

2 cups milk
2 eggs, beaten
1 tsp vanilla
2 egg whites
1/2 cup sugar
1/3 cup walnuts, chopped

Mix rusk, sugar, butter and cinnamon. Place evenly against the bottom of an 8" x 8" pan or pie plate, reserving some for the top.

Mix sugar, corn starch and salt in a sauce pan. Gradually stir in milk. Stir over moderate heat until it boils. Remove from heat, stir half the mixture into eggs, then return to the rest of the mixture in the pan. Boil 1 minute more, stirring constantly. Add vanilla. Pour into the crust. Beat the egg whites until soft peaks form. Add the sugar gradually, still beating. When thick, spread the meringue on the filling. Add walnuts to the remaining crumb mixture and sprinkle on top. Bake 5 minutes in a preheated 450° oven.

Corn Flake Cookies

1 cup butter
1 cup sugar
1 1/2 cups flour
1 tsp baking soda

1 tsp cream of tartar
1 tsp vanilla
1/2 cup pecans, chopped
2 cups corn flakes

Mix butter, sugar, flour, soda, cream of tartar and vanilla together. Add pecans and corn flakes. Mix. Drop by teaspoons onto a cookie sheet. Bake at 350° for 8 to 10 minutes. Let cool a little before removing from sheet.

Editor's note: Suggest greasing the cookie sheet.

Corn Flake Macaroons

2 egg whites
1 cup sugar
1/2 cup walnuts

1 cup coconut
1 tsp vanilla
2 cups corn flakes

Beat egg whites stiff. Add sugar gradually, continuing to beat until very stiff. Fold in nuts, coconut, vanilla and corn flakes. Drop by teaspoon on greased sheet. Bake 15 to 18 minutes at 350°.

Cracker Cookies

About 35 saltine crackers
2 sticks margarine

3/4 cup dark brown sugar
12 ozs chocolate chips

Line 15" x 10" pan with foil and lay crackers side by side in the bottom. Mix margarine with 3/4 cup dark brown sugar. Boil for 3 minutes and pour over crackers. Bake 5 minutes at 375°. On taking out of oven, put 12 ounces of chocolate chips over all. Let melt and spread evenly. Cut and separate between the crackers when cool.

Kourabiedes

2 cups sweet butter
3/4 cup powdered sugar
1 egg yolk
1 jigger brandy

4 1/2 cups sifted flour
2/3 cup chopped (finely) walnuts or pecans
Powdered sugar for topping

Cream butter until very light (almost white). Gradually beat in sugar. Beat in egg yolk and brandy. Gradually blend in flour to make a soft dough. Add nuts and mix well. With floured hands, shape dough into 1/2" balls. Place on a baking sheet. Bake in 350° oven for 15 to 20 minutes. Upon removing from the oven, place cookies on sifted sugar. Sift sugar over top and sides. Cool thoroughly before storing. Makes 4 to 6 dozen.

Meringue Cookies

3 egg whites
1/8 tsp salt
1/2 tsp cream of tartar
3/4 cup sugar

6 ozs semi-sweet chocolate morsels
1 cup walnuts, chopped (optional)
Butter
Flour

Beat egg whites until foamy. Add salt and cream of tartar. Beat until whites form soft peaks. Add sugar and beat until stiff. Fold in morsels and nuts. Line a cookie sheet with wax paper, spread with butter and dust with flour. Drop batter onto sheet by teaspoons. Bake in 200° preheated oven for 1 hour. Turn off heat and leave cookies in the closed oven for a few hours or over night.

Editor's note: After the whites have formed soft peaks, sprinkle in the sugar while continuing to beat.

Nut Cookies

1 cup butter
4 tblsps sugar
1 3/4 cups flour
1 tsp vanilla

1/4 tsp salt
2 cups finely chopped nuts
Powdered sugar

Cream butter and sugar. Add flour, vanilla, salt and nuts. Form into balls about 1" across. Place on a cookie sheet. Bake at 350° about 15 minutes. Do not brown. Roll in powdered sugar. Makes about 40.

Rice Krispies® Melt Cookies

1 cup white sugar
1 cup brown sugar
1 cup margarine
1 cup oil
1 egg, slightly beaten

1 tsp vanilla
3 1/2 cups flour
1 tsp cream of tartar
1 tsp soda
1 tsp salt

Mix sugars, margarine, oil, egg and vanilla together. Mix flour, cream of tartar, soda and salt together. Mix both mixes together.
Add:

1/2 cup chopped nuts
1 cup coconut

1 cup Rice Krispies®
1/2 cup oatmeal, uncooked

Mix all together. Drop on a greased cookie sheet by teaspoons full. Flatten a little. Bake at 350° until golden. This makes a large batch. Freezes well.

Sinful Cookies

2 cups flour
1/2 tsp baking powder
1/2 tsp baking soda
1/2 cup butter or margarine
1/2 cup shortening
1 cup sugar
1 cup brown sugar
2 eggs

1/2 cup milk
1 tsp vanilla
2 cups rolled oats
1 cup raisins
1 cup chocolate bits
1 cup chopped nuts
1/2 cup honey
Confectioners sugar (optional)

Stir ingredients together and beat. Chill for 2 hours. Drop by tablespoons onto an ungreased cookie sheet. Bake at 375° for 12 minutes. Use a spatula to remove onto wax paper. Sprinkle with confectioners sugar, if desired. Makes 60 cookies.

Sunflower Seed Cookies

1 cup butter or margarine
1 cup firmly packed brown sugar
1 cup granulated sugar
2 eggs
1 tsp vanilla
1 1/2 cups unsifted all-purpose flour

3/4 tsp salt
1 tsp baking soda
3 cups quick cooking oats
1 cup raw sunflower seeds
1/2 cup chopped walnuts

Cream together butter, brown and white sugars. Add eggs and vanilla and beat well. Add flour, salt, soda and oats. Mix thoroughly. Gently blend in sunflower seeds and walnuts. Form in long rolls about 1 1/2" in diameter. Wrap in clear plastic and chill well. Slice 1/4" thick and arrange on ungreased cookie sheet. Bake in a 350° oven for 20 minutes or until lightly browned. Cool and store in airtight containers. Makes about 6 dozen.
Note: These may be dropped from a teaspoon after mixing. Also, raisins may be added.

Peanut Butter Twinkles

2 cups granulated sugar
2 cups white corn syrup
2 cups peanut butter

1/4 cup butter or margarine
1 (18 oz) box of plain corn flakes

Bring sugar and corn syrup to a rolling boil. Take off heat. Stir in peanut butter and margarine until dissolved. Pour over corn flakes and, using ice cream scoop, drop immediately on to a cookie sheet which has been greased with margarine. Do not bake. Cookies will be ready to eat in 10 minutes.

Maine Crunchies

2 cups sugar
3 tblsps cocoa
1/4 lb margarine
1/2 cup milk

1 tsp vanilla
1/2 cup peanut butter
3 cups dry quick cooking oatmeal

Mix together sugar, cocoa, margarine and milk. Bring to a boil and boil hard for 2 minutes (no more, that's the secret to the recipe). Remove from heat and add vanilla, peanut butter and oatmeal. Mix well and drop on wax paper with teaspoon. Ready to eat when cool.

Apricot Balls

1 1/2 cups dried apricots, ground
2 cups shredded coconut

2/3 cup sweetened condensed milk
Confectioners sugar

Mix apricots and coconut. Add condensed milk. Blend well. Shape into balls. Roll in confectioners sugar and let stand until firm. Makes about 32 balls.

Bananas Iceberg, Quick & Easy

Ripe bananas
Sugar and cinnamon, mixed

Heavy cream

Peel ripe bananas and wrap in plastic wrap, twisting ends tightly. Store in the freezer 4 to 5 hours. When ready to serve, cut bananas into diagonal slices. Sprinkle liberally with sugar and cinnamon. Serve immediately with heavy cream poured over. As soon as the cream is poured on the bananas, it freezes almost instantly.

Lemon Dainty

1 lemon, the peel grated and the juice strained
3 tblsps butter
1/8 tsp salt
3/4 cup sugar

2 tblsps flour
2 eggs separated
1 cup milk

Combine the butter, salt, sugar and flour and mix well. Beat the egg yolks lightly. Add to the mixture the egg yolks, milk, lemon juice and lemon peel. Beat the mixture with an egg beater until smooth. Beat the egg whites until stiff. Fold whites into the mixture. Pour the mixture into a buttered 4 cup baking dish, set the dish in a shallow pan partly filled with water and bake in a preheated 350° oven for 45 minutes until golden brown. There will be cake on top, pudding on the bottom. Serve warm or at room temperature.
Makes 4 servings.

Lemon Soufflé

4 egg yolks, beaten
4 tblsps sugar
3 tblsps hot water
Grated rind of 2 large lemons

Juice of 2 large lemons
4 egg whites, stiffly beaten
2 tblsps sugar

Beat the yolks in the top of a double boiler. Add the 4 tblsps sugar, water, rind and juice. Continue beating over hot boiling water (water must not touch the top pan) until the mixture is thick. Add the stiffly beaten egg whites, beaten with the 2 tblsps sugar. Pour into 6 dessert glasses and let chill in the refrigerator. Makes 6 servings.
Editor's note: If dessert glasses are not available, a bowl may be used and the soufflé spooned out at the last minute.

Senior Citizen Orange Delight

1 lb carton cottage cheese, large or small curd
1 box orange Jell-O® (3 cups)
1 (11 oz) can mandarin oranges, drained

1 (20 oz) can crushed pineapple, drained
1 (8 oz) container Cool Whip®

Mix well cottage cheese and Jell-O®. Cut mandarin orange pieces in half. Put the oranges and pineapple in strainer. With fork, squeeze most of the juice out. Then fold all ingredients into Cool Whip® until well blended. Makes 10 to 12 servings, 1/2 cup each.

Peaches Cardinal

4 to 6 ripe peaches
2/3 cup sugar
1 cup water

2 slices lemon
1 tsp vanilla

Peel, halve and pit peaches. Cook sugar, water and lemon until the sugar is dissolved. Simmer peaches in syrup until barely tender. Remove from heat and add vanilla. Serve warm or cold, as a side dish or fruit dessert.

Pistachio Pudding Dessert

2 small pkgs instant pistachio pudding
1 large Cool Whip®
2 large cans crushed pineapple, drained

3 jars maraschino cherries (2 red, 1 green)
1 bag mini marshmallows

Prepare pudding per package instructions. Let set. It is best to do this a day ahead if time permits. Add fruit. Fold in Cool Whip® and marshmallows. Let set in refrigerator for at least 1 hour.

Prune Whip

3 egg whites
1 tblsp grated lemon rind
2 tblsps lemon juice
2 tblsps prune juice
1 tsp salt

1/3 cup sugar
1 cup finely chopped cooked prunes
Light cream or custard sauce (see soft custard recipe in recipe for trifle)

Combine egg whites, lemon peel, lemon juice, prune juice, salt and sugar in the upper part of a double boiler. Set over boiling water in the bottom pan (water must not touch bottom of top pan). Beat with a rotary beater 10 minutes or until the mixture holds its shape. Remove pan from boiling water. Fold in prunes. Let cool. Chill. Serve in dessert dishes with a little light cream or custard sauce.

Frosty Strawberry Squares

1 cup flour
1/4 cup brown sugar

1/2 cup chopped walnuts
1/2 cup melted margarine

To make crumb mixture, stir together the ingredients above. Spread evenly in shallow pan. Bake at 350° for 20 minutes, stirring occasionally. Cool. Should be a crumbly mixture.

2 egg whites
1 cup sugar
2 cups sliced fresh strawberries (may use one 10-oz pkg frozen berries partially thawed; reduce sugar to 2/3 cups)

2 tblsps lemon juice
1 cup whipping cream

Combine egg whites, sugar, berries and lemon juice in large mixer bowl and beat with electric beater at high speed until stiff peaks form, about 10 minutes. Fold in whipped cream.

Sprinkle 2/3 of the crumb mixture in a 9" x 13" pan. Spoon strawberry mixture over crumbs. Top with remaining crumbs. Freeze 6 hours or over night. Cut into 10 to 12 squares. Garnish with whole strawberries.

Frozen Fruit

1 cup water
1 cup sugar
6 oz can frozen orange juice, undiluted
2 tblsps frozen lemon juice

1 (29 oz) can apricots, pitted and drained
30 ozs frozen strawberries, not drained
1 (20 oz) can crushed pineapple, drained
3 bananas, diced

Heat ingredients until sugar dissolves. Cool, then stir in fruit. Cover and freeze. (May be put in plastic or muffin cups.) Take out 1/2 hour before serving.

Old Fashioned Boiled Custard

1 tblsp corn starch
4 cups milk
4 eggs

4 tblsps sugar
1/2 tsp salt
1 1/2 tsps vanilla flavoring

Dissolve corn starch in a little cold milk. Bring remainder of milk to a boil. Add corn starch mixture. Stir in smoothly and cook slowly for 10 minutes. Beat eggs and sugar and salt together and pour boiling milk over mixture. Blend all together and return to stove. Cook slowly until thick enough to mask spoon. Take off heat at once. Set in pan of cold water and stir often so as to cool custard down quickly. Then add flavoring. Pour into serving dishes if eaten at once, or into jars for refrigeration.

Editor's note: Pour the boiling milk mixture over the egg mixture little by little in order not to scramble the eggs.

Hot Fudge Pudding

1 cup flour
2 tsps baking powder
3/4 cup sugar
1/4 tsp salt
2 tblsps cocoa

1/2 cup milk
2 tblsps margarine
1 cup brown sugar
4 tblsps cocoa
1 3/4 cups hot water

Sift into a bowl the flour, baking powder, sugar, salt and 2 tblsps cocoa. Stir in milk and margarine. Spread in a 9" square pan. Sprinkle with a mixture of brown sugar and the 4 tblsps cocoa. Pour hot water over the entire mixture. Bake at 350° for 45 minutes. Invert pan on a plate and serve warm.

Pistachio Salad or Dessert

1 pkg instant pistachio pudding
1 cup milk
1 regular size Cool Whip®

1 pkg mini-marshmallows
1 cup crushed pineapple

Mix pudding and milk until thick. Add Cool Whip® and mix. Add pineapple and mini marshmallows and mix. Chill.

Swedish Rice Pudding

1 qt milk
1/3 cup rice (not instant)
Salt to taste
1/2 cup sugar
3 eggs, beaten
1/8 tsp cinnamon

1/8 tsp nutmeg
1 tsp vanilla extract
1/2 tsp almond extract
1/4 cup raisins
1 cup milk

Cook the milk, rice and salt in double boiler 3/4 hour. Mix together the sugar, 3 beaten eggs, flavorings, raisins and 1 cup milk in a casserole dish. Combine this with the cooked rice mixture. Bake 1 hour at 350° or until custard is set. Serve warm or cold.

Dulce con Leche (Caramel Pudding)

1 large can sweetened condensed milk
1 large pot boiling water

Cream (unsweetened whipped, or coffee cream)

Put the can of milk in the pot of boiling water. Cover and, over moderate heat, boil the can for 4 hours. Cool the can before opening; place in refrigerator. For each serving, scoop out a heaping soup spoon of the pudding and place in a bowl. Cover with unsweetened whipped cream or pour on a little coffee cream. A small serving is sufficient. If there is any left over, scoop it out of the can, put it in a small bowl, cover closely with plastic wrap and refrigerate. It will keep a long time.

Chocolat Pots de Creme

2 to 3 squares unsweetened chocolate, shaved
3 cups milk
2/3 cup sugar
1/4 tsp salt

5 egg yolks
1/2 tsp vanilla extract
Cream or whipped cream

Melt chocolate in milk over low heat. Add sugar and salt; cook until chocolate is completely melted. Remove from heat. Add egg yolks gradually, stirring. Cook over very low heat until pudding thickens, stirring constantly. Remove from heat. Stir in vanilla. Pour into custard cups or serving dishes. Chill until set. Serve with cream or whipped cream.

Editor's note: To be safe, it might be wise to cook this in a double boiler. These custards separate quickly.

Kolaches

Filling

1 cup pitted finely chopped prunes
2 slices lemon
1 tsp cinnamon

1/4 tsp ground cloves
2 tblsps white corn syrup

Cook on low heat and stir like a jam for just a few minutes. Take out lemon slices and set aside to cool.

1 cup milk
1 pkg or 1 cake yeast
1/2 tsp sugar
1 1/2 cups sifted flour
1/2 cup margarine

1/3 cup sugar
1 to 1 1/2 tsps salt
1 egg, beaten
2 to 2 1/4 cups more sifted flour
Powdered sugar

Scald milk and cool until tepid. Beat in yeast and sugar. Add flour and mix well. Set in a warm place and let rise to double, about 45 minutes.

In a large bowl, cream margarine and sugar together. When yeast mixture has risen to double its size, add to margarine and sugar. Add salt, egg and 2 to 2 1/4 cups sifted flour. Mix well and let rise again, covered with a tea towel, about an hour or so.

Turn out on floured board. Take pieces of dough and, with light fingers, form into round, fat buns, about 18 or 20 in all. Let rise again 1/2 hour on a greased baking sheet in a warm place. When fat and soft, make a dent in center with 2 or 3 fingers and fill centers with filling, a tblsp or more to each bun. Bake at 400° for 25 to 30 minutes. Sprinkle with powdered sugar. Eat while warm or warm up and top with sour cream.

Editor's note: It is absolutely necessary to check the date on the yeast. If it is old or nearly old, discard it and buy fresh yeast. Yeast keeps better in the freezer.

Scottish Shortbread

1/2 lb butter, softened (2 sticks)
1/2 cup sugar

2 1/4 cups all purpose flour
2 (9") Pyrex® pie plates

Mix sugar and butter until creamy. Add flour 1/2 cup at a time and mix with your hands until all the flour is added and the mixture does not stick to your hands. Form into a ball and cut in half, evenly. Press each half into a 9" pie plate. Prick with fork all over and press with fork around edges. Bake at 325° for 30 to 40 minutes or until golden brown.

IMPORTANT: Cut while it is still hot.

Editor's note: Butter is essential in this recipe; it furnishes the flavor. Some recipes call for sweet butter.

Gum Drop Bars

4 eggs, well beaten
1 tblsp water
2 cups light brown sugar
2 cups flour

1/2 cup chopped nuts
1 cup gum drops (not spiced), chopped
Salt

Mix in order given. Put in well-greased, floured baking pan. Bake for 30 minutes at 350°. While still hot, ice with the following:

2 tblsps orange juice
2 tblsps butter

Enough powdered sugar to spread.

Cut into bars.

Trifle

Thick slices of sponge cake
1 1/2 cups sweet sherry or sweet white wine
Soft custard
Raspberry or strawberry jam

1 pint whipping cream
1/2 cup sugar
1/2 tsp vanilla

The sponge cake may be bought. If not obtainable, pound cake will do. Make the custard.

Soft Custard

4 eggs, slightly beaten
1/2 cup sugar
1/4 tsp salt

1 qt milk
1 tsp vanilla

Mix well the eggs, sugar and salt. Combine thoroughly with milk. Place mixture in the top of a double boiler. Put hot water in the bottom of the boiler but not touching the top. Cook over moderate heat, stirring constantly until it coats the back of a silver spoon. Remove from heat and cool, stirring occasionally to keep a skin from forming. Chill.

Push raspberry or strawberry jam through a fine sieve to remove the seeds.

Whip the cream using the 1/2 cup of sugar and 1/2 tsp of vanilla.

Assemble the trifle. Layer the bottom of a large bowl with sponge cake slices. Sprinkle the wine over the cake until it is soaked. Spread the jam over the cake. Pour custard over the jam. Cover with whipped cream. Chill thoroughly.

A clear glass bowl is preferable since the layers will show through. Serves 8.

Editor's note: Some people use vanilla pudding, but the artificial vanilla can be tasted plainly.

Candy Bar Surprises

(Tastes just like a well-known candy bar)

12 ozs of white chocolate
12 oz box of Cheese-Its®

Peanut butter

Melt white chocolate in the microwave or over a double boiler according to the directions. Make Cheese-It® "sandwiches" with two crackers filled with peanut butter. Dip in white chocolate completely. Refrigerate.

Baklava

1 lb ground nuts (blanched almonds, walnuts or pecans)
1 cup sugar
1 1/2 tsps cinnamon
Pinch of powdered clove and powdered nutmeg

1 lb phyllo sheets (in frozen section; follow directions on box)
2 cups melted butter

Mix nuts, sugar and spices in a bowl. Place 8 sheets of phyllo dough in the bottom of a an 8" x 14" pan, brushing each sheet with melted butter. Sprinkle top with nut mixture; put 2 buttered phyllo sheets on top, sprinkle again with nuts. Continue alternating phyllo sheets and nuts until all the nuts are gone. Place remaining phyllo on top, buttering each sheet. With a very sharp knife, cut the baklava in diamond-shaped pieces. Put baklava pan on the middle shelf of the oven; put a pan with water on the lower shelf. Bake at 300° for 3 hours.

1/2 cup sugar
1 cup honey
2 cups water

1 1/2 tblsps lemon juice
Rind of a lemon, cut into strips

Combine all the ingredients, boil over medium heat for 15 minutes. Cool. When baklava is baked, pour cool syrup over it. Cool before serving. Serves 30.
Editor's note: It is obligatory that the phyllo sheets be kept between 2 damp towels while in reserve and waiting to be used. They dry out and crumble very quickly.

Chrusciki (Angel Wings)

5 egg yolks
1/2 tsp salt
3 tblsps sugar

1 tblsps brandy or cognac
5 tblsps sour cream
2 1/2 cups flour

Add salt to eggs and beat until thick and lemon-colored. Add sugar and flavoring and continue to beat. Add sour cream and flour alternately, mixing well after each addition. Knead on floured board until the dough blisters. Cut in halves, roll very thin and cut into strips about 4" long. Slit each piece in center and pull end through the slit. Fry in hot lard until lightly browned. Drain on absorbent paper and sprinkle with powdered sugar.

Cold and Crunchy Dessert

2 1/2 cups Rice Krispies®
1 cup pecans, broken
1 cup flaked coconut

1 stick butter
3/4 cup brown sugar
1/2 gallon ice cream

Toast first four ingredients in oven for 20 minutes, stirring. When slightly brown, remove and stir in brown sugar. Pat 1/2 mixture in bottom of 9" x 13" pan.
Slice 1/2 gallon peppermint (or any flavor) ice cream in 6 slices and place on mixture in pan. Spread remaining mixture on top. Cover and place in freezer until served.

Peanut Butter Ice Cream Cups

1 qt vanilla ice cream
1/2 cup crunchy peanut butter
1 cup Cool Whip®

Graham cracker crumbs
Muffin cups

Soften ice cream. Fold in peanut butter and Cool Whip®. Place 1 teaspoon graham cracker crumbs in bottom of muffin cups. Add mixture and freeze in muffin tins until firm.
Also may be made in a pie using graham cracker crust.

Lagniappe (A Little Something Extra)

Upper terrace, showing glass pages

Asparagus. Starting at the bud end, peel asparagus stalks with a vegetable parer. The stalks will be tender.

Biscuits. Leftover biscuits are still good. Split and butter them, then place them under the broiler until they are brown and crisp.

Bisquick®. Not a new product, but it was and still remains a superb base for many varieties of foods. Read the box.

Bleu Cheese. The Agricultural Department of Clemson University in South Carolina sells 10 oz cartons of Bleu Cheese Crumbs from October to December. They are very helpful in stuffing celery, making salad dressings, etc. A little goes a long way, and, refrigerated, they keep practically forever. For information, write:

Uniquely Clemson
Agricultural Product Sales Center
118 Newman Hall, Clemson University
Clemson, SC 29634-5345

Bread baking. If baking powder bread seems to be browning too much before it is done, cover the pan loosely with foil.

Canapés. When preparing the canapés, spread the bread with a very thin layer of softened butter or margarine. This will keep the toppings from soaking the bread.

Celery. Use a vegetable parer to peel celery, thus removing annoying strings.

Chicken. If only a small amount of chicken is desired, Swanson sells a 5 oz can.

Clarified butter. Place the desired amount of butter (not less than 1/4 lb) in a small pan over a low flame and let it melt slowly. When melted, skim off the foam that rises to the surface. Remove from fire, let it settle for a few minutes and then ladle or pour off the clear butter oil, being careful not to include any of the milky sediment in the bottom of the pan. Cover and refrigerate. Butter oil will stand much higher cooking temperatures than plain butter. The sediment may be used to flavor vegetables.

Confectioners sugar. Be sure to sift confectioners sugar before using to avoid lumps.

Fruits. To freeze fruits, sprinkle with Fruit Fresh and mix gently. They will stay their normal color and not turn dark.

Garlic. Fresh garlic is important, not dried out heads in a plastic bag. When you get fresh garlic, peel the cloves, place them in an airtight jar, cover them with sherry or olive oil, close and put the jar in the refrigerator. They keep a very long time.

Leftovers. Many leftover vegetables may be combined with seasoned canned chicken broth to make satisfying soups. Use your imagination.

Mushrooms. In many cooked dishes, mushroom bits and pieces will serve just as well as the more expensive whole mushrooms.

Olive oil. The editor prefers SASSO from Italy. It is very delicate and can be used for cooking or salad dressing.

Parer. Williams-Sonoma has a vegetable parer that is superb. The small protrusion on the upper right is for removing eyes from potatoes.

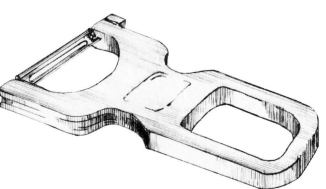

For a catalogue, write:
Williams-Sonoma
Mail Order Department
PO Box 7456
San Francisco, CA 94120-7456

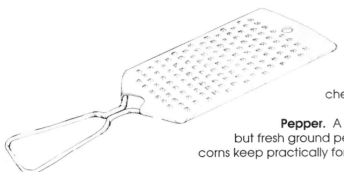

Parmesan cheese should be bought in a block. There is all the difference in the world between fresh grated cheese and the shaker containers. A block of Parmesan cheese in a plastic bag in the refrigerator will keep a very long time. Cheese in the shaker container becomes stale. A very good hard cheese grater looks like this drawing shown here.

Pepper. A pepper mill is a good investment. It need not be fancy, but fresh ground pepper has a taste and aroma that is special. Peppercorns keep practically forever.

Potatoes. If raw sliced or diced potatoes are not to be used at once, place them in cold water immediately. To use, remove and pat dry. Exposed to the air, they will turn brown very quickly.

Rice. An easy way to cook rice is to put it in a large pot of slightly salted boiling water. While cooking, test the rice by biting into a kernel. When it is just tender, pour it into a colander and drain. Put the colander back into the empty pot and cover to keep warm until serving. Cooked down, the rice water makes a very good light starch.

Rolled sandwiches. Use ordinary bread and cut off the crusts. Roll the bread as flat as possible with a rolling pin. Put on filling and roll up.

Salads, molded. Place salad in either lightly oiled mold or a mold that has been rinsed in cold water, but not dried. To unmold, put a slight film of cold water on the plate on which the salad is to be served. If the salad is not centered, the water will allow it to be moved until centered.

Scallion brushes (just for fun). Trim roots and green parts from scallions, leaving about 1 1/2" stalks. Make 1/2" lengthwise cuts at both ends of the stalks and spread fringed ends gently. Put the scallions in a bowl of ice cold water and chill 2 hours or until fringed ends have curled. Drain well. Small ends of celery stalks may be treated the same way.

Spices. Paul Prudhomme's Magic Seasoning Blends™ mixed spices are now being carried in many supermarkets (on the spice shelf). There are spices for meat, vegetable, pork and veal, poultry, seafood, etc. Just a dash will add zest to many dishes.

Stack pans for hors d'oeuvres. Buy cheap baking sheets. Buy a strip of wood 1" x 1". Have it sawed into 1" lengths (for taller canapés, use 1 1/2" length). Secure one block of wood to the top corner of a pan with tape. Turn the pan over and drive a short nail from the bottom of the sheet into the wood. Remove the tape.

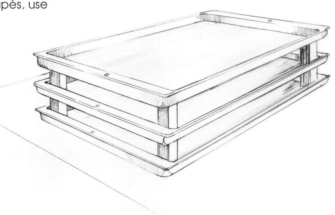

Continue for the other three corners of the pan. You now have a stack pan. Do this with as many pans as you like. Perhaps one person would not care to do it, but a group of friends could and pass the pans around as needed.

Make the canapés. Line the pans with plastic wrap. Put the canapés in the pans, closely touching each other. Cover with plastic wrap. Continue with other pans. Make sure that each pan contains a variety of canapés. Clean out the bottom of the refrigerator. Stack the pans one on top of another. The canapés will keep fresh for hours or over night. These will save last minute rushes prior to cocktail parties.

Tomato paste. If at all possible, buy tomato paste in a tube. It keeps a long time in the refrigerator. A tablespoonful of tomato paste is instantly available. How many cans of tomato paste have been thrown away, just because you needed a little?

Zip. Don't forget a dash of Tabasco® sauce. The people in New Orleans swear by it and use it by the gallons. Just a little adds pep.

Mrs. Lavonne "Sally" I. (Lusk) Abbott, Arvada, CO
US Navy, WW II

Mrs. Frances (Miller) Arnold, Seneca Falls, NY
US Navy, WW II

BG Mildred Bailey, Alexandria, VA
US Army, Retired

Mrs. Marguerite Ann (Langacher) Bardon, Merritt Island, FL
US Navy, WW II

Ms. Eleanor E. Beaudry, Houghton, MI
US Navy, WW II

Mrs. Imogene (Mellen) Bennett, Seaside Heights, NJ
US Marine Corps, WW II

Capt Katrina Bentler, Alburquerque, NM
US Air Force Reserve, 1983-1992

Mrs. Beulah (Watters) Bessmer, Mishawaka, IN
US Army Nurse Corps, WW II

Mrs. Maud (Hollowell) Black, Crowley, LA
US Army Nurse Corps, WW II

Mrs. Terrie Ann (Hoffman) Black, Columbia, MO
US Army, 1981-1990

Ms. Beatrice Blakly, Bronx, NY
US Coast Guard, WW II

Mrs. Marie (Knotts) Bogovich, Industry, PA
US Army, 1976-1985

Lt Col Jo Ann Bolitho, Port Charlotte, FL
US Air Force, Retired

Mrs. Albena (Starvinsky) Bolsar, Colmar, PA
US Navy, WW II

Mrs. (Lyda) Vera R. (Rowe) Bonnette, Neeses, SC
US Army Nurse Corps, 1941-1943

Dr. Olga Bonke-Booher, MD, Indianapolis, IN
Memorial Supporter

Mrs. Helen J. (Shanline) Bonnell, Watsonville, CA
US Army, WW II

Ms. Betty Bothe, Los Angeles, CA (Decased 1994)
US Coast Guard, WW II

Mrs. Glenda (Taylor) Bowling, Aberdeen, MS
US Marine Corps, 1958

Mrs. Pamela (Waddell) Bradbury, Fort Worth, TX
US Army Medical Specialist Corps, WW II

Mrs. Doris (Palm) Brander, Avon, MT
US Navy, WW II

TSgt Janis Brant-Walker, Costa Mesa, CA
US Air Force Reserve

Lt Col Norma V. (Vanderheide) Breedlove, San Antonio, TX
US Air Force, Retired

Mrs. Gertrude "Trudy" (Sternberger) Briere, St. Petersburg, FL
US Army, WW II

Mrs. Essie (Raney) Brock, Phoenix, AZ
US Air Force, 1951-1952

Mrs. Helen (Murphy) Brooks, Robbinston, ME
US Army, 1955-1956

SGM Beverly Butzer, Garland, TX
US Army, Retired

Ms. Mary Alice Campbell, Jamestown, NY
US Army, WW II

LCDR Pauline (Peters) Carr, Miami, FL
US Navy Nurse Corps, Retired

Ms. Madeline J. Cegelske, Minneapolis, MN
US Navy, WW II

Mrs. Justifa Chase-Jones, Radcliff, KY
US Army, 1965-1967

Ms. Karen Christian, La Selva, CA
WIMSA Supporter

Maj Sherry (Hoyt) Cline, Apple Valley, CA
US Air Force Nurse Corps, Retired

Mrs. (Eleanor) C. "Jo" Corwin, Federalsburg, MD
US Navy, WW II

Mr. Barney Cosgrove, Lake Oswego, OR
In memory of his late wife, Marjorie (Bothe) Cosgrove
US Army, WW II

Mrs. M. Jeanne (Merten) Costa Lakeland, FL
US Coast Guard, WW II,

Mrs. Mildred (Tiller) Covell, Montrose, VA
US Navy, WW II

Mrs. Marian (Long) Cox, Albuquerque, NM
US Army, WW II

Mrs. Kathryn (Kossel) Dale, Grosse Pointe, MI
US Navy, WW II

Mrs. Nina E. (Stafford-Wetmore) Daly, Grand Rapids, MI
US Army, WW II

Mrs. Janina S. (Smiertka) Davenport, Amherst, MA
US Navy Nurse Corps, 1938-1943

Mrs. Dorothy R. (Rushbrook) Davidson, Carrollton, IL
US Army Nurse Corps, WW II

Ms. Grace Decker, Dunedin, FL
US Navy, WW II

MSgt Beth Demel, Hoisington, KS
US Air Force, Retired

Ms. Gene Theresa Dighera, Milwaukee, WI
US Navy, WW II

Mrs. Jan Stefan Donsaach, Indiana
WIMSA Supporter

Mrs. Katherine "Kay" (King) Dorsey, Surprise, AZ
US Army Nurse Corps, WW II

Mrs. Alice (Clark) Douglass, Montgomery, AL
US Army Air Corps Nurse, WW II

Ms. Elizabeth Dunne, Boston, MA
WIMSA Supporter

Ms. Patricia Dupuy, Lutcher, LA
US Army, 1972-1976

Mrs. Helen V. (Weinman) Dyson, Steubenville, OH
US Army, WW II

Mrs. Jeanne R. (Malko) Edwards, Akron, OH
US Army, WW II

Bob and Darlyn Efferson
WIMSA Supporters

Mrs. Louise "Lou" (Graul) Eisenbrandt, Overland Park, KS
US Army Nurse Corps, 1967-1970

A1C Alma (Gauss) Eklund, Burke, VA
US Air Force

SP4 Beverly (Johnson) Enix, El Dorado, ARNG
US Army,1979-1990

Mrs. Chris (Martinez) Erla, Cass City, MI
US Navy, WW II

Mrs. Alice Eubanks, DuQuoin, IL
Mother of retired Navy servicewoman

Mrs. Ernestine H. Fagan, Colorado Springs, CO
WIMSA Supporter

Ms. Kathleen "Kay" Fearon, Forest Park, IL
WIMSA Supporter in memory of her mother, Mary K. Wesley,
US Army, WW II

Miss Jeanette Fetter, Kansas City, MO
US Navy, WW II

Mrs. Rita (Rounds) Forsythe, Santa Rosa, CA
US Army Nurse Corps, WW II

Mrs. Rachel (Gilbert) Francis, 1941-1955, Hill, NH
US Army Nurse Corps

SFC Sandi (Nelson) Franklin, Grand Prairie, TX
US Army Reserve

Mrs. Beatrice V. (Rivers) Gallagher, Spring Hill, FL
US Navy Nurse Corps, 1943-1948

Ms. Eveline Gallagher, Alexandria, VA
US Army, WW II

Mrs. Nancy (Stuart) Gallegos, Colorado Springs, CO
US Army, 1958-1960

CPT Jacqueline Garrick, Silver Spring, MD
US Army, Medical Specialist Corps

Mrs. Dolores (Sleicher) Gates, Waynesboro, PA
US Navy, 1953-1954

Ms. Wanda Gilchrist, Hydro, OK
US Navy Nurse Corps, 1950-1957

Mrs. Anna Marie (Olup-Bauer) Giese, Fayetteville, AR
US Navy, WW II

PN2 Lynette (Mauer) Glass, Waterford, CT
US Naval Reserve

Ms. Helen Grady, Hingham, MA
US Navy, WW II

Mrs. Elaine (Gordon) Griffin, Corpus Christi, TX
US Marine Corps, WW II

Ms. Doris C. Gross, San Jose, CA
US Army, WW II

Mrs. Aline A. (Maas) Hamblen, Park Ridge, IL
US Air Force Nurse Corps, 1952-1954

Mrs. Louise S. (Steinbrink) Harris, San Antonio, TX
US Air Force Nurse Corps, 1970-1972

CAPT Mileva Hartman, Arlington, VA
US Naval Reserve

Ms. Sandy Hartmann, DuQuoin, IL
IL GFWC, Veterans Affairs Chair

Mrs. Esther M. (Jungmann) Halverson, Nevada, IA
US Army Nurse Corps, WW II

Mrs. Estella (Bloemer) Hasting, St. Louis, MO
US Army, WW II

Ms. Caroline M. Hayden, Coronado, CA
US Marine Corps, WW II

MAJ Mary Jo Helfers, Augusta, GA
US Army Nurse Corps, Retired

Mrs. Agnes (Kucz) Henley, Lansing, MI
US Public Health Service, WW II

Maj Patricia Hester, La Coste, TX
US Air Force Nurse Corps, Retired

Capt Jennifer "Jenni" (Whitnack) Hesterman, Alexandria, VA
US Air Force

Mrs. Linda Ann (Brown) Hill, Winter Park, FL
US Army, 1975-1976

MAJ Helen (Freudenberger) Holmes, Guthrie, OK
US Army Retired

Mrs. Inez R. (Combites) Hood, Wagoner, OK
US Army Nurse Corps, WW II

Mrs. Dorothy (Meetze) Hooss, Chapin, SC
US Army Nurse Corps, 1948-1952

Mrs. Helen (Martin) Horner, Port Charlotte, FL
US Army Nurse Corps, 1940-1943

Mrs. Murielle (Montroy) Horskey, Hilton Head, SC
US Marine Corps, WW II

Mrs. Hughena (Hecht) House, Spokane, WA
US Navy, WW II

Mrs. (Marion) "Bing" (Bingham) Howard, Port Charlotte, FL
US Navy, 1944-1948

Mrs. Mari (Hitchcock) Hughes, Lake Worth, FL
US Army Air Corps, WW II

Mrs. Pearl (Koerner) Hughes, Anderson, SC
US Army, WW II

LT (JG) Suzanne C. Isham, Vienna, VA
US Navy

Mrs. Margaret (Karl) Jasinski-Dalton, High Falls, NY
US Army, 1950-1952

Mrs. Betty (Schrack) Johnson, San Pedro, CA
US Navy, WWII

Ms. Harriet Johnson, Augusta, ME
US Army Nurse Corps, WW II

Mrs. Gloria (Eberhardt) Jorgenson, Red Lodge, MT
US Army Medical Specialist Corps, 1950-1955

Mrs. Margaret (Flannes) Junemann, San Clemente, CA
US Coast Guard, WW II

YNC Doreen Kasprinski, Winnetka, CA
US Naval Reserve

Mrs. Margie (Pearce) Kiefer, Shell Knob, MO
US Marine Corps, WW II

Mrs. Madeline (Sebasky) Kirby, Capron, VA
US Army & US Air Force Nurse Corps, 1943-1953

Mrs. Victoria C. (Overton) Kirkwood, Hilton Head, SC
US Marine Corps, 1978-1981

Ms. Violet Knotts, Grafton, WVA
WIMSA Supporter

Ms. Paula Koslosky, Silver Spring, MD
US Army, WW II

Mrs. Beverly (Bookwalter) Krick, Etters, PA 717 938 6346
US Army, 1967-1970

COL Josephine M. (Scaparrotti) Landes, Staten Island, NY
US Army, Retired

Mrs. Rebecca (Smith) LaPehn, Indianapolis, IN
US Navy, WW II

Mrs. Mary (Hageman) Lawson
WIMSA Supporter

Mrs. Donna (Bianco) Leet, Niles, OH
US Army, 1973-1974

Mrs. Elsie Livengood, Ventura, CA
Mother of Navy Veteran, WIMSA Supporter

Mrs. Kathleen (Benner) Lockwood, Fairfax, VA,
US Army Nurse Corps, WW II

Mrs. Dorothy (Fekite) Lookabaugh, Pontiac, MI
US Navy, 1943-1950

Ms. Jean Lorenzetti Hollywood, FL
US Army Nurse Corps, WW II,

Mrs. Rose M. (Canal) Lowery, Highland, NY
US Marine Corps, WW II

Mrs. Ingrid E. (Frisell) Magnuson
US Army Nurse Corps, WW II, Merrifield, MN

Mrs. Dorothy (Looby) Manfredi, Rockville, MD
US Army Nurse Corps, 1941-1952

Ms. Mary Adele Manley, Elko, GA
WIMSA Supporter

Ms. Albina L. Marek, San Antonio, TX
US Army Nurse Corps, WW II

Ms. Frances Martin, Johnstown, PA
WIMSA Supporter

Mrs. (Mary) Alice H. (Hamill) Matyjasik, Apache Junction, AZ
US Navy, 1943-1950

Mrs. Ann C. (Church) Mays, Quincy, IL
US Army, WW II

Mrs. Jeanne M. (Huettl) McCann, Carlsbad, CA
US Navy, WW II

Mrs. Elwanda "E.P." (Bright) McClain, St. Louis, MO
US Air Force Nurse Corps, 1950-1955

Mrs. Lynette (Mobley) McClain, Sierra Vista, AZ
US Marine Corps, WW II

Mrs. Anita M. (Stierle) McGredy, Brookside, NJ
US Coast Guard, WW II

Mrs. Frances (Turner) McKinney, Green Valley, AZ
US Army Nurse Corps, WW II

Mrs. Elsie Melms, Goodells, MI
WIMSA Supporter

MSgt K C Mendenhall, Driftwood, TX
US Air Force

Mrs. Diane (Ballard) Michael, Boothbay Harbor, ME
US Navy, 1951-1952

Mrs. Jean Miles, Concord, NC
WIMSA Supporter

Mrs. Betty M. (Heckert) Miller, Harrisburg, PA
US Coast Guard, WW II

Ms. Debra A. Miller, Sandwich, MA
WIMSA Supporter

Mrs. Violet (Woods) Mills, Waldoboro, ME
US Navy Nurse Corps, WWI

Mrs. Willa (Miover) McCormick, Hemet, CA
US Navy, WW II

Mrs. Dolores (Wells) Mistretta, Fort Myers, FL
US Army, WW II

Mrs. Maxine (Knowles) Montgomery, R.N., Ashton, MD
US Nurse Corps Cadet, WW II

Ms. Charlotte Morehouse, Upperville, VA
US Army, WW II

Mrs. Marion (Monteforte) Nadrchal, Duncan, NE
US Marine Corps, 1958-1985

Ms. Lenora I. Nagel, Tampa, FL
US Air Force, 1953-1956

Mrs. Helen (Slusarick) Nord, Brookhaven, PA
US Army Nurse Corps, WW II

Mrs. Clotilde (Vargas) Novak, Lake City, PA
US Air Force, 1953-1956

Mrs. Patricia (Resse) Patton, Jal, NM
US Air Force, 1952-1954

Maj Mary (Smith) Payrow-Olia, TX
US Air Force, Lackland AFB

LTC Dorathea (Kercher) Pease, Merritt Island, FL
US Army, Retired

Ms. Margaret Peterson, Glendale, CA
WIMSA Supporter

Mrs. Marjie L. (Boettcher) Peterson, Blue Earth, MN
US Navy, WW II

Col Nelda M. Peterson, Trimont, MN
US Air Force, Retired

Mrs. Edith-Joyce Petrikat, Seymour, MO
US Army, WW II

Mrs. Pauline (Smith) Phillips, Vallejo, CA
US Army, WW II

Mrs. Elinor S. (Sherman) Prescott, St. Petersburg, FL
US Army Medical Specialist Corps, WW II

Mrs. June (Swadley) Provini, Seabrook, MD
US Navy, WW II

Lt Col Lillian (Bailey) Puckett, Windcrest, TX
US Air Force Nurse Corps, Retired

Mrs. Helen (Lingin) Pytlewski, Lemont, IL
US Navy, WW II

Mrs. Mary (Ervin) Quick, Tucson, AZ
US Navy, WW II

Mrs. Robin L. (Brooks) Ramsey, Oakdale, CT
US Air Force 1977-1981; US Air Force Reserve 1983-1985;
Army National Guard 1985-1988

Mrs. Mary (Hollyfield) Rapalje, East Aurora, NY
US Army, WW II (Deceased April 1994)

Mrs. Patricia "Pattie" (McManus) (Long) Reber, Marietta,
GA
US Army, 1962-1965

Mrs. Ruth (Jones) Redjives, Richfield Springs, NY
US Army, WW II

Ms. Anne K. Reifsneider, Oxon Hill, MD
US Coast Guard, WW II

Mrs. Viola "Lolly" (Eastlund) Ripperger, Cincinnati, OH
US Navy, WWI I

Mrs. Alice (Radigan) Roche, Sacramento, CA
US Army Nurse Corps, WW II

COL Gloria C. Rojas, Pompano Beach, FL
US Army Nurse Corps, Retired

Mrs. Estelle (Brassil) Roper, Germantown, TN
US Marine Corps, WW II

Mrs. Vivian (Weyland) Rose, Menomonee, FL
US Navy, WW II

Col Rose Salem, Kenwood, CA
USAF, Retired

Ms. Peggy Sandstrom
WIMSA Supporter

Ms. Tracy Sargant, Rome, NY
WIMSA Supporter

Mrs. Judith A. (Mormillo) Schaut, Covina, CA
US Marine Corps, 1962-1963

Mrs. Eileen (Bankston) Schiavone, Vero Beach, FL
US Army, WW II

Mrs. Marie (Gerds) Schulz, Harper Woods, MI
US Army, WW II

Lt Diane Schunemann, Brooklyn, NY
US Air Force Reserve Nurse Corps

Miss Charlotte Scripture, Suncook, NH
US Army Medical Specialst Corps, WW II and Korea

Mrs. Thelma (Swarner) Segebartt, Seattle, WA
US Army Nurse Corps, WW II

Mrs. Helen (Roden) Shatynski, Downey, CA
US Army Nurse Corps, 1954-1956

SSG Merilyn K. Sherrill, Albuquerque, NM
US Army

Mrs. Velma F. (Campbell) Shiffler, Franklin, VA
US Navy, WW II

Mrs. Lois Siminski, Burbank, CA
WIMSA Supporter

Mrs. Dorothy (Nesbit) Slott, Lava Hot Springs, ID
US Army Nurse Corps, WW II

Ms. Dorothy Small, Bayonet Point, FL
US Navy, WW II

Ms. Bessie J. Smith, Weston, OH
US Army, WW II

Mrs. Cleoma (Schneider) Smith, Des Moines, IA
US Navy, WW II

LTC Dianne L. Smith, Lorton, VA
US Army

Ms. Janet W. Smith, CA
WIMSA Supporter

Mrs. Joyce (Hamilton) Smith, Omaha, NE
US Army, WW II

Mrs. Sophie (Negomir) Smith, Charles City, IA
US Army, WW II

Mrs. Theresa (Darge) Smith, Oceanside, CA
US Navy, WW II

Mrs. Dottie (Markham) Snell, Hot Springs, AR
US Army, WW II

Mrs. Irene (Davis) Snyder, Masontown, PA
US Army, WW II

Mrs. Rhonda Snyder, Orange Park, FL
WIMSA Supporter

Mrs. Mary M. (Sherrill) Southworth, Laguna Hills, CA
US Navy, WW II

Mrs. Beth (Mackey) Stiffler, Macomb, IL
US Navy, WW II

Mrs. F. Jean (Spackman) Stratton, West Sedona, AZ
US Air Force, 1952-1959

Ms. Leota Striplin, Mariposa, CA
US Army, WW II

Mrs. Frances T. (Trott) Sweat, Fernandina Beach, FL
US Army, WW II

SSgt Grace Tate, Howard AFB, Panama
US Air Force

Mrs. Florence Thiele, Walden, NY
WIMSA Supporter

Ms. Priscilla Thomson, York Beach, ME
WIMSA Supporter

Mrs. Lillie F. (Hanson) Thoreen, Everett, WA
US Navy Nurse Corps, WW II

Mrs. Domenica "Sunny" (Cardinale) Thornton, Fallston, MD
US Army, WW II

Mrs. Mary Jo (Carden) Tolan, Prospect Harbor, ME
WIMSA Supporter

Mrs. Constance (Gunderson) Totten, Bloomington, MN
WIMSA Supporter

Mrs. Genevieve (Strauss) Tweedy, Brookfield, WI
US Navy, WW II

Mrs. Eleanor F. (Cheplak) Unverzagt, West Allis, WI
US Army Nurse Corps, WW II

Mrs. Kathryn "Kay" (Sheen) Van Hook, Santa Ana, CA
US Marine Corps, WW II

Mrs. Florence E. (Benson) Vanidestine, Monroe, ME
US Army, WW II

Mrs. Josephine F. (Miller) Velding, Grand Rapids, MI
US Marine Corps, WW II

SMSgt Georga Vickery, Mansfield, TX
US Air Force

Col Marilyn A. Walker, Upper Marlboro, MD
US Air Force Medical Service

Ms. Sarabel D. Wardle, Palo Alto, CA
Woman Airforce Service Pilot, WW II

CDR Pat Warner, Howey-in-the-Hills, FL
US Navy, Retired

Mrs. Alice (Bender) Watkins, Largo, FL
US Army Medical Specialist Corps, 1946-1957

Mrs. Mary M. (Earnest) Weaver, Savannah, GA
US Army Nurse Corps, WW II

Ms. Arline Wertz, Millington, TN
WIMSA Supporter

Mrs. Marcella (Montgomery) Wilkes, Denton, TX
US Navy, WW II

Ms. Pamella Windham, Marietta, GA
US Coast Guard, WW II

DP2 Rene Wiesner, US Navy

Ms. Mary Ellen Withrow
WIMSA Supporter, Treasurer of the United States

Ms. Dorothy Worsham, Stilwell, OK
US Coast Guard, WW II

Ms. Leta Wright, Fort Meade, FL
WIMSA Supporter

Ms. Roberta Wright, Austin, TX
WIMSA Supporter

Mrs. Martha (Dunn) Adams Yeh, Buffalo, NY
US Army Nurse Corps, WW II

Mrs. Alice M. (Martin) Younger, Thousand Oaks, CA
US Navy, WW II